FIGHT

FIGHT

HOW GEN Z IS CHANNELING THEIR FEAR AND PASSION TO SAVE AMERICA

JOHN DELLA VOLPE
FOREWORD BY DAVID HOGG

ST. MARTIN'S PRESS
NEW YORK

First published in the United States by St. Martin's Press, an imprint of St. Martin's Publishing Group

www.stmartins.com

Designed by Gabriel Guma

Library of Congress Cataloging-in-Publication Data

Names: Della Volpe, John, author.
Title: Fight : how Gen Z is channeling their fear and passion to
    save America / John Della Volpe.
Description: First edition. | New York : St. Martin's Press, [2022] |
    Includes bibliographical references and index.
Identifiers: LCCN 2021037801 | ISBN 9781250260468
    (hardcover) | ISBN 9781250260475 (ebook)
Subjects: LCSH: Generation Z—Political activity—United States. |
    Generation Z—United States—Social conditions. | Young
    adults—Political activity—United States. | United States—
    Social conditions—1980- | United States—Politics and
    government—1989-
Classification: LCC HQ799.9.P6 D45 2022 | DDC 305.2420973—
    dc23
LC record available at https://lccn.loc.gov/2021037801

First Edition: 2022

10 9 8 7 6 5 4 3 2 1

For Linda,
and our family of fighters,
and to the memory of
Jim Della Volpe

CONTENTS

List of Figures

Author's Note

I am using this platform to give and amplify the voice of the many Zoomers and millennials I've had the good fortune of meeting, listening to, and learning from over my career. Their words and experiences have left an indelible impression on me. Many of the interviews for this book were conducted in research settings—sometimes individually, often in groups. To protect the persons' privacy, I use pseudonyms when referring to specific people, conversations, or events. The cities or towns in which subjects reside are unchanged.

This book was written in my personal, independent capacity and is not formally connected to Harvard University in any way. The Harvard Kennedy School Institute of Politics polling data that I reference is included with permission from the president and fellows of Harvard College.

Foreword

To my fellow young people who feel let down and abandoned by the nation's leaders; to parents and teachers struggling to understand their children; to the politicians looking for our votes; and to the businesses seeking our loyalty, understand this: we are a generation forged by trauma and loss, but we are not defeated.

We are a generation forced to grow up in fear of becoming victims of gun violence in our neighborhoods and schools. Heavily in debt, we enter an economy that reduces young people to commodities and squeezes us for profit. We inherit a natural world that may have already reached its tipping point. At every turn, our institutions are failing us, and we are paying the price. Half of our generation reports feelings of depression and/or anxiety. The government reports our stress levels are twice those of adults over thirty.

But rather than becoming cynical or retreating from these challenges, we fight back. For me, that fight started on February 14, 2018, when a gunman murdered seventeen students and staff in my school and tore my community apart. A month later I stood cold and numb with my classmates before a crowd of millions, determined to end the scourge of gun violence in the country. My message that day was that when people say that your voice doesn't matter, we say: no more. We say to those who underestimate us: get your résumés ready.

The work and determination of our generation has resulted in stricter gun laws in states across the country and led to record levels of participation in elections that cost many who oppose our political beliefs their jobs. But it is not enough. Violence pervades our cities and towns, and our fellow citizens continue to be gunned down by militarized police departments across the country.

Every day I am emboldened by the courage, compassion, and commitment of our community. Never before has a generation been so devoted to serving justice and solving the underlying issues that hold so many in America back from pursuing their best lives. Never before has a generation been as connected as ours, with an ability to turn a simple school strike into a global movement that has upended politics as we know it.

To young people who aspire to join our fight, know that the challenge will not be easy. The increasingly sophisticated use of technology employed to promote conflict, sow discord, divide us, and spread distorted and extremist views makes it easy to distract us from our goals. But every day we are winning. Every day, when an eighteen-year-old registers to vote or fights for the rights of someone they've never met, we are winning.

Whatever role you choose to play to make your community and our country stronger—whether you are young or old—know that you are not alone. I encourage you to be conscious of your own health, both mental and physical. Reach out and stay connected to your community and friends. Listen and be open to the advice and wisdom of others whose experiences are different from your own.

After the Parkland shooting, when I was meeting with

local activists from Chicago, I was introduced to Martin Luther King, Jr.'s Six Principles of Nonviolence. The final principle states that "the universe is on the side of justice. The nonviolent resister has deep faith that justice will eventually win." Today I am more confident than ever. As a generation, our faith has often been tested, and our resolve continues to grow.

Peace,
David Hogg

FIGHT

Introduction

Families, tribes, sects, classes, cliques, clubs, and associations are all groups of individuals organized by either vital, existential ties of "proximity" or on the basis of one's own free choice. Generations are fundamentally different. One cannot disassociate, leave, or pass from one to another. You don't choose them. They choose you. Some are tight-knit; others have less solidarity. They don't start and end on particular dates or flow in a certain predestined cycle or rhythm. Their lines are gray. Generations are what happen when a group of people coming of age share the experience of living through certain historical events. Values naturally emerge. They inform worldviews, ways of thinking that are carried for a lifetime.

This is the story of Generation Z.* Its members include a group of about seventy million young people in America born in a roughly twenty-year period beginning in the mid-1990s. They are the most diverse and most educated generation in history. Approximately half are white (non-Hispanic),

---

* I interchangeably refer to Generation Z as "Gen Z," "Gen Zers," and "Zoomers" in this book. Originally "Zoomers" was a play on "baby boomers," but since these young people have spent a significant portion of the last year attending school, social events, and work through a computer monitor, the moniker "Zoomers" has taken on new meaning in the era of COVID-19.

a quarter are Hispanic, 14 percent are Black, 6 percent are Asian, and 5 percent are either of mixed race or another background.[1]

Zoomers are more likely than any other generation to be raised in a household where at least one parent has a bachelor's degree, and a majority of recent high school graduates are enrolled in a two- or four-year college or university.

Less than 80 percent of Gen Z put themselves in the straight or heterosexual bucket. Those in Gen Z are more than twice as likely (12 percent) as millennials to self-identify as bisexual, and six times as likely as Generation X.[2] About one-third of Gen Zers say they know someone who prefers to use gender-neutral pronouns; this compares to a quarter of millennials and 16 percent of Gen Xers who say the same.[3]

Tethered to their screens and connected to the world, Gen Zers have never known their country at peace. The oldest Zoomers, including my own children, were just starting their education when nineteen terrorists hijacked four airplanes on September 11, 2001, killing almost three thousand people. They are old enough to have voted for or against Donald Trump in two presidential elections. The youngest Gen Zers were forced to attend elementary school from home during the COVID-19 lockdown. Many learned to write and solve math problems through Zoom; the joy that recess and play dates with non–socially distant friends can bring delayed.

Millennials, sometimes referred to as Generation Y, can be thought of as their older cousins. The oldest millennials, born when Reagan was president, are now settling into careers. Less likely than previous generations to have a spouse or children at this stage of their lives, those that do are snapping up suburban and exurban homes wherever they can. With community service and volunteerism in their DNA, many continue to serve their country, at home and through military service abroad. One even made a pretty good run for the Democratic nomination for president in 2020 and now serves in the Biden cabinet.

The parents of Generation Z were mostly born in the 1960s and 1970s. We know them as Generation X, a label used at various times since the 1950s to describe alienated youths. In the 1980s, it finally stuck on a generation that displays "centrist tendencies in a political climate that celebrates the extremes"[4] and is sandwiched between the larger "baby boomer" and millennial cohorts. Solidly middle aged, many are currently shepherding their children through high school or college, while caring for aging parents during their peak earning years. Gen X is shouldering much stress. Gen X writer Alex Williams reminds us that less than half of people born during this time consider themselves part of the generation;[5] they lack the strong ties and central identity other generations have in common.

Generation Z's grandparents commonly straddle two generations. Those in their sixties and early seventies represent baby boomers, so named after the uptick in the post–World War II birthrate that began in the mid-1940s. Others, who are now in their mid-seventies or older, are part of the silent generation, a relatively small bunch, born between the Great Depression and the start of the Second World War, that birthed rock and roll, the civil rights movement, and our current, forty-sixth president.

To understand Generation Zers—who they are and why they do what they do—we need to understand who raised them, who came before, and who are still present in their lives. Millennials, Gen X, baby boomers, and the silent generation are coexistent with Generation Z. Zoomers are

America's younger cousins, children, and grandchildren. The values, actions, and attitudes of these older generations continue to shape, oppose, and, increasingly in turn, be shaped by those of Generation Z.

I have traveled for about half my life through dozens of states and about as many countries to learn the stories of the young people and emerging generations shaping tomorrow. As a dad, coach, and mentor—working with undergraduates as polling director at the Harvard Kennedy School Institute of Politics (IOP), as an Eisenhower Fellow, the founder of a public opinion research company, a pollster and advisor to President Biden's 2020 campaign—I have lived with, worked with, and studied countless members of Generation Z. Simply put, it's my job. Before that, I focused on millennials.

At the end of each journey, whether I was visiting Nashville, Tennessee, or Kaesong, North Korea, I would always return home optimistic and more fired up about our future than when I left. During the summer and fall of 2017, though, that changed. The America I found in coffee shops and courtyards, in high schools and on college campuses had darkened—altered in a way that wasn't reflected by many of the traditional gauges of our country's health and direction. Generation Z was feeling increasingly uneasy in Trump's America. It was the support of Gen Xers, along with majorities of baby boomers and the silent generation, especially in the battleground states of Michigan, Pennsylvania, and Wisconsin, that allowed for his ascension to the White House.[6] Scores of older Americans did not much care what Generation Zers thought. It wasn't their turn to speak up. They hadn't paid their dues.

Through both in-depth and informal conversations, focus

groups, and surveys, I learned that despite an extended period of economic growth following the Great Recession, Generation Z was struggling. Teenagers and twenty-somethings opened up to me in ways millennials never had at that age. They shared the heavy burdens of anxiety, fear, and pain they were carrying.

Just a few years earlier, the attitudes of young Americans seemed markedly different. During the age of Obama, millennials were acutely aware of the difficulties facing their communities and our country. Still, there was a recognition, or at least hope, that the opportunities uniting us eclipsed the divides among us. Even during the administration of George W. Bush, when our country was engaged in war overseas and battling the Great Recession at home, I would visit some of the neediest urban centers and least-resourced rural counties and reservations and still find faith and optimism for a brighter tomorrow.

Spending time with young people of all backgrounds, I sensed confidence during the early and mid-2010s. When conversations turned to America, millennials would use words and phrases like: "progress," "strong," "diverse," "free," "land of opportunity," "abundance," and "the world's big brother." In 2015, three years into President Obama's second term, even when a majority of Americans were losing faith in Washington's ability to get things done, it was not uncommon for me to hear the guarded optimism of a then twenty-two-year-old:

> People will get angry, and the problems will be fixed, because they'll vote the problems out of office. So, in the long run, I tend to trust the American people. I trust the government.

In 2017, a few months into the Trump presidency, I returned to some of these same neighborhoods and asked similar questions. This time, though, the reactions were different. Questions that for years drew upon hopeful responses now induced an unmistakable heaviness. Standing beside an easel with a giant Post-it note, ready to transcribe the responses of a focus group, I'd ask, "What is the biggest challenge facing America?"

- gun violence
- school shootings
- unchecked rise of hate speech and hate groups
- racism
- surging levels of disrespect and incivility
- inequality
- sexual assault
- drugs
- the potential of crippling debt associated with the pursuit of higher education

These were the answers I received—urgent, sad, dark, painful, and far different in tone from what I'd heard in the past. They did not change much regardless of which town I was in or the race, gender, or education level of those I met.

I'd follow up with more direct questions, such as, "Does anyone know someone who's been a victim of gun violence?" In an instant, most of the African American hands would go up, along with a smattering of others.

"Does anyone have a friend or family member who's been a victim of sexual assault?" Across cities, suburbs, and small towns, nearly every hand was raised before I could even finish my question. It was the same when I asked about those suffering from mental health challenges, about thoughts of suicide, use of opioids, or other drug abuse and addiction.

Generation Z wasn't looking for pity. Gen Zers were not retreating from the reality in front of them. They were ready to engage directly on these issues—the underlying elements of what was stifling their generation. They were looking to fight.

For many reasons that I will outline in the chapters ahead, I soon became confident that young Americans were connecting the dots between the troubles now facing them, the generations of leaders who were disregarding their concerns, and a president who was uninterested in even paying lip service to the idea of national unity. They would soon turn their personal trauma into purpose that would upset politics as we know it.

A year later, after the heinousness of the shooting at Marjory Stoneman Douglas High School in Parkland, Florida, and with the fighting spirit of Generation Z already taking hold, I identified, through the release of the Harvard IOP youth poll—a project I've directed since 2000—a once-in-a-generation attitudinal shift about the efficacy of participating in the political process. These findings, I believed, were the precursors of increased political participation and presence of young voters in the upcoming 2018 midterm elections.

At the time, respected political analysts and friends dismissed these conclusions, which were featured in a May 2018 *New York Times* article. Their analysis told a different story; they were not buying that young people would show up for a midterm election. I was reminded by them of the overhyped baby boomer, Generation X, and millennial youth voter waves of the past, that more often than not never fully crested. They weren't wrong on that score. Missing from their calculus, though, was that every generation of young voters is unique—and I believed three (not equally weighted) factors stood this moment apart.

First and foremost was Donald John Trump and his extraordinary talent for making politics tangible, while tapping into and bringing out the very best and the very worst of people. His young, mostly white, and rural supporters were giddy. Borders were closing, and concrete was being poured on the southern border; their vote mattered. Hillary Clinton supporters were distraught: Obamacare was jeopardized, the environment imperiled, and white supremacists were marching in Charlottesville—again, the consequences of politics on full display.

Second, a powerful, purposeful, and diverse grassroots movement was forged from the literal and figurative assault on their generation in Florida—a movement committed to registering and turning out a new generation of voters with access to the technology and tools to turn their goals into reality.

Third, there was evidence that the actions of both Trump and the grassroots organizers were already having a discernible impact, as measured by spikes in Generation Z's voter registration and increased participation in primary campaigns, like the one that toppled the chair of the US House Democratic Caucus and brought Alexandria Ocasio-Cortez (AOC), a then-twenty-nine-year-old activist, former waitress, and bartender from the Bronx, to Washington.

Unlike other election cycles, when young people were detached and struggled to discern the difference between the values of one party and the other, I could both feel Gen Z's passion and also objectively measure its impact. In November 2018, Generation Z and other young Americans exceeded even the rosiest expectations and turned out in historic fashion to vote Trumpism out of office, though they would have to wait two more years to do the same for its namesake. Voters under age thirty doubled their participation relative to the last midterm election four years earlier; they also increased their share of the electorate by nearly one-third.[7]

After listening to their concerns, tracking their progress, and seeing these election results, I became convinced that we were witnessing the earliest days of the members of a new generation facing their fears and claiming their stake in America. That's when I knew I had to write this book.

Generation Z, the youngest members of the under-thirty youth cohort, was the catalyst for turning a good outcome into a great one for Democrats as they seized control of the

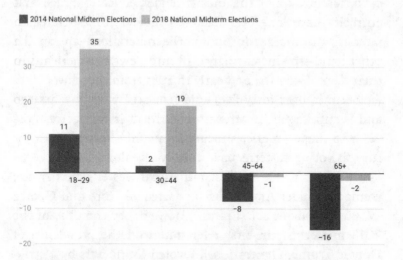

Figure 0.1. Percentage point margin of support for Democratic candidates in the 2014 and 2018 midterm elections for the US House of Representatives. For example, in 2018, among 18–29-year-olds, Democrats 67 percent, Republicans 32 percent (+35).

Source: 2014 and 2018 exit polls, CNN.com

House from Republicans in 2018. The 6-point margin Republicans received in 2014 shifted into an 8-point deficit four years later, a stunning 14-point turnaround. And no subgroup in the electorate shifted more in Democrats' favor than young voters. According to analysis of the CNN-published exit polls, in 2014, voters under thirty supported Democratic candidates by 11 percentage points (54 percent to 43 percent);[8] by 2018, the margin of support from this group more than tripled, to 35 percentage points (67 percent to 32 percent).[9]

While participation in politics was narrowing the turnout gap between Generation Z and older generations, their views on bedrock American issues like capitalism, racial justice, inequality, democracy, climate change, the role of government, and our presence in the world were quickly diverging. Political differences along the lines of gender, education, race, and ethnicity have long been factored into electoral strategies, politics, and market forecasts. The generation gap, on the other hand—the increasingly differing views of Americans in their teens, twenties, and early thirties from those over sixty (sometimes over forty-five)—did not exist twenty years ago and is still largely underexamined. Yet it is the factor most likely to shape America's future in the mid-twenty-first century, as voting patterns have quickly revealed.

In 2000, when the first millennial was eligible to vote, young and older Americans supported Al Gore and George W. Bush at about equal rates.[10] However, by the time of the 2018 midterms, the first referendum on the presidency of Donald Trump, Generation Z favored Democrats by a striking 37 points. Among voters slightly older, between the ages of twenty-five and twenty-nine, the Democratic margin was 33 points.[11]

In the 2020 general election, as greater numbers of Gen Z came of age, modern youth-turnout records were broken.

The share of the youth vote increased, and Joe Biden's share of the under-thirty cohort was larger than in every other Democratic campaign this century, with the exception of Obama's in 2008.

A values-based ideological gap that divides Americans by year of birth, mostly nonexistent in 2000, is now a driving force in local and national political contests. Every day younger and older Americans wake up to different Americas. Many older people still see their country as the "shining city on a hill" that Puritan John Winthrop envisioned almost four hundred years ago and that twentieth-century presidents John F. Kennedy and Ronald Reagan invoked at key junctures in their political careers. The coming-of-age experiences of Generation Z, on the other hand, marked by rising inequality, discrimination, an endangered environment, and

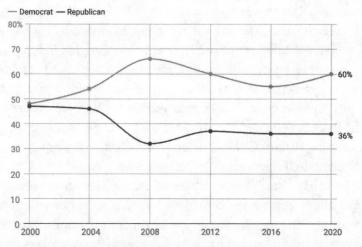

Figure 0.2. Preferences of 18–29-year-old voters in presidential elections, 2000–2020.

Source: Exit polls, Roper Center for Public Opinion Research, 2000–2020

a fractured politics, comprise a conscious rejection of American exceptionalism.

One of the most challenging questions I ask Gen Zers today is to name the time in their lives when they were most proud to be American. More often than not, I get blank stares, or examples of random sporting events like the USA soccer team finally beating Ghana in a 2017 friendly match. I've found that young Americans have no such trouble answering my follow-up question about a time when they were ashamed of their country.

Young people vote, or engage in any activity, when they seize upon the material difference participation can make. That is the first lesson I learned from studying millennials before 9/11 and through the Bush, Obama, Trump, and now Biden years. Stifling economic inequality, Donald Trump's presidency, the March for Our Lives movement, George Floyd's murder, and the specter of climate change have made politics come alive for this generation.

Generation Z knows the difference it made in the 2018 Democratic takeover of the House, in electing Joe Biden and Kamala Harris in 2020, and in Democrats regaining control of the Senate in January 2021. Gen Zers are also aware that youth involvement in 2016 nearly anointed Bernie Sanders as the leader of the Democratic Party, while their lack of enthusiasm for Hillary Clinton helped elect Donald Trump.

Social-change-theory experts Stephen Vaisey and Omar Lizardo say that "if we want to make our best guess (net of age) about what a person thinks or what kinds of practices he or she engages in, we would be better off knowing what year the person was born than what year we are observing them."[12] Following this approach argues against the theory that today's young voters will abandon progressive values for conservatism as they age. My research, too, suggests that this won't happen. Instead, Generation Z has placed the issues raised from my 2017 focus groups—the ones keeping Gen Zers up at night, and the ones holding America back—at the forefront of our national agenda.

They will change America more than growing up in America will change them.

When I was outlining the book and sharing the thesis with friends, I was asked more than once, "So, why does Gen Z fight?" We are fortunate to live in the "richest" society the world has ever known. A place where a biracial son of a single mother can be president, and a Black, Asian American woman can be vice president. Millions of Americans are doing just fine, living out the American Dream, struggles and all. But what Generation Z understands, even at this young age, is that others are not doing well. Tens of millions of Americans are struggling in important and consequential ways. We have raised Zoomers to be an uncommonly empathetic generation.

They may see things that others do not. They may feel obliged to "correct us" during a family dinner or challenge what we have grown to accept. There's nothing wrong with this. We can talk it out. They love a debate. But don't be fooled; change is in the air.

What I hope you will learn is that as a consequence of an unfolding climate crisis, economic upheaval, gun violence, civil unrest, and increasingly brazen displays of intolerance, white nationalism, and hate, Zoomers have endured more adversity than any generation of young Americans in at least seventy years. And they know it. The failure of older generations to resolve these challenges weighs heavy on them. For them, America at times has resembled a dystopia. But they won't sit back and take it. They've decided to fight their own war against injustice and inequality right here at home. They can be this century's "Greatest Generation." Every day, they are fighting for America's future. And they're already winning, causing a sea change in politics, the economy, society, and the ways we live, love, and work.

If you want to understand what America will be like ten, twenty, thirty years from now, it starts with Generation Z.

I

UNITED BY FEAR

These are the words and phrases Generation Z uses to paint the picture of the America that raised them:

terrifying
broken
declining
fake
close-minded
divided
aggressive
dystopic
off the rails
a bloody mess

These postmillennials, the roughly seventy million Americans born in the mid-1990s through the early 2010s, suffered—like previous generations—the problems, dangers, and uncertainties of the world. Unlike those in previous generations, however, they've enjoyed few of the glories and hopes that define America's promise.

Baby boomers saw JFK, RFK, and MLK assassinated and cities crumble. They watched their country ripped apart over Vietnam, and they suffered the ideals-shattering betrayal of

Watergate. But they (especially white Americans) saw their incomes rise while enjoying the highest standard of living the world has ever known, the American middle class. And with it came Beatlemania and Woodstock, the moon landing, the civil rights movement, the Great Society, Springsteen, and disco.

Generation X, America's middle child and my own cohort, remembers Americans as hostages; Gen Xers suffered from AIDS (or the fear of it), the Iran-Contra affair, Reagan's betrayal of government and his embrace of the "greed is good" ethos, the *Challenger* disaster, and the Los Angeles riots; but many of us were also there for the "Miracle on Ice," MTV, the PC revolution, the fall of the Berlin Wall, and, for some—particularly white suburbanites—increased opportunity and wealth.

In their formative years, millennials saw the Clinton impeachment, Columbine, Timothy McVeigh's bombing of a federal building in Oklahoma City, the First Gulf War, and Kurt Cobain's suicide. They were also the first to use iTunes and were part of Facebook from the beginning, although they would eventually come to view it as more of a negative than a positive. In 2008, they were the spark that delivered Barack Obama to the rest of us.

Let's compare that to the life and collective memory of Generation Z.

When the oldest Zoomers were in preschool, George W. Bush won the presidency by less than a thousand votes, amid claims of fraud and suppression. Within a year, the 9/11 attacks occurred. Then there ensued a search for WMDs that did not exist, Hurricane Katrina, and the beginning of America's longest war. Next, the 2008 financial crisis, the housing crisis, and bailouts for those who caused the crises, while Main Street, which suffered it, was ignored. On top of this,

Gen Z endured the opioid epidemic and witnessed the militarization of police and national borders, an explosion of white nationalism, frightening red-alert active-shooter drills and school lockdowns, increasingly frequent and deadly mass shootings, the accelerating and genuine threat of climate change, and a global pandemic and lockdown with a yet-undetermined impact on Zers' mental health and education. And most recently, a conspiracy-fueled insurgency has been bent on tearing down our institutions and kidnapping and assassinating our elected leaders.

Even the bright spots of Obama's historic election in 2008 and the official end of the Great Recession in 2009 turned dark. In 2010, Senate Majority Leader Mitch McConnell declared that "the single most important thing we want to achieve is for President Obama to be a one-term president." Washington, DC, became a battleground.

The following year, in terms every once-closeted racist heard loud and clear, Donald Trump—and soon Roger Ailes's Fox News—fully embraced "birtherism," suggesting that the only president Generation Z really knew wasn't even an American. "Maybe he's a Muslim; I don't know,"[1] said our future commander in chief, perpetuating wildly racist depictions of Muslims as anti-American terrorists.

Social media has connected the like-minded in ways their parents who remember CompuServe could never have dreamed of. It helped give rise to the #MeToo movement and Black Lives Matter, to Bernie Sanders and AOC, but it also enabled the rise of bots, trolls, QAnon, Russian interference, and alt-right terrorists, while Silicon Valley titans Mark Zuckerberg and Jack Dorsey looked away, counting their billions.

By 2017, researchers had already reported that rates of depression and anxiety, especially among youths, were higher than at any other point in history.[2] And then Trump blew everything up, further dividing America, fueling racism, undermining the justice system, destroying trust in science, creating even greater gaps between the rich and the poor, before he oversaw the early response to COVID-19, which has claimed more than seven hundred thousand American lives.

Except for maybe Netflix, reruns of *The Office*, Amanda Gorman, Halsey, Simone Biles, and Lil Nas X, Gen Z hasn't caught much of a break. Even uploading new dance moves or pranks on TikTok was deemed a national security threat, enabling Chinese cyber-warriors.

For most of their lives, Gen Zers have been failed by our nation.

As I write this in the summer of 2021, nearly half of Generation Z is suffering from depressive symptoms requiring professional treatment. The chronic stress from worrying about school, future education and employment, gun violence, economic insecurity, political instability, personal relationships, and social media has weighed down Zoomers just as they should be preparing to fly. Ellen Burstein and Alan Zhang, two Harvard undergraduates who work on the Harvard Public Opinion Project with me, wrote for *The Boston Globe*:

> There needs to be open conversation about mental health, and families, parents, and friends need to be aware of troubling symptoms in their loved ones.[3]

Before the coronavirus isolation and stress made everything worse, youth suicide (in ten- to twenty-four-year-olds) was already on the rise in every one of fifty states and was the second leading cause of death for Americans under age thirty-five (as it was for younger age groups, as well).[4] From

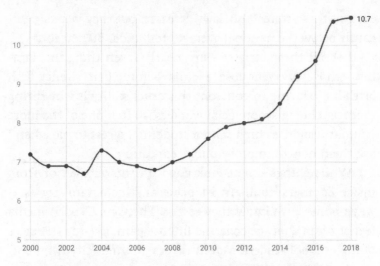

Figure 1.1. Suicide death rates among 10–24-year-olds in the United States. Rates per 100,000 population enumerated as of April 1 for 2000 and 2010, and estimated as of July 1 for all other years.

Source: National Center for Health Statistics, National Vital Statistics System, Mortality

an eight-year period of stability (2000 to 2007), the suicide rate began increasing as Gen Z aged into adolescence. When government researchers compared the period of 2007–2009 with 2016–2018, they found that suicide rates among youths increased by 47 percent.[5]

Every state saw an increase; in forty-two states the growth rate was statistically valid and not the result of random error. In the other states, suicides also rose, but the change was not statistically significant. At an increase of 110 percent over that time frame, New Hampshire saw the largest escalation by far. The Granite State was followed by Oregon, Georgia, Missouri, Oklahoma, and Michigan, which recorded spikes of at least 70 percent in youth suicide rates during this period. On the other end of the spectrum are Maryland, Mississippi, and Florida;

each of these states also saw increases, but they were significantly below the national average, and under 30 percent.[6]

Behind these statistics are nearly seven thousand families who every year lose a child before their twenty-fifth birthday.[7] Having to confront this cruel reality is why hiring more psychologists or social workers is often one of the more popular responses high school students suggest to me when I ask them how to improve public education.

While things might look good on the outside, or from inside Zoomers' ebullient Snapchat and Instagram stories, if we're honest, we know they're not. The Gen Z social media feed is often a facade covering intense pain, like the struggles of high school student Marcus, from an inner-city neighborhood in Atlanta:

> A lot of people have different mental problems and stuff like that, and depression's a common one, but others have PTSD, and when that triggers, it just turns into a whole different problem, and that caused a lot of suicides. It's just bad really.

According to IOP polling, for at least several days within a two-week period in March 2021, 53 percent of Zoomers said they had little interest or pleasure in doing things; 51 percent felt down, depressed, or hopeless; 49 percent had a poor appetite or were overeating; 48 percent had trouble concentrating on things, such as reading the newspaper or watching television; and 28 percent had thoughts that they would be better off dead, or thoughts of hurting themselves in some way. Some 5 percent say these thoughts cross their mind every day.[8] While there are certain subgroups of youth that have heightened levels of stress, anxiety, or suicidal thoughts, no group is immune.

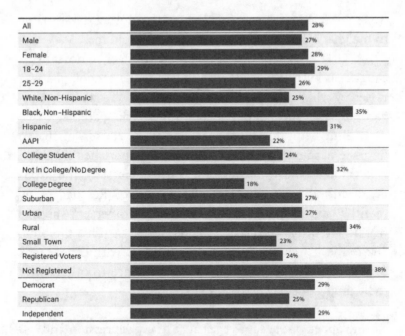

All	28%
Male	27%
Female	28%
18-24	29%
25-29	26%
White, Non-Hispanic	25%
Black, Non-Hispanic	35%
Hispanic	31%
AAPI	22%
College Student	24%
Not in College/No Degree	32%
College Degree	18%
Suburban	27%
Urban	27%
Rural	34%
Small Town	23%
Registered Voters	24%
Not Registered	38%
Democrat	29%
Republican	25%
Independent	29%

Figure I.2. 18–29-year-olds who indicate that they have been bothered by the following problem at least several days in the last two weeks: "Thoughts that you would be better off dead, or thoughts of hurting yourself in some way."

Source: Harvard IOP Youth Poll, April 2021

Zoomers are twice as likely as Americans over thirty to be afflicted by mental health challenges like these. The health care system in the United States, and in most parts of the world, is unable to keep up with demand.

Before the pandemic, I met Katherine, a then-nineteen-year-old young woman from one of Georgia's wealthiest communities. I was interested in speaking with her about current events. She quickly turned the conversation personal, however. In front of two dozen other teens from surrounding schools, she opened up and shared a period of her life that was so dark, she felt incapable of facing another day—unable to make another human connection, she told me.

A gifted student when she was younger, whose peers caught up with her academically by middle school, she was raised by what she describes as affluent "you're going to Harvard, or some super-fancy school, super-strict parents."

Falling behind in more than one of her classes, unable to find the academic and mental health support her situation necessitated, she was overcome with depression and anxiety, eventually dropping out of high school. Rescued many months later by the grace of a teacher, at nineteen, she was working to finish the classes she needed to earn her diploma. She found it important in our focus group with other teens to reflect and offer hope and some guidance to others who sadly might one day walk in her shoes:

> I dropped out because the cause of my depression and anxiety was taking so much of my time that I wasn't getting any work done. My new homeroom teacher was really, really supportive, and helped me find hope so I could actually get towards (*sic*) graduating and take that stress off my shoulders. But you just find someone to talk to. Like if you're not capable of getting professional help, just having someone to talk to saved me.

Generation Z's American Dream isn't to own a house and raise a family with an eye toward living more comfortably than their parents. That's a fantasy in a nation that has mortgaged their children's future to fund their own present. For many of the Zoomers I talk to, their dream includes an education that prepares them to live a full and happy life, managing four-, five-, and sometimes six-figure student debt, and not having to resort to the back pages of the internet to find the four roommates they need to avoid being priced out of housing after graduation. The fortunate ones, they tell me, are able to save enough money for therapy.

Being conscious of Generation Zers, their stressors, the life they've led, and where they will lead us all is far from a trivial pursuit. To inspire them to action, whether it's in the arena of politics, or any commercial or cultural venture, requires an understanding, if not appreciation, for what has shaped them to this point.

Competitive, well-fought political campaigns for the presidency are often the prism through which a generation determines what they feel is right and what is wrong

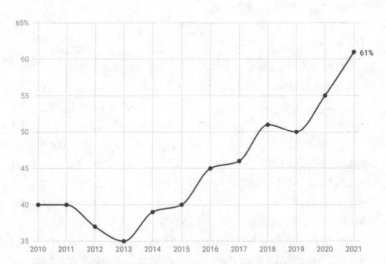

Figure I.3. 18–29-year-olds who strongly or somewhat agree that "the government should spend more to reduce poverty."

Source: Harvard IOP Youth Poll, 2010–2021

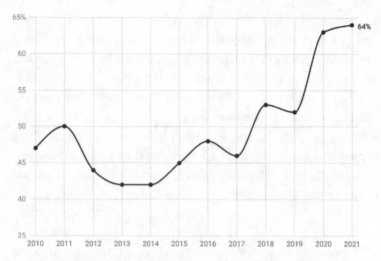

Figure I.4. 18–29-year-olds who strongly or somewhat agree that "basic health insurance is a right for all people, and if someone has no means of paying for it, the government should provide it."

Source: Harvard IOP Youth Poll, 2010–2021

in society. Like our quadrennial obsession with Olympic sporting events, there is heightened attention on public policy that just does not exist otherwise. Every four years, millions of young Americans are welcomed into a debate about their future. And while most will not be able to articulate the details of tax, climate, or foreign policy, they are more than prepared to form opinions on which of the myriad issues are of greatest importance to them—and on which side they sit.

As the group of young Americans eligible to vote has evolved from millennials to Generation Z over the last six years, we have found a cohort that is more engaged, displays more progressive values, and favors a more active federal government.

Whether you praise him or wished he was impeached, it is impossible to overestimate the influence Donald Trump has had on the personal and political development of Generation Z. Transformational leaders, for good and for evil, have that effect. They serve as orienting points or touchstones for generations of youths, allowing for ideas and movements to coalesce into a coherent vocabulary and goal. The Germany of the late 1920s and 1930s saw the indoctrination and rise of Hitler Youth. JFK inspired a generation to service in the 1960s. Reagan created a contemporary conservatism attractive to young baby boomers and Gen Xers in the 1980s. Obama held sway over millennials in the 2000s. And then Trump.

Given the significant levels of youth support President Obama enjoyed in 2008 and 2012, and their preference for a third Democratic term in 2016, President Trump had his work cut out for him if he was to truly succeed in his inaugural pledge to "lift our sights, heal our divisions"[9] and establish a rapport with Generation Z. The divisions between his politics and the politics of Generation Z were measured not in feet but miles. In the first Harvard Kennedy School Institute of Politics youth survey of his presidency, taken within the first one-hundred-day window, only a third (32 percent) of voters under thirty approved of his performance.[10] His ratings were underwater with Generation Z regardless of gender, race, geography, and education level.

On trade and immigration—two of the policy issues President Trump seemed most invested in—after several years of stability in Harvard IOP polling, youth opinion turned sharply away from Trump and the Republican Party. Between 2016 and 2021, the number of young Americans who agree that "our country's goal in trade policy should be to eliminate all barriers to trade and employment so that we have a truly global economy" increased by 12 percentage points.

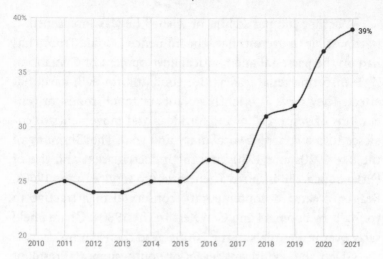

Figure I.5. 18–29-year-olds who strongly or somewhat agree that "our country's goal in trade policy should be to eliminate all barriers to trade and employment so that we have a truly global economy."

Source: Harvard IOP Youth Poll, 2010–2021

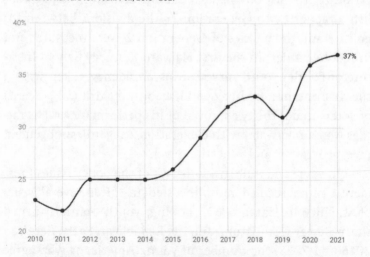

Figure I.6. 18–29-year-olds who strongly or somewhat agree that "recent immigration into this country has done more good than harm."

Source: Harvard IOP Youth Poll, 2010–2021

Youth agreement that "recent immigration into this country has done more good than harm" increased by 8 points over the same time frame. In other words, if Trump was advocating for it, young Americans were not; almost every time, Gen Z would lead others in taking the opposite tack.

When our 2017 IOP spring survey asked Zoomers for one piece of advice they would offer the president in order to move the country forward, the message two students and I delivered to Trump counselors Kellyanne Conway and Bill Stepien in the White House was clear and prescient: "uniting our country should be the top priority." Other open-ended responses from our survey included:

> I would say that he's already done a lot to change the way things are handled in our country. But to move it forward we need to work on becoming one as a country.

> Be strong against America's enemies, and compassionate to the American people.

> Do whatever you can to ease racial and religious tensions because if not, something terrible is going to happen.

Trump's unpopularity among young and old alike (he received the lowest ratings for an incoming president in modern polling history, according to Gallup[11]) was soon demonstrated by a crowd far larger than the one that had attended his inauguration. On the second day of his presidency, between three million and five million people in the United States took to the streets in hundreds of locations to support the Women's March, a multigenerational outpouring of support for women, organized on Facebook in the immediate aftermath of the 2016 election.[12]

The largest single-day march up to that point in US history, the Women's March was, according to its organizers, a struggle "for the protection of our rights, our safety, our health, and our families." Unsurprisingly, these were the same concerns Zoomers would express to me in my interviews, focus groups, and town meetings that I held later that year and throughout the duration of Trump's presidency.

Also, on day two of the presidency, White House press secretary Sean Spicer insisted in his first official briefing that Trump had "the largest audience to witness an inauguration—period—both in person and around the globe."[13] It was obviously not true, and after leaving government seven months later, Spicer said that he "absolutely regretted it."[14]

Gen Zers' outrage at what they believed—since the election and transition—to be a plot to strip away objective truth, our rights, and democracy continued into the following week. On January 27, 2017, Trump announced the first of four "Muslim bans," which prevented individuals from seven Muslim-majority countries from visiting the United States for 90 days, banned Syrian refugees from entering the country indefinitely, and prohibited any other refugees from coming into the country for 120 days.

Soon after, while visiting CPAC,* Trump's 2016 chief strategist Steve Bannon (who three-plus years later would be the recipient of a last-minute presidential pardon) boasted to those who seemed surprised by the rapidly rising xenophobia from the White House that "It was all in the speeches. He

---

* The Conservative Political Action Conference, the country's most influential annual gathering of conservative politicians and activists.

went around to these rallies, but those speeches had a tremendous amount of content in them, right?"[15]

Speaking in the third person at a campaign rally late in 2015 in Mount Pleasant, South Carolina, Trump said:

> Donald J. Trump is calling for a complete shutdown of Muslims entering the United States until our country's representatives can figure out what the hell is going on![16]

The old adage that elections have consequences had rarely before seemed more apt. Suddenly borders were closed, decades-long multilateral relationships fractured, opportunities for a more peaceful and just world felt squandered— just as Trump had promised and planned. According to the Harvard IOP youth poll, most members of Generation Z believed administration priorities of building a wall and repealing and replacing Obamacare would do significant harm to the country, their family, or both. And while Trump and his party were enjoying the early spoils of their election victory, 62 percent of Black Zoomers were telling us that they felt seriously under attack, with nearly half of Hispanics feeling the same way.[17]

The Trump presidency made Generation Z feel less secure in just about every sense of the word; rather than acknowledging this, Trump and his cabinet only exacerbated problems already present. Day after day, young Americans saw their country and government breaking into a million little pieces. We were in "disarray" and headed "downhill," Columbus, Ohio–area students told me in the late spring of 2017 when I visited.

In addition to enacting that first travel ban, within his first *ten* days in office President Trump

- issued executive orders to scale back the Affordable Care Act and begin construction of a border wall;

- reversed the Obama administration's halt on the Keystone XL and Dakota Access Pipelines;

- announced his intention to investigate alleged voter fraud from the 2016 presidential election;

- added political aide Steve Bannon to the National Security Council;

- initiated his first international dispute, hanging up on Australian prime minister Malcolm Turnbull; and

- fired acting attorney general Sally Yates, who refused to defend the travel ban, which she argued was unconstitutional.

It was, by all measures, as audacious an entry into government service as there's ever been. His supporters were delighted; most Zoomers were devastated.

By the beginning of month six, Trump had told the country of his intention to withdraw from the Paris Agreement on climate change, reminding an already anxious nation, "I was elected to represent the citizens of Pittsburgh, not Paris."[18] Ironically, Hillary Clinton beat Trump handily in Pittsburgh's Allegheny County, 56 percent to 40 percent,[19] and in 2020 Biden would win 60 percent of the vote there.[20]

Trump would find public opinion staunchly opposed to this action, as was the case for so many of his acts in office.

A *Washington Post*/ABC News poll found that opposition to Trump's exit plan for Paris outpaced support by nearly a two-to-one margin, 59 percent to 28 percent. Among the under-forty cohort of Gen Z and millennials, opposition was marked at two-thirds.[21]

While the norm-busting transition and early months of the Trump presidency were jarring for many, for Generation Z—whose members became politically conscious during the age of "No Drama Obama"—the change was seminal. In a January 2019 article for *Pacific Standard,* Jared Keller explained:

> Two years later, the physiological effects of the Trump administration aren't going away. A growing body of research has tracked the detrimental impacts of Trump-related stress on broad segments of the American population, from young adults to women, to racial and LGBT communities.[22]

Other studies confirmed these insights, showing how major sociopolitical events can affect individuals' psychology and physiology, with age-related vulnerability as a factor.[23] "Although young adults usually think of stressors as the personal problems, imminent threats, or daily hassles that penetrate their everyday lives,"[24] Fordham University professor Lindsay T. Hoyt noted that her 2016 study "suggests that macro-level events (at a national scale) can influence their health and well-being."[25]

Through social media, Gen Zers have been exposed to, and feel a connection to, the climate and their peers in all parts of the world. As children, the world for baby boomers and many Gen Xers often began and ended on their block; for Gen Z, there is no limit, and with this brings an unparalleled understanding of humanity and empathy. Therefore, attacks on the environment, whole groups of people, and Muslim bans are fundamentally at odds with who they are.

As if existing as an adolescent isn't challenging enough in itself, especially with the enhanced pressures created by mobile phones and social media, the nature of our politics added a dangerous and toxic level of anxiety. Higher levels of cortisol, a pathway to headaches, sleep problems, digestive ailments, concentration impairment, anxiety, and depression were forming a "pit of despair" in millions of Americans, according to Keller.

Transitioning from the calm, thoughtful assuredness of President Obama to a reality-show president elected without majority support was a most unsettling way for Generation Z to come of age. I came face-to-face with this anxiety and uneasiness during the first in a series of in-depth conversations I hosted with small groups of high school and college students from across the country that summer of 2017.

When I asked my standard question, "What unites us as Americans?" Katie, a nursing student from Southern Illinois, quickly answered, "Fear unites us."

Before I could even follow up with "Fear of what?" she continued:

Let's see, fear of death. Fear of our rights being infringed upon. Fear of the future for our kids. Fear for our family. Fear for our health.

Chris, a rising college senior from Northern Kentucky echoed her sentiment. "The thing that really brings us together as Americans," he said, "is being afraid and paranoid of ab . . . so . . . lute . . . ly everything. Sandy Hook and the club shootings, when those happened, everybody lost all of their shit at the same time. This is happening to everyone!"

Fear for their future. Fear for our future. Fear was on its way to seizing the soul of the next generation before most of its members reached adulthood. In dozens of similar conversations from that moment forward, the extreme levels of stress and anxiety I witnessed in Columbus were impossible to miss. To this day, few moments in a focus group have had a greater impact on me than when I asked for an explanation of what older generations don't get about Generation Z. Grace, a biology student about to turn twenty-one at the time, told me:

> An older generation would not understand walking into a classroom and thinking about how easy it would be for someone to shoot it up. The same daily weight on an adult's shoulders over bills or taxes is what children feel about living or dying.

While many in Washington and on cable TV were fixated on the seemingly bizarre notion of using psychoanalysis and the Twenty-Fifth Amendment to remove President Trump from office his first summer in Washington, it was apparent to me that our attention should instead be on the fragile mental health of Generation Z.

Not long ago, young people told me that "opportunity" was the thread that connected us as Americans; by 2017 I was reminded that it "now divides us because not everyone can have it." For Generation Z, fear, stress, and anxiety were the dominant forces shaping the generation.

The young people I spoke with that summer spent

surprisingly little time railing against President Trump, however. Generation Z recognized and voiced more quickly than others that it was structural deficiencies in our institutions, and not any one individual, that were to blame for the position in which they, and our nation, now found themselves. Trump was a symptom, not the root problem, they would tell me. The failure of older generations of elected officials from both parties to address myriad concerns related to systemic inequality, and an economy leaving too many behind, were among the ailments these young Americans sought to cure. Generation Z is introspective. Its members are comforted and not burdened when they challenge our leaders, traditions, the meaning of exceptionalism, and even themselves.

In what the Republican Party might one day consider a cruel twist of fate, Donald Trump single-handedly removed one of the most challenging barriers to political engagement. Generation Z learned a lesson that some never do. Its members now know extremely well the difference politics can make in the health of our democracy—and also in their own day-to-day lives.

Things would get far worse, however, before Gen Zers could begin to make them better.

2

JUST A STUDENT

The oldest members of Generation Z were in high school when a protest targeting economic inequality took shape two blocks north of New York City's Wall Street in September 2011. The encampment that embodied the early days of the Occupy Wall Street push did not include much of a Gen Z presence in those days. But by firmly establishing a set of facts about the inequities of the US financial and political systems, constructing a simple "us against them" narrative—and through the long tail of its cause—Occupy became the first of five landmark events interwoven with Generation Zers' personal experiences that shaped their political value set—and will in turn shape America's in the days and decades ahead. The Trump presidency, Parkland, the George Floyd murder, and Greta Thunberg's School Strike for Climate are the other four.

When the financial crisis struck in 2008, none of Gen Z and only about half of the millennial generation were in the workforce, but neither were they shielded from the messy aftermath that the market collapse wrought. The Great Recession eliminated 20 percent of the net worth from four in every five American families.[1] By some measures, over thirty million individuals lost their jobs.[2] Ten million homes were taken.[3] Largely unrecognized by older generations, millions more Zoomers bore the disquieting memories and cognitive impact of suffering loved ones.

Tommy, a Zoomer from Chicago, told me in 2010:

> Throughout the past few years, I've had to see a lot of family members lose their homes because they were out of work. Most of my family does construction and that's all they know. . . . Construction took a hard hit and there were points when they wouldn't work for three, four weeks at a time. And it only goes down from there. So, like I said, a lot of my family members . . . they lost their homes, their cars and all that. So, yes, I was involved personally.

Like their older millennial cousins who experienced the trauma of 9/11, Generation Z was (and is) at greater risk for emotional and behavioral troubles because of the 2008 financial crisis.[4] Developmental psychologists know that the aftereffects of the Great Recession resulted in a cohort of children having a more challenging time trusting others and relating to their peers. Researchers from Columbia and Princeton universities found that boys in particular were at greater risk for behavior problems such as vandalism and drug and alcohol abuse. Gen Z's overall sense of well-being is frail—a diagnosis well established before they were compelled to confront active shooter drills, the coronavirus pandemic, and other realities of adolescent and young adult life in an increasingly confusing and chaotic America.[5] In response to the financial crisis, Zoomer boys living with single mothers, in particular, proved the most vulnerable.[6]

One of the greatest legacies of the Occupy Wall Street movement was that it recognized and gave voice to the millions of hardworking people of every generation who were still trying to recover and decode the disorder triggered by Wall Street three years earlier. "I gave a lot of stuff away, man," Billy, a Gen X single parent of a Gen Z high school student (whose teenage girlfriend also lived in the same home), told me at the time.

> Things that I liked, my motorcycle, guitars . . . I had to sell. But I had to do it for them; to keep a roof over their heads. It's been a hell of a ride for me, man, . . . you know, trying to keep them on track.

He shared in our Memphis focus group that he was ready and willing to do anything for his family, but when the recession hit, opportunities closed in all around him.

"Watching the family car get 'repo'd' is not something that I, or my kids, should ever have to see! The impact on our children had to be significant" is what Fred, a Gen X dad of three Zoomers living in Cobb County, Georgia, emailed me in 2019, after I shared research on attitudes related to the American Dream on *Morning Joe*.[7]

Countless intergenerational experiences like these drove then-twenty-year-old Josh Dworning to drop $300 on an Amtrak ticket taking him from Florida to New York City so he could, like thousands of others, set up camp in Lower Manhattan's Zuccotti Park and fight for a more responsible capitalism. "I'm no crazy radical or something," he said in September 2011. "I'm just a student who believes in something."[8]

Occupy Wall Street was a sort of gift from the old to the young. Kalle Lasn, a silent-generation Canadian magazine publisher and radical provocateur, was inspired to kick-start the movement by California college students who occupied campus buildings to protest rising tuition—and the pro-democracy and anti-austerity uprisings in Iran, Spain, Tunisia, and Egypt—during the first decade of the 2000s.

Occupy was referred to in its early days as a sort of "charming mess"[9] because what the movement lacked in leadership, it enjoyed in verve and passion. Activists would say that their ultimate goal was to level the playing field between "the ultra-rich and the rest of the population."[10] The dream scenario for Lasn was even more grandiose: "a total rethinking of western consumerism that throws into question how we measure progress."[11]

From the beginning, its organizing thesis was mocked by political leaders and pundits on the right. This derision played into Occupy's hand, which above all pitted the self-interest of the 1 percent against the other 99 percent. "No candidate is going to win by catering to the alleged Occupy Wall Street vote," then senator Jim DeMint, a Tea Party Republican from South Carolina, crowed in early 2012.[12] Kayleigh McEnany, who would later become President Trump's fourth press secretary, labeled the young activists "prodigal protestors" at the time, writing for the Daily Caller that their demands were extraordinary and predicting they would "squander the very wealth they seek."[13]

While history shows that Occupy Wall Street was unable to score significant policy victories and had a difficult time organizing itself coherently—once refusing to let civil rights icon Congressman John Lewis address an Atlanta gathering[14]—its impact on Generation Z was nevertheless profound. The attention concentrated on corporations and the super-wealthy who don't pay their fair share, the fight for a living wage, Generation Z's critique of the unchecked capitalism of today—all find their roots in the soil of Zuccotti

Park. As Occidental College professor Peter Dreier explained: "the one percent versus the 99 percent—redefined the decade and our politics. It put a target on the back of Wall Street, corporate America, and the super-rich. . . . The news media also began paying more attention to these issues."[15]

From the strategic use of art, fashion, and memes, Lasn and his team created an unmistakable street-style aura to Occupy, allowing the movement to connect with and speak to young people worldwide.[16] It was the substance measured in the human suffering, however, that galvanized the movement as it swept across hundreds of US cities. Leading into the protests:

- Youth unemployment reached modern highs at close to 20 percent.[17]

- Student debt levels were soaring.[18]

- Nearly half of those under thirty were living with their parents.[19]

- Investors and credit were hard to come by.[20]

- First-time home ownership had sunk to modern lows.[21]

While tens of millions were barely hanging on, Americans learned that Wall Street firms Citigroup and Merrill Lynch paid $9 billion in bonuses after losing a combined $54 billion and receiving federal bailouts worth $55 billion.[22] They were hardly the only ones. A report from the New York State attorney general summarized the situation plainly:

When the banks did well, their employees were paid well. When the banks did poorly, their employees were paid well. And when the banks did very poorly, they were bailed out by taxpayers and their employees were still paid well. Bonuses and overall compensation did not vary significantly as profits diminished.[23]

Two recoveries to the same crisis had exposed two Americas. The net wealth of the top 10 percent was rising again, as the recession ended, while the opposite was true for the more than 150 million in the bottom half. The majority of working-class Americans were seeing their already trifling slice of America's wealth contract from 1.7 percent in early 2009 to only .3 percent two years later.[24]

Facing the harsh reality of the government's complicity in allowing corporate greed to run amok—and attacking it at its source to shield future generations from the indignities of their parents—became a unifying cause. It is now elemental to Generation Z.

Within weeks of the Zuccotti Park kickoff and marches that closed the Brooklyn Bridge and other parts of Manhattan, our Harvard IOP youth survey found that one-third of young Americans under thirty were following the demonstration, and through open-ended response questions, we found evidence that the Occupy voices were indeed carrying and influencing the opinions of the next generation.[25] Historian and writer Jon Meacham surmised that America's wealth gap was "once again becoming an organizing political principle in the country,"[26] after a generation or more of politicians, from Richard Nixon to Sarah Palin, favoring cultural over economic populism.

By early 2012, as the eldest Zoomers were preparing for life after high school, the Harvard IOP youth survey found that addressing income inequality was of greater importance for them than climate change, the rising influence of China, conflicts between Israel and Palestine, and promoting stable democracies in the Middle East and North Africa. This was further evidence of the impact Occupy had in shaping public opinion and influencing the hearts and minds of the next generation at this critical stage in its members' maturation.

Despite all of these activities and shifts in public sentiment, much of the political establishment was still unprepared and ill-equipped in 2015 for the groundswell of support Bernie Sanders and his populist message would have among Americans less than one-third his age. When Senator Sanders first indicated he was running for president, it was treated with incredulity in both political parties. In Washington, DC, where he was a backbencher in the House and the Senate, it was regarded as a joke. Gen Zers didn't get the joke, however, and they would soon say to their elders, including the traditional wing of the Democratic Party, something equivalent to "The joke's on you!"

The day before he announced his first presidential run in 2015, Senator Sanders questioned the very underpinnings of our political and economic system and did so in plain language Generation Z could understand and soon rally around.

> Ninety-nine percent of all new income generated today goes to the top 1 percent. The top one-tenth of 1 percent owns as much wealth as the bottom 90 percent. Does anybody think that that is the kind of economy this country should have? Do we think it's moral?[27]

These convictions, which would come to be shared by an eclectic set of activists, scholars, athletes, entertainers, and even Pope Francis—who characterized modern capitalism as "immoral and unsustainable"[28]—ultimately were not enough

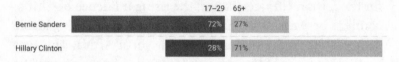

	17–29	65+
Bernie Sanders	72%	27%
Hillary Clinton	28%	71%

Figure 2.1. 2016 Democratic primary and caucus preferences by age.

Source: Public Opinion Strategies analysis of exit polls, *The Wall Street Journal*

to outlast Hillary Clinton in her second bid for the Democratic nomination in 2016. It is acknowledged, however, that Sanders and his legions of youthful, passionate supporters exerted more influence over the Democratic Party's future, its platform, and the country than any losing candidate in modern times.

"The central dynamic in this really was age as much as anything," Sanders strategist Mark Longabaugh said in a postelection debrief.[29] With 72 percent of primary and caucus voters under thirty in his corner, Sanders won a higher share of the youth vote than even Obama did in 2008.[30]

Without this near wholesale support of Gen Z in 2016, Sanders would have been a less relevant factor moving forward—and expanding health care, making college accessible, raising the minimum wage, and tackling climate change would not have been as dominant as they were in framing the 2020 Democratic primary debates. Now these issues are, along with the White House's expansive COVID-19 relief package and the ambitious and far-reaching infrastructure and jobs plan, the pillars of a transformative Biden domestic agenda.

Spurred on by progressive periodicals like *The Atlantic* and *The New Yorker* restoring the phrase "late capitalism," if not the original meaning, into the lexicon of the young left, the image of American capitalism suffered as a wide swath of youths grew more comfortable shaking up what labor movement expert Richard Yeselson calls "the big, giant, totalistic system that is underneath everything."[31] According to Gallup, positive views of capitalism among Generation Z and millennials shrank from 66 percent the year before Occupy Wall Street was birthed in 2010, to only 51 percent a decade later. Among the youngest members of that cohort (eighteen- to twenty-nine-year-olds), support was even lower.

Whether it was based on rebounding 401(k)s, or a blindness to the unforgiving path ahead for the next generation—older, purportedly wiser Americans did not share these same views. In 2019, 61 percent of Gen Xers reported positive views toward capitalism (+3 points since 2010), and the combined baby boomer and silent generation category rated capitalism 10 points higher in 2019 than they did a decade earlier.[32]

"Children grow up to work until they're mentally unstable and call it normal" is how a Generation Z voter described capitalism to me in early 2020.

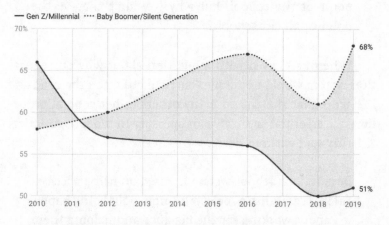

Figure 2.2. Positive views toward capitalism by age, 2010–2019.

Source: Gallup

Another first-time Gen Z voter said, "Capitalism leaves too many people homeless, sick, and jobless. You lose your job and then you lose your home and health care. And then you get sick and die. Capitalism does not have enough protection for the workers, the lifeblood of our economy."

Even when the subject in one of my Gen Z focus groups isn't free-market democracy, capitalism almost invariably finds itself in the conversation. In the summer of 2020, I met Kristina, a bright, then-sixteen-year-old rising high school junior who attends both a technical high school and an art school in Ohio. I have little doubt that she will soon fulfill her dream to "make it somewhere." When talking about the quality of her state's and our nation's schools, Kristina quickly connected her concerns about education to what she sees as the uneven and warped incentives of modern capitalism.

> We're not learning things that we're going to apply in real life. I go to a vocational school and that's the point of the school, but why wouldn't that be the point of all the schools?

When I followed with a question about why our education system would not design curricula to teach the civic and life skills that she and so many others in her generation believe are essential to survive and prosper in modern America, Kristina said without delay:

> Because our school system is based on being successful in a capitalistic society. It's not about being happy, it's about working for the big guys and helping them make money and then you can spend your money on their products.

The lack of responsiveness and empathy baby boomer officials bring to Gen Zers' perspective enrages Zoomers. The cost of college, the cost of housing, the cost of health care, the ability to save some money for tough times are all among the everyday stressors for Generation Z. All of this was, of course, far less daunting to baby boomers at a similar life stage.

From the 1960s until the early 1980s, it was not uncommon for baby boomers and Gen Xers to work summer jobs and, in those thirteen to fourteen weeks, save enough money for one year of college tuition, without taking on student loans. By the early 2000s, it would take at least a year while working a minimum-wage job to earn enough for one year of tuition (based upon an averaging of the cost of all public and private four-year colleges).[33]

Young Americans are angry and anxious because they know the clock for their families and their futures is ticking. They are sweating it. Steven Pearlstein, in *Can American Capitalism Survive?*, argued that inequality is near impossible to overcome as you age—it is connected to physical and mental health, educational achievement, and marriage rates.[34] Generation Z is connecting the dots between political and economic policy decisions that protect the standing of the very few, while millions in this generation struggle for a shot at making their own best life in America. Without addressing the systemic inequalities now, their futures are less bright than they should be. This is the urgency behind their fight.

Free-market capitalism is under renewed pressure from a generation willing to examine underlying premises of US society. They perceive that they are living in an age of narrowing opportunities and perilous consequences. Not since President Harry S. Truman's Fair Deal policy of the late 1940s, which argued that prosperity cannot be maintained without a fair distribution of opportunity, was economic justice squarely at the forefront of American politics. Gen Z is unmoved by statistics showing that aggregate wealth has increased in this country. Although less overtly religious than any previous generation, Zoomers take more seriously the biblical admonition that if one suffers, all suffer. And they are acutely aware that when the economic data are analyzed through the lens of race, the differences in suffering are staggering. The median and mean wealth of Black families in America are more than 85 percent less than the wealth of white families.

According to the Federal Reserve, the median net worth in 2019 of white families in America was $188,200, while it was $24,100 for Black or African American families. Among Hispanic and Latino families in the United States, median net worth, at $36,100, was far closer to that of Black families than white.

Measuring average net worth tells a similar story. Mean net worth in 2019 for white families was nearly $1 million; but for Hispanic and Latino families it was $165,500, and for Black or African American families it was $142,500.[35]

Among the Generation Z and millennial cohorts in the Federal Reserve Board data set,[36] the picture is even more bleak. Median wealth of white families thirty-five and younger was $25,400, while that of Hispanic and Latino families was $11,200. The median wealth of the youngest Black families in America was $600—roughly the cost of two months of groceries in a place like St. Louis, Missouri.[37]

"Capitalism in America is too discriminatory. It isn't fair at all," said Jamie, a Gen Z voter from Albuquerque in a 2019 focus group. "Anyone that is poor, or of color, has to work harder to get to the same place." No one needs data from the Fed to come to that conclusion today. That capitalism was supported by only about one in three African Americans

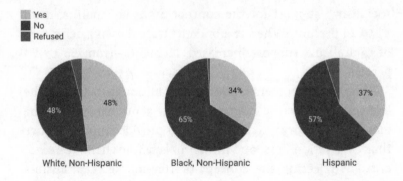

Figure 2.3. Support of capitalism among 18–29-year-olds by race and ethnicity.

Source: Harvard IOP, April 2020

under thirty in the spring 2020 Harvard IOP youth survey, therefore, was unsurprising.

Years of Harvard IOP polling data, as well as reviews from Gallup and other sources, show that while a majority of Generation Z do not support capitalism, the traditional form of socialism is also not viewed as a panacea. Despite what media pundits often lead us to believe, only 15 percent of Americans under the age of thirty identify as socialist. Thirty percent support socialism, more broadly. Capitalism (at 45 percent support), with all its flaws, is still far more popular than socialism.

In 2018, my students and I conducted an experiment in which half of survey respondents in our youth poll were provided a dictionary definition for both socialism and capitalism before we asked for their opinions. The other half was asked for their opinions without being given definitions. Among the respondents who were presented a definition of socialism,* support for the concept dropped 7 points, from 31 to 24 percent. When respondents were shown a definition of capitalism,† support increased 11 points—from 43 to 54 percent.[38]

The more Zoomers knew about traditional socialism, the less they liked it; the more they knew about capitalism, the more promise they saw. These findings provided more evidence that Generation Zers, and millennials before them, were not outright rejecting the concept of free-market capitalism—they were telling us that they disapprove of the manner in which it is practiced today.

With majorities of young Americans rebuffing capitalism, and even more renouncing classic forms of socialism, what do Zoomers want? When I first put this question to a dozen undergraduates at Franklin & Marshall College in Lancaster, Pennsylvania, they succinctly explained that young Americans are seeking a better, modern form of capitalism that rewards the industriousness and innovation of all Americans, not just the shrinking slice of privileged whites graduating from college with a network of connections and little debt. They are looking for a plan that holds Wall Street and monopolies accountable, while also creating a social safety net for those willing to work but unable to keep up—Square Deal meets New Deal, they told me.

First are the Square Deal principles shared by President

---

* Socialism: any of various economic and political theories advocating collective or governmental ownership and administration of the means of production and distribution of goods.

† Capitalism: an economic system characterized by private or corporate ownership of capital goods, by investments that are determined by private decision, and by prices, production, and the distribution of goods that are determined mainly by competition in a free market.

Theodore Roosevelt on a trip to Osawatomie, Kansas, in 1910:

> I mean not merely that I stand for fair play under the present rules of the game, but that I stand for having those rules changed so as to work for a more substantial equality of opportunity and of reward for equally good service. . . . Now, this means that our government, National and State, must be freed from the sinister influence or control of special interests. Exactly as the special interests of cotton and slavery threatened our political integrity before the Civil War, so now the great special business interests too often control and corrupt the men and methods of government for their own profit. We must drive the special interests out of politics.[39]

Second is the New Deal ethos outlined twenty-three years later by T.R.'s fifth cousin. In President Franklin Delano Roosevelt's first inaugural address, he could not "deny the dark realities of the moment":

> The measure of the restoration lies in the extent to which we apply social values more noble than mere monetary profit. Happiness lies not in the mere possession of money; it lies in the joy of achievement, in the thrill of creative effort. The joy and the moral stimulation of work no longer must be forgotten in the mad chase of evanescent profits. These dark days, my friends, will be worth all they cost us if they teach us that our true destiny is not to be ministered unto but to minister to ourselves and to our fellow men. . . . Restoration calls, however, not for changes

in ethics alone. This Nation is asking for action, and action now.[40]

Generation Z lives today in a world both presidents would recognize, and as the Franklin & Marshall students explained to me, politicians who are able to meld these two ideas would easily win the hearts and minds of this generation. As the Biden administration endeavors to expand the conventional political definition of American infrastructure from roads, rails, runways, and bridges to now include the underpinnings of a caring economy, Democratic policy makers are as close as they've been in decades to meeting the economic demands of America's youths.

Dubbed a "lost generation" by the Federal Reserve Bank of St. Louis,[41] incessantly reminded by politicians and pundits that the American Dream was nonexistent, "dead," and "a nightmare,"[42] why wouldn't Generation Z question and search for ways to improve capitalism? As Diego, a computer programmer from Pima County, Arizona, put it to me not long before the 2020 election:

> I'm thirty, and there have been two recessions and we live in a dystopia now. I'm pretty fearful.

While the prospects of the next generation earning more than the last faded over the last half century in the United States,[43] citizens of Northern European countries like Finland, Denmark, Norway, and Sweden, along with Germany and New Zealand, were all showing greater opportunity for upward mobility.[44]

Zoomers yearn for a capitalism open to everyone and do not shy away from debating the merits of other political and economic systems. The data-driven outcomes from the modern Nordic version of market-driven social democracies—less poverty, more innovation, more family time, and overall a more relaxed, healthy, and satisfied citizenry[45]—are worth exploring and learning from, they tell me.

In a group discussion I held with a few dozen Zoomers in early 2020, one of our participants, Hannah, originally from Norway, preemptively defended her generation's decidedly loose definition of socialism, leading to a robust and unexpected exchange with a young African American car salesman struggling to afford an apartment in his hometown due to gentrification.

> *Hannah:* I'm Norwegian. I know what socialism actually is in a country, and it's being thrown around in America like it's an awful, evil thing. Maybe it won't work for this country completely like it would for Norway, but if not, we shouldn't be demonizing this word without people fully understanding what that even means.

> *Jay:* I feel like we should be demonizing capitalism. It's a terrible way to live. Everything's about money, money, money. It's terrible.

I have found the exchange between Hannah and Jay to be commonplace in the college towns I've traveled to over the last decade or more. For as long as I have been conducting surveys, young Americans have never been comfortable with traditional ideological labels and boxes. Millennials, and now Zoomers, have been fiercely independent in this way. Generation Z is in search of the right amalgam of devices to begin eradicating the systemic injustices holding us back as individuals and a nation. This includes conversation and debate around the size and priorities of government, how other countries develop productive partnerships between the public and private sectors, and what we can learn from other democracies that have earned the trust of their citizens.

During the Great Recession, overall trust in the US federal government fell across the board and has hovered around 20 percent ever since.[46] In the 2021 spring Harvard IOP youth poll, 20 percent of Zoomers said the same for Wall Street.[47] For billionaires in 2020, trust was 16 percent.[48]

It's no wonder that in the most recent wave (2017–2020) of the World Values Survey, only less than a quarter of Generation Z reported having confidence in "the [US] government." Three times that number showed little to no confidence (74 percent), meaning that the net confidence rating of government is negative 50 for Zoomers—giving the United States a 41st ranking of out of 54 nations analyzed. Other national governments that lack youths' confidence on the same scale as the United States include: Serbia (net confidence, −45), the Czech Republic (−46), Brazil (−47), Hungary (−48), Nicaragua (−50), and Italy (−53).[49]

Generation Zers will continue to search, protest, and fight until they are confident that our public and private institutions are on track and reflective of their values.

W e know that Americans generally seek a more active Rooseveltian-style government but worry that due to what they see as the stranglehold big business has on politicians, the changes necessary to reform these systems will be exceedingly difficult to accomplish. So, with little confidence in our government and the business sector, Generation Zers are taking things into their own hands by linking their political values to their burgeoning influence as consumers. To borrow a phrase from the late Randy Shepard, an award-winning advertising strategist and guardian of the United States Marine Corps brand for more than two decades, "We once lived in a time when consumers voted; we now live in an era where voters consume."

Trivialized as "woke" capitalism and the "vanguard of un-freedom" by conservative opinion shapers,[50] consumer politics has been the device of political actors for as long as we've had a republic. From the Boston Tea Party, to the Quaker-led abolitionist "free produce" movement of the eighteenth and nineteenth centuries, to the activism of Rosa Parks in 1955—"boycott," a term not coined until 1880 in Ireland, has been an integral element to nudge civil society forward in the United States and elsewhere.

Rooted in centuries of movements that changed policy, and sometimes history, Generation Z- and millennial-led consumer activism is a central component to the politics of the future, according to Cornell University historian Lawrence Glickman.[51] In many ways, the future is now, as woke capitalism is practiced to some extent by all sides and all demographic groups.

In a February 2020 survey I conducted for *RealClear-Politics*, I found that nearly half of all American adults (48 percent), and a majority from Generation Z say that the political positions of a company have affected their purchasing habits—some buying more, others buying less, based on their connection to a company's or a brand's values. Increasingly, Americans—led by both Democrat and Republican Zoomers and millennials—expect and have a desire for American businesses to take positions on the consequential political or social issues facing the nation.[52]

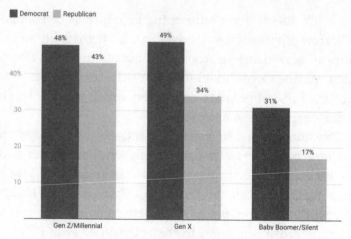

Figure 2.4. Voters who agree that "American businesses have a responsibility to take positions on political or social issues facing the country," by age and party.

Source: RealClear Opinion Research, February 2020

During the Trump presidency, especially after the period that followed the 2017 Las Vegas and 2018 Parkland mass shootings, youth-fueled consumer engagement and activism led to numerous and significant corporate moves toward supporting progressive causes. As youths began organizing after the Parkland shooting in 2018, Dick's Sporting Goods chairman and chief executive Ed Stack started devising a plan to remove assault-style weapons from his shelves, while recognizing that crossing the gun lobby would cost him employees and sales in the short term. Two weeks after the shooting, Dick's, one of the country's largest sellers of firearms, with nearly nine hundred stores in the United States, announced it would no longer sell assault-style weapons while also halting gun and ammunition sales to anyone under the age of twenty-one.[53]

Fortune 500 CEOs grasped which way the political and

economic winds were blowing, and they soon followed Ed Stack's lead. The next day, Walmart also raised the age restriction for purchasing firearms and ammunition to twenty-one.[54] Months after these and other gun-sales restrictions were enacted, a solid majority of both young Democrats and Republicans alike told us that they believe the decisions by Dick's and Walmart to change gun policy were credible and done for the right reasons. Time will tell, but the lasting effect will likely benefit both companies' corporate reputations and their bottom lines. Gen Z and millennial Democrats, in particular, tell us that they are now much more inclined to frequent Dick's and Walmart because of these policy stances (46 percent of Gen Z and millennial Democrats say they will buy more, 28 percent of Republicans say so as well).[55]

Following Dick's and Walmart, which made additional changes to store policy after the El Paso mass shooting in 2019,[56] major American companies stood with the Parkland survivors, severing ties with the NRA, including Delta Air Lines, United Airlines, Enterprise Holdings (the parent company of car rental brands Enterprise, Alamo, and National), Hertz, Avis, Budget, Symantec, TrueCar, MetLife, SimpliSafe, First National Bank of Omaha, and others.[57]

Certainly, consumer boycotts and corporate acts like these are not the sole domain of progressives. One of the more visible examples of grassroots consumer activism during this century was from the right and aimed at country music's Dixie Chicks (now, simply The Chicks) for their criticism in London of President George W. Bush and his imminent invasion of Iraq.[58]

Over its fifty-year history, Hobby Lobby has faced a great deal of scrutiny for applying the conservative values of CEO David Green and his family to its employees and customers. One of its most recent examples was in March 2020, in the early days of the pandemic. At a time when more than ninety major retailers in the nation were temporarily shuttering to prevent community spread of COVID-19, Hobby Lobby resisted, arguing they were an essential business. The decision, they said, was based on a message from God.[59]

While in office, President Trump used the weight of his presidency to publicly call for a boycott of Goodyear tires, which saw its stock immediately drop by 4 percent after the announcement, as well as to endorse boycotts against Macy's, Harley-Davidson, the National Football League, AT&T, Glenfiddich scotch, Comcast, HBO, *Rolling Stone, The Wall Street Journal,* CNBC, Univision, *The Dallas Morning News,* and *The Arizona Republic.*[60]

In April 2021, Trump and numerous members of his party called for a boycott of Major League Baseball, Coca-Cola, and other companies that expressed outrage at Georgia voting-rights restrictions. In the summer of 2020, President Trump and first daughter Ivanka endeavored to counter a boycott from the left and used White House resources to heartily endorse Goya Foods.[61]

What many conservatives label as woke capitalism today, multinational corporations have been calling "corporate social responsibility" for decades. In an increasingly competitive era for customers and talent, most of corporate America recognizes that aligning its values, products, and services to the most diverse, educated, and progressive market entering its prime earning years is not just good PR or good business, but essential to survival. Not long after the 2020 election, a team of analysts from Brookings noted that the 509 counties that voted for Biden accounted for 71 percent of America's economic activity. Meanwhile, Trump's base of 2,547 counties represented only 29 percent of the economy.[62]

The arrival of Generation Z as a political and cultural

force—and an emerging economic one—will only supercharge these efforts. Zoomers know that government alone cannot fix all that ails us, and they expect the private sector to play an integral role in helping to solve both the everyday and more intractable challenges we face. As Zoomers become a larger part of the workforce, the private sector will begin to more closely mirror these values.

Understanding that President Biden, as well as the two Georgia Democratic senators—millennial Jon Ossoff and Raphael Warnock—were elected largely because of the support of Generation Z and historically disenfranchised people of color, corporate America has stepped up the pace with which it is engaging on public issues. Already, Zoomers are modernizing some aspects of capitalism. The more than one hundred American CEOs who spoke out through the Civic Alliance against restricting Georgia voting laws is evidence. Gen Z–forward brands like Abercrombie & Fitch, Lyft, Reddit, and Snapchat were joined by institutionalists JPMorgan Chase, BP, Bain & Company, the World Bank, and dozens of others calling on "elected leaders in every state capitol and in Congress to work across the aisle and ensure that every eligible American has the freedom to easily cast their ballot and participate fully in our democracy."[63]

"C.E.O.s have become the fourth branch of government. They're trying to hold the country together," Jonathan Greenblatt, chief executive of the Anti-Defamation League (ADL), said in reference to business leaders pausing political contributions to certain Republican members of Congress after the January 6, 2021, storming of the Capitol.[64]

Generation Z and the coalition that elected Democrats in 2018 and 2020 are influencing policy to a greater degree than they may realize. Without pressure from thousands of college students who "believed in something," Walmart,

Target, and Amazon likely would not feel the pressure to boost the minimum wage they offer their employees. If not for Generation Z and the political pressure it brought to bear, it's a good bet that the NRA would be on a much better financial footing, and Dick's and Walmart would still be selling deadly weapons to minors. Americans whose names we will never know may be alive today because some teenager couldn't conveniently purchase an assault rifle from his local sporting goods store.

Led by two large generations with similar values and interests, analysts see an economic "youth boom" on the horizon that could be more pronounced and dynamic than the growth led by boomers in the 1990s.[65] In the crassest of capitalistic terms, with the youngest baby boomers close to sixty, their generation is quickly turning irrelevant as the world focuses on Generation Z and millennials.

When General Motors tells us that it is "acutely aware of the responsibility and opportunity to use our scale and resources to drive a better, more inclusive future for all,"[66] it's responding to the values and the market potential of Gen Z. The same goes for Nike, whose extraordinarily successful 2018 advertising blitz featuring Colin Kaepernick could easily have been swapped out for the motto of a high-minded political campaign: "Believe in something. Even if it means sacrificing everything."[67]

In 2019, months after decisive moves by Dick's, Walmart, Nike, and others, the Business Roundtable, a Washington, DC–based association of CEOs, issued a statement recognizing that the American Dream is "fraying" and that the most promising way to build long-term value is by redefining the purpose of a corporation to "promote an economy that serves all Americans—and not just shareholders."[68]

Whether or not that declaration was prompted to soothe

critics on Capitol Hill and an anxious generation of employees, or a genuine indication that the private sector is committed to partnership with all of their stakeholders will take years to discover. It's a marker, though, that the engagement of Generation Z can lead to the recognition of societal concerns and to tangible results when the political process fails or progress is slowed. In the decade since millennials occupied Wall Street parks and numerous college campuses, there's measurable progress toward a modern capitalism wherein the rewards, and not just the losses, are shared by all who contribute.

3

SIX MINUTES IN PARKLAND

During a spring semester that saw Massachusetts hit by four feet of snow and three nor'easters, Valentine's Day in 2018 brought a moment of sunny relief. It was a typically bustling Wednesday at the Institute of Politics, located across from the sprawling Kirkland House, where Facebook was born, and a block north of the icy Charles River separating Cambridge from Boston. Resident fellows, students, and staff were preparing for late-afternoon study groups; my team of undergraduates and I were working on what we thought would be the final touches of the Harvard IOP's thirty-fifth youth survey.

Entering through the frosted glass doors in the newly decorated IOP reception area, where two television monitors were recently installed, I stopped stock-still around 3 P.M. as CNN was beaming footage from a helicopter circling a Florida town that was not yet familiar to most Americans. A female voice was breaking news that Broward County officials had confirmed those three dreaded words: *"Shots were fired."*

About an hour earlier, fifteen hundred miles away from us in Parkland, Florida, an Uber driver took what she thought was a quiet, "normal person" on a thirteen-minute drive from his neighborhood to the school[1] matching the lettering on his burgundy-colored shirt, MSDHS JROTC.[2]

Calmly, the then nineteen-year-old cleared out of the car at 2:19 P.M. with a large backpack the size of a guitar case that contained a lawfully purchased AR-15, magazines, and bullets. The Uber driver thought the young man had a music lesson. She had no idea he was soon to be responsible for one of the deadliest school shootings in history.[3]

Less than two minutes later, at 2:21 P.M., inside Marjory Stoneman Douglas High School (MSD) building 12 (the freshman building), the gunman raised his rifle and unloaded his first rounds in a hallway, killing three students and wounding one.[4]

Three seconds later, he trained his rifle toward a classroom, killing three more and wounding five from inside the doorway.

Investigators reported that the "speed with which the attack happened prevented some students from even having a chance to respond and at least one student was struck while seated at his desk."[5]

At 2:22 P.M. the first call to 911 was placed from the school. The campus-wide fire alarm was activated. Many students thought it was someone playing a Valentine's Day prank following a fire drill from earlier that day.[6] By 2:23 P.M. the alarm was shut off.

Boys and girls were screaming and crying hysterically. Some of the upperclassmen were in hallways telling younger students to "Stop running, guys, it's fine," while in other sections of the school, ashen-faced adults began screaming "CODE RED! CODE RED! Get into your classrooms, now!"

Students who barely acknowledged each other minutes earlier were now holding hands praying, and hiding wherever they could find some cover.

Group texts were flying:

Oh my God, what's that noise? It sounds like somebody's shooting.

Someone's running down our hall with a gun shooting. I love you guys so much!

Someone's shooting into my class, there's smoke in the air, it's so thick.

Oh my God, he's shooting down our hallway.

He's shooting into my room. . . . I love you guys so much. . . . Tell my parents I love them.

Oh my God, our teacher's dead. . . . Bleeding out on the floor.

Oh my God, I think Alyssa's dead.[7]

One minute after police received confirmation that there was an active shooter at MSD, the last round was fired. The gunman placed his rifle, vest, and 180 live rounds on the ground before running down the stairs. Within thirty seconds, the gunman vacated the building. It was only 2:27 P.M.

In six minutes—about the time it takes to order a drink at Starbucks—seventeen lives were taken: Alyssa Alhadeff (age 14), Scott Beigel (35), Martin Duque Anguiano (14), Nicholas Dworet (17), Aaron Feis (37), Jaime Guttenberg (14), Chris Hixon (49), Luke Hoyer (15), Cara Loughran (14), Gina Montalto (14), Joaquin Oliver (17), Alaina Petty (14), Meadow Pollack (18), Helena Ramsay (17), Alex Schachter (14), Carmen

Schentrup (16), and Peter Wang (15).[8] Sixteen others were wounded that day.[9] Not much more than a month past the one-year anniversary of the massacre, Sydney Aiello (19)[10] and Calvin Desir (16), two students who survived the shooting, took their own lives.[11]

One hour and ten minutes after he walked out of his school for the last time, the gunman was detained nearby by the Coconut Creek Police Department, after stopping at Subway for a drink.[12] More than three years after the crime, he remains in jail awaiting trial and a team of prosecutors who are intent on seeking the death penalty.[13]

Having retreated down the hallway to the solitude of my IOP office, I stared at my screen as CNN cameras trained on hysterical parents searching for their children. Some would have to wait ten hours to find out their child had died.[14] News photographers beamed images from a helicopter of the always-heartbreaking human chain we have become all too accustomed to seeing: dozens of young souls in a state of horror and shock few ever know—arms raised like zombies, resting on the sinking shoulders of a classmate, slowly marching toward the nearby middle school. What moments earlier was a high school filled with chocolates, flowers, and notes in celebration of Valentine's Day, was now a bloodstained murder scene. Soon, a global shrine.

It did not take long that afternoon for those images to join the other historic encounters—often violent, though not always—that I remember watching on television throughout my life. They sit alongside my first memories of Watergate coverage, the Iran hostage crisis, the inauguration and then failed attempt to assassinate Reagan, Howard Cosell's announcement of John Lennon's murder, the *Challenger* disaster, Tiananmen

Square, the Berlin Wall, the start of the First Gulf War, 9/11, and the Boston Marathon bombing.

As I did on the day a young Tunisian fruit vendor's self-immolation ignited the Arab Spring, I knew that this day would change America. The survivors of the shooting were not content being victims or soothed by the "thoughts and prayers" of the political establishment. To Generation Z, a spiritual, but not overtly religious generation, "thoughts and prayers" is anti-rhetoric. The idiom is a parody of religion that many Zoomers don't even understand.

If the carnage were ever to stop, the students of Marjory Stoneman Douglas, part of a student body that ethnically and economically looks a lot like America's future, realized they would have to do it themselves.

Remarkably, they were as prepared as anyone could reasonably expect them to be. The group of students who would get the movement off the ground were already comfortable storytellers and public speakers. Many had recently taken AP Government, a popular class that, hours before the shooting, ironically included class discussions about guns, politics, the Second Amendment, and the National Rifle Association.

At home, frustrated and helpless because he could not comfort his younger sister, Lauren, who was grieving the loss of her best friend, then-seventeen-year-old David Hogg needed to do something. As he headed out the door to go back to MSD, his parents—an elementary school teacher and former FBI agent—physically stopped him. "I need to do this," David pleaded. "If they [reporters] don't get any stories this will just fade away. I have to make sure this stays in the news."[15]

Two of David's favorite classes were Debate and TV Production. Those kinds of academic opportunities were among the reasons why his parents chose Parkland as their home when they relocated from Southern California a few years earlier. His was a family of news junkies. David, Lauren, and their parents would watch the evening news every night during dinner; *60 Minutes* was not to be missed. After homework was completed or before school, David would obsessively take in as much as he could—*Vox, Last Week Tonight with John Oliver, Vice News Tonight,* and Hank Green's *SciShow* on YouTube were among his favorites.[16]

While the gunman was roaming the halls of his school, David was recording footage on his phone. He interviewed those he was hiding alongside. "I want to show these people exactly what's going on when these children are facing bullets flying through classrooms and students are dying trying to get an education," he said. "If I was going to die, I wanted to die doing what I love, and that's storytelling," he recalled. "And this is a story that needed to be heard. . . . At least our echoes, our voices, would carry on and possibly make some action."[17]

Against their better judgment, David's parents eventually relented, and he rode his bicycle back to MSD, where news media from around the globe were setting up coverage. Less than eight hours after the shooting, David's first interview was on Fox News with primetime host Laura Ingraham. At the closing of the almost-eight-minute segment in which David praised an unnamed female janitor and the school staff and administration for saving hundreds of lives that day, he politely asked if he could "say one more thing to the audience."

Seizing every moment of an opportunity to tell a story he wished he never had to tell, David paused, trained his eyes on the few million Americans watching that evening, and said:

I don't want this to be another mass shooting. I don't want this to be just something that people forget.

This is something that people need to look at and realize that there is a serious issue in this country that we all need to face. It's an issue that affects each and every one of us and if you think it doesn't, believe me, it will. Especially if we don't take action to step up and stop things like that.[18]

As Ingraham tried to interrupt him when he suggested we "take action," David pushed forward:

For example, going to your Congressman and asking them for help and doing things like that.[19]

Unintentional in the moment, the opportunity Laura Ingraham granted David Hogg that evening already changed and will continue to transform America.

While David was reporting his account on television, others like Cameron Kasky, who started the #NeverAgain hashtag,[20] turned to social media. On Facebook he asked people not to "pray for me. Your prayers do nothing. Show me how you care in the polls."[21] Later, on Twitter, he posted, "I want people talking about this. I can't let this die like all the others. I need this to be the end. Everybody needs this to be the end. Talk to me."[22]

Fearless, with a sharp independent streak, comfortable in the spotlight and with the ability to teach himself just about anything—including reading and swimming as a child—Cameron used his home as the launching pad for the organization we know today as March for Our Lives. Within a few days, classmates Ryan Deitsch, Delaney Tarr, and Emma González were fully on board. Emma connected the others with her friend David Hogg, and knowing that the group needed an organizer in chief, Cameron recruited junior class president Jaclyn Corin, who was already planning a trip to meet with lawmakers in Tallahassee.[23]

On February 16, a member of the local school board made a decision that changed everything. She asked Emma González to speak the next day at a gun-violence-prevention rally in Fort Lauderdale. Working on her speech from the time of the invitation through the moment she took the lectern, Emma bared her soul and lifted the cause to another level, connecting with America like few other teenagers ever have. Nervously rubbing the sweat off her soon-to-be-famous buzz cut, she unlocked the door to political and social action for her generation.

The AP Government class notes Emma waved in her hands proved useful. She explained that a year before the massacre, President Trump signed legislation passed by Congress that repealed an Obama-era regulation that made it easier to block the sale of firearms to people with certain mental illnesses. She continued by calling out Republican senator Chuck Grassley (who more Americans would soon become familiar with as he chaired the Kavanaugh hearings) for hypocritically criticizing the FBI's failure to conduct background checks on mentally ill people, while at the same time being the sole sponsor of a bill that stops just that.[24]

Ultimately, in a speech that spanned just twelve minutes, Emma took aim at a generation of mostly baby boomer leaders serving both in government and private enterprise for repeatedly lying and making caricatures of Generation Z. She declared:

> Companies trying to make caricatures of the teenagers these days, saying that all we are self-involved and trend-obsessed, and they hush us into submission

when our message doesn't reach the ears of the nation, we are prepared to call BS.

Politicians who sit in their gilded House and Senate seats funded by the NRA telling us nothing could have been done to prevent this, we call BS.

They say tougher guns laws do not decrease gun violence. We call BS.

They say a good guy with a gun stops a bad guy with a gun. We call BS.

They say guns are just tools like knives and are as dangerous as cars. We call BS.

They say no laws could have prevented the hundreds of senseless tragedies that have occurred. We call BS.

That us kids don't know what we're talking about, that we're too young to understand how the government works. We call BS.[25]

Emma closed with purpose and direction for what was to come next, imploring Zoomers to vote and engage with their local member of Congress.

What Emma, who would soon see her Twitter follower count increase from zero to more than the NRA's, did while standing in solidarity with David, Cameron, Delaney, and their classmates, was give both voice and a foil to millions of Zoomers who'd grown up with near omnipresent coded-red-active-shooter drills and the related anxiety-, stress-, and depression-inducing issues that follow.[26] In TIME's cover story, Charlotte Alter underscored the generational nature of the fight the Parkland students were waging. They "painted the NRA and their allies as the mortal enemies of the roughly fifty million schoolkids growing up in what Kasky calls 'the mass-shooting generation.' They took the mantle of 'personal protection' from the gun lobby, while reframing the larger gun debate along generational lines," she wrote.[27]

Within weeks, we found that not only were the Parkland students swiftly winning the hearts and minds of Generation Z—a group ready and awaiting a call to action—but they were also following through. In the two months after the Parkland shooting, "young registrants represented a higher portion of new voters in Florida, North Carolina and Pennsylvania, among other states," according to reports by Michael Tackett and Rachel Shorey of *The New York Times*.[28] An ominous sign for the NRA and Republicans in the upcoming midterm elections, to be sure.

Along with calls for a modern, moral capitalism, the movement coming together out of Parkland was an added reactant stirring the fight among Generation Zers. On guns, Zoomers already stood apart from millennials. Through the IOP poll, we found that Newtown's Sandy Hook Elementary School massacre did not materially affect the way millennials approached gun policy. In 2011, the year before that shooting, net support among millennials under thirty for stricter gun laws was 34 percent (46 percent stricter, 12 percent less strict);[29] three months after twenty young children and six adults were murdered, net support was unchanged, remaining at 34 percent (49 percent stricter, 15 percent less strict).[30]

However, between Sandy Hook in 2012 and Parkland in 2018—a time that covered more than two thousand mass shootings,[31] including the Pulse nightclub, Las Vegas' Mandalay Bay, and dozens on public school campuses[32]—we found double-digit increases for stricter prevention measures and a growing antipathy toward the NRA.

Student efforts brought tangible legislative results, as

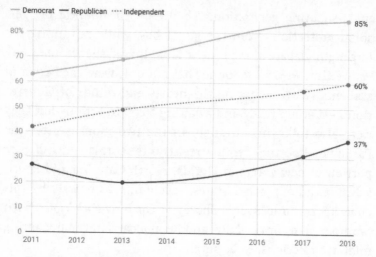

Figure 3.1. 18–29-year-olds who agree that "gun control laws should be made more strict."

Source: Harvard IOP Youth Poll, 2011, 2013, 2017, 2018

well. Three weeks after the day of the shooting, Florida governor Rick Scott signed a comprehensive bill that raised the age requirement to purchase a gun and banned bump stocks.[33] The legislative victories were not confined to Florida. By summer 2018, fifty new gun-safety laws were passed, including fourteen in states with Republican governors, like Florida. Speaking to the pragmatism of state lawmakers and governors, Allison Anderman, the managing attorney at the Giffords Law Center, an organization founded by former US Representative Gabby Giffords to prevent gun violence, said, "Legislators are starting to realize that mass shootings can happen in their state anytime, and they don't want to be in a position that this kind of thing can happen in their state at all."[34]

Yet Generation Z's problem is not with the Second

Amendment, per se. As is the case with capitalism, Zoomers' objections are rather with the way it is being practiced. National research I conducted in 2019 shows that a quarter of Generation Z already plans to own a gun in the future, and another 15 percent say there is a good chance they will own one. When we expand the choices to include the possibility of ownership, it's clear that Zoomers are not anti-gun at all. It's a fact that disappoints many on the left, but the data are consistent and unlikely to swing dramatically one way or the other anytime soon.

By a three-to-one margin, Zoomers also believe that having a firearm in the home makes the homeowner more, not less, safe. Despite these views, and across party lines, Generation Z overwhelmingly believes that our current laws should be stricter.

A review of the platform the Parkland students assembled illustrates a holistic approach to gun violence, while still respecting the rights of the overwhelming number of law-abiding Americans. In short, the Parkland students' ten-point plan advocates for:

1. funding for gun violence research;
2. digitizing of Bureau of Alcohol, Tobacco, Firearms, and Explosives records;
3. universal background checks;
4. banning high-capacity magazines;
5. an assault weapon ban;
6. funding for intervention programs;
7. red-flag laws;
8. blocking people with a history of domestic violence;
9. a federal solution to interstate gun trafficking; and
10. safe storage and mandatory theft reporting.[35]

Unsaid, of course, in all of this is that even with new laws in place, we have to rely on law enforcement to do its job, and friends, family, and the larger community to do theirs, as well. Sadly, what we learned from Parkland is that federal law enforcement and local authorities can't always be counted upon. "The FBI could have and should have done more to investigate the information it was provided prior to the shooting," David Bowdich, deputy director of the FBI, said when questioned by Congress. "While we will never know if we could have prevented this tragedy, we clearly should have done more."[36]

In the period leading up to the March for Our Lives, the unprecedented and game-changing rally that was held on March 24, 2018, in Washington, DC, and more than eight hundred other locations around the globe, my polling team of Harvard undergraduates and I spent an hour with many of the Parkland student-activists and their families during a visit they made to Harvard. Over breakfast, we shared data from the gun-related polling questions we asked in our previous surveys, plus a roundup of other publicly available data collected within the short window between February 14 and their visit. I remember two things clearly from that morning. First, the innocence and vulnerability of Emma González, who in alternating breaths was both the wide-eyed teenager sharing her college plans with me over eggs, and one of the most inspirational and influential individuals on the planet. Following her values and being true to herself, she inspired a generation to identify, stand up, and fight through the injustices holding them back. Second, I was struck by the raw intelligence and reasoned perspective of David Hogg and Ryan Deitsch, whom I escorted back to campus. Bundled up to protect ourselves from the harshness of early March in New England, we talked about their upcoming meeting with Nancy Pelosi and their understanding that the fight they were embarking on would not be over in a year or an election cycle. They were preparing for a generational battle, knowing that progress in defeating the NRA and reducing gun violence in America would be measured in decades, not years.

Back on the road that summer, it did not take me long to witness the influence of the March for Our Lives movement and, specifically, the echoes of Emma González. In my focus groups and town meetings, I sensed a more confident cohort of young Americans. Their stress and anxiety were still present, but so too were voices that were increasingly comfortable calling out the "BS" they were witnessing in their personal and our public lives. "People are finally able to take a stance on a lot of stuff like gun control, or race, or equality," Raiyan, a slight, bespectacled, studious-looking high school junior from Los Angeles, told me. He continued, "It's good that people are finally thinking about it, as opposed to just being in a corner."

No matter where I was during the rest of 2018—Ohio, Tennessee, Georgia, California—when I spoke with Zoomers, fear for their physical and mental well-being was still palpable.

> Thousands and thousands of people die each year on the streets or in accidents . . . if people getting shot in a school doesn't rile everyone up, nothing will.

> School shootings and gun violence is a major topic that should be discussed more. . . . It's getting to the point where it is almost out of control.

> We've had multiple threats. My school is serious about it, but at the same time they want to avoid it.

During the same time, the American Psychological Association, sponsor of the Stress in America survey, found that on every current events–related issue tested, Generation Z reported a higher level of stress than older adults. Zoomers were most likely of all generations to report poor mental health, and also significantly more likely to seek professional help for mental health issues, the report authors noted.

- Seventy-five percent of Generation Z felt stress because of mass shootings (13 percentage points higher than adults overall).

- Sixty-two percent were concerned about the rise in suicide rates (+18 compared to adults overall).

- Fifty-eight percent were anxious about climate change and global warning (+17 compared to adults overall).

- Fifty-seven percent were stressed due to the separation and deportation of immigrant and migrant families (+12 compared to adults overall).

- Fifty-three percent, at the time, reported stress related to widespread sexual harassment and assault reports (+14 compared to adults overall).[37]

In a September 2018 survey that Jonathan Chavez and I conducted at SocialSphere, our public opinion research company, we found that three-quarters of Zoomers had been affected or had someone close to them affected by mental health issues. Whether they were in college or not; living in a city, suburb, or in rural America; regardless of race—mental health transcended everything. We also found that 26 percent of all Zoomers, including nearly half of young Black Americans, were affected by gun violence.

Of more than fifteen issue priorities measured in our survey, school shootings ranked number one when Zoomers were asked to "indicate the importance of certain issues related to America's future." Gun violence prevention, a far more pressing concern with young Black people (net important: 71 percent) than white (net important: 46 percent), was in sixth position overall; access to higher education, health care reform, job creation, and mental health funding were also in the top five.

From a roundtable conversation at the University of Chicago Institute of Politics, which I hosted with more than a dozen Zoomers representing both Chicago's predominantly Black South Side and the nearby white neighborhoods and suburbs, a young Black woman spoke up for her community and the millions of unrecognized Black Zoomers like herself affected by gun violence:

> The country only pays attention when white bodies droppin', in my opinion. There's always an uproar and outrage when a mass shooting happens in a school with white kids, but mass shootings are happening every day. Every day on the South Side of Chicago people are getting killed for nothing. It just baffles me that the country is saying that "the only people that matter are these people, and you don't."

Parkland students knew the power of their platform as well as they knew their own pain. From its outset, their movement was focused on working with all communities impacted by gun violence—especially in underresourced urban areas. Although an early skeptic, *The Root*'s Jason Johnson noted that the March for Our Lives protest in Washington was open to everyone. There were Black kids from Chicago, Latino kids from Los Angeles, and minorities from other big cities, suburbs, and inner cities. "The March for Our Lives was one of the most organized, intersectional, disciplined and integrated protest marches I've ever seen, and I've been to a lot of marches," he said.[38]

Leading up to the fall election, Emma González had a final message to those who still viewed politics as folly and were not quite ready to engage in the fight: "You might not be a big fan of politics, but you can still participate. All you need to do is vote for people you believe will work on these issues, and if they don't work the way they should, then it is your responsibility to call them, organize a town hall and demand that they show up—hold them accountable. It's their job to make our world better."[39]

Proving the power of her persuasion, we found that like Emma herself, scores of Zoomers were leaning in to their stressors, taking initiative, and voting for something they believed in. In the end, midterm-election-turnout records for youths were broken and a record number of Trump- and NRA-backed politicians were defeated in November 2018. Our analysis from previous surveys showed that Zoomers with the highest levels of anxiety were the most likely to vote. Young Americans under thirty turned out at twice the rate they had in the previous midterm election, an unprecedented milestone. In his postelection wrap-up, *FiveThirtyEight*'s Nate Silver reported, "Turnout among young voters was high by standards of a midterm, voters 18 to 29 chose Democratic candidates for the House by 35 points, a record margin . . . in the exit-poll era. . . . This was a really big story."[40]

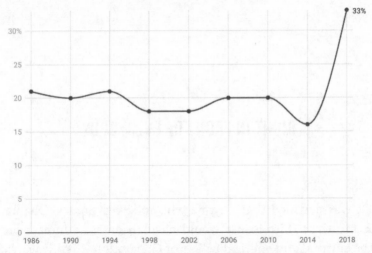

Figure 3.2. 18–29-year-old turnout in midterm elections, 1986–2018.

Source: United States Elections Project (based on US Census Bureau Current Population Survey and using Census Weight for Vote Overreport Bias Correction)

With Parkland a new catalyst, Generation Zers were finding community and strength in the failure of their leaders and the trauma of their generation. A first-year college student I met along the way shared a message he offered to those holding the seats of power and influence in Washington:

My generation, though we may be young, has a strong voice. We have shown it already. We are not going to back down until something changes and our country is safe. . . . Someday change will come. We are ready. Are you?

4

RIGHT IN FRONT OF EVERYBODY

It was destined that anyone who followed Barack Obama into the White House would have an outsized impact on the cultural and political beliefs of Generation Z. As Reagan's small-government doctrine shaped Zoomers' parents' ideologies and views of civic life during similarly impressionable years, the views and actions of the winner of the 2016 election would influence the vision and values of Gen Z. For the tens of millions of teenagers and young adults tuning in to current affairs and politics in the summer of 2015, Donald Trump brought America's unsettled racial history to the foreground.

Trump's path from the world of celebrity real-estate maven and reality-TV host into the arms of the nativist wing of the Republican Party had been greased by his obsessively mendacious claim that President Obama was born in Africa. And once he commanded the megaphone, Trump centered his campaign around the notion of erecting an enormous wall on America's southern border, a regressive fixation he heralded in his June 2015 announcement speech denigrating Mexican immigrants as "rapists" and drug mules.

Bookended by a tiki-torch-fueled march of white supremacists in Charlottesville, Virginia—with "very fine people on both sides"—and a global movement for racial justice during the summer of 2020, Gen Z's perceptions of race will be forever shaped by the words and deeds of Donald Trump and the policies of his administration.

Before Trump entered the arena, only 16 percent of American adults told Gallup (2005) that they were worried "a great deal" about race relations in the United States. But by the end of Trump's presidency sixteen years later, nearly half of the nation's adults were seriously concerned about race relations.[1]

Likewise, the number of Americans who indicated they were *very* dissatisfied with the way our society treated Black, Hispanic, and Asian Americans tripled during this period. Adults citing serious concerns about the treatment of Black or African Americans increased from 14 percent in 2005 to 46 percent in 2020. Meanwhile, those very dissatisfied with the treatment of Hispanic Americans rose from 10 percent to 32 percent; while those very dissatisfied with the treatment of

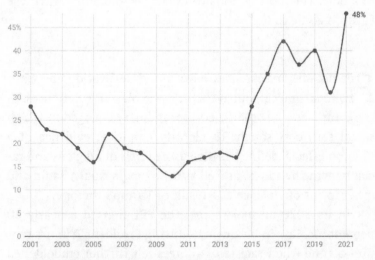

Figure 4.1. Americans worried a "great deal" about race relations.

Source: Gallup

Asian Americans also tripled, from 5 percent to 16 percent.[2] Younger Americans, more likely than their parents and grandparents to interact with and befriend members of an increasingly diverse society, are unsurprisingly more concerned than older groups with the treatment of others in society.

As Zoomers were coming of age, the air was filled with media commentators—from both the left and the right—who argued that the "21st century is a post-partisan, post-racial society."[3] America had elected Barack Obama twice, after all; or so the logic went. By the end of 2017's summer, the raggedy veneer was now fully stripped away. "A messed-up Rubik's Cube" is how one then eighteen-year-old described America in a town meeting I moderated. "Everything's off," he told me. Another student, about to start his first semester at a state university in Southern California when I interviewed him, said that America post-Charlottesville was like a giant hole "because you don't know what's in the bottom of a hole. The more actions you take, the more unknown the future's going to be."

For decades, researchers have found correlations between political and campaign rhetoric and bias-based offenses. In the Trump era, however, a cottage industry emerged in which social scientists sought to identify empirical evidence of a "Trump Effect," defined as increasing levels of religious and racial bullying by adults, as well as misogyny, sexual assault, and other forms of violence as a result of Trump's rhetoric.

In its 2020 annual report, the FBI charted a nearly 20 percent increase in hate crimes during President Trump's tenure—a time when racists of all ages felt further emboldened and protected. Hate-motivated murders spiked to a record-setting total of fifty-one in 2019, which doubled the previous record set the year before, when twenty-four murders were categorized as hate-motivated. An analysis of the more than seven thousand hate crimes in the database found that the greatest increases were crimes targeted against Black people, Jewish people, gay men, and Latinos.[4]

"Politics plays a role," Brian Levin, who directs the Center for the Study of Hate and Extremism at California State University, San Bernardino, told The New York Times. "The president's rhetoric has been identified in a series of actual attacks, but moreover the day-by-day ticks of F.B.I. hate crimes show there are increases after sustained and fervent remarks by the president that enter into an online feedback loop that also ends up in other discourse, both at the water cooler and on television."[5]

Prior to Trump's arrival in Washington, the overall violent crime and hate crime rate in the United States had been on a downward trajectory for decades. The only exception came in the wake of Osama bin Laden's September 11, 2001, attack on America. Since 2001, no discernible spike in hate crimes was identified until Trump's political rise in 2015 and 2016, when rates increased by 13 percent, while the overall crime rate dipped by 2 percent.[6] This study's authors, Professors Stephen Rushin and Griffin Edwards, conclude:

> President Trump's election coincided with a statistically significant surge in hate crimes, even when controlling for alternative explanations. And counties that voted for President Trump by the widest margins experienced the largest increases in reported hate crimes.[7]

Of particular concern to millions of Zoomer schoolchildren and teenagers—and their parents and teachers—was the rapid increase in youth bullying that also coincided with

Trump's politics.[8] In a comprehensive study published in *Educational Researcher* of more than 155,000 seventh- and eighth-grade students across every one of Virginia's school districts, bullying rates among middle school students in the spring of 2017 were 18 percent higher in localities where Donald Trump supporters outnumbered Hillary Clinton voters. While the report showed that in 2015 there was no difference between red-Trump and blue-Clinton school districts in the incidence of race- or ethnicity-based harassment, after the election, race-based bullying increased in the districts that favored Trump. It decreased in those that voted blue.[9] The authors were careful to note that while there was not enough evidence in this particular study to prove direct causation, they advise politicians to be "mindful of the potential impact of their campaign rhetoric and behavior on their supporters and indirectly on youth."[10]

To combat the disturbing trends leading to a growing number of Americans comfortable expressing, and therefore passing down, blatantly racist views to young Gen Zers, the California Department of Education launched the "Education to End Hate" initiative in 2020. Its goal is to empower their state's students and teachers to "confront the hate, bigotry, and racism rising in communities across the state and nation."[11]

About a year before this initiative was announced, I met Moses, then a talented sixteen-year-old African American musician raised near Los Angeles International Airport. In just a few minutes, he brought those troubling statistics from the Virginia study to life for me.

Moses explained that his parents recently thought it best for him to commute outside his Inglewood neighborhood to a new, mostly white high school just on the outskirts of Culver City. Some know Culver City today as home to many of the great cinema and television production companies of our time, but a hundred years earlier, it was a "sundown town" sold to tourists and newcomers as a "model white city."[12]

Reserved by nature, Moses feels more comfortable in smaller groups than in large settings, where he tells me he feels a lot of pressure to be someone he's not. Still, Moses, like many Zoomers, has grown to understand the importance of standing up for something.

Softly, measuring each word, he would tell me that his parents grew up in the sixties, and "in those days, they were like . . . kids were supposed to be seen, not heard." Today, though, he says, "kids have more power in their voice."

In a two-hour conversation I facilitated with twenty-nine other high school students representing a diverse set of greater Los Angeles communities, Moses pulled up a chair close to mine.

Diving into a discussion about life as a teenager in Los Angeles, Moses shared that while he was fortunate to live in one of the better parts of Inglewood, he's had a number of friends drawn into gangs, carrying guns into school, "showing off their pieces on Instagram."

Casually, Moses mentioned that a childhood friend was recently shot multiple times in the back, just steps from his home. "Sadly, he's dead," Moses sighed, swiveling gently in his seat, staring at his shoes, resting his elbows on his knees.

It was not until the discussion turned to the subject of "tough conversations," though, that I would feel the weight of his story or understand for a minute his reality as a Black teen in a country where racial discrimination is long sanctioned by our institutions.

Moses started: "I was sitting at my friend group, and they were talking about this other Black kid who was across the way, who I think has some mental disorder. I'm not sure. And he had headphones on, and he was standing by a tree."

He continued with a certain dry matter-of-factness to his delivery I have yet to forget. "First, they said, 'Oh, look at the ape in his natural habitat.' And I'm the only Black kid at the table.

"And these are all white kids, and they're talking about this other Black kid, calling him an ape! And they don't even realize how racially insensitive it is. Or they pretend not to. And then another kid says, 'Oh yeah,' and they see his head-phone cord, and they call it a noose!"

"What do you do in a situation like this?" I asked, floored.

"First, I confronted them," Moses said. "'I'm not sure if you understand, but what you said is very racially insensitive. You called him an ape, and you said that's a noose.'

"And it's funny because they tried to turn the conversation on me, and they were like, 'Moses, why are you bringing up race? Nobody brought up race.'"

As I quickly scanned the room for reaction, I locked eyes for a moment with Jasmine, a mixed-race high school basketball player from a nearby high school. She was blunt: "I just fin-ished my third year. It's been that way since I was a freshman."

Not long after those conversations in Los Angeles, I asked Albert, a veteran public-school teacher from St. Louis, to ex-plain the increasing levels of bigotry and racism he witnesses in his community.

Well, I think it's from the leadership of Donald Trump. What Trump was able to say and do on his platform—don't take this the wrong way—I think it's given white America more confidence to do and say things to Black people. Donald Trump came in and did the opposite of what Obama was trying to do. You got a president who talks about different races like he does, that's not good leadership. Now people are more comfortable with being disrespectful to other races.

Makayla, a then-sixteen-year-old high school student from Albert's St. Louis community who'd been working at Popeye's in her still largely redlined* neighborhood to save for college, had no shortage of race-related incidents she could share:

It's been multiple situations that I have seen racism in my job. When a Caucasian person has something wrong with their food and they talk to one of my Black managers: attitude, disrespect, all that. But when one of my Caucasian managers was talking to them and they have a problem with it, they would just talk regular and respectful. It's a different vibe when it's Black people.

A January 2020 study of Black Gen Zers like Moses and Makayla, but who were living in Washington, DC, helped quantify these experiences. Researchers found that the 101 middle school and high school students living in the District endured more than fifty-six hundred experiences of racial discrimination in two weeks. The authors found that racial microaggressions of every conceivable description—as well as documented assumptions of criminality, intellectual inferiority, the universality of the Black experience, inferior status, and second-class citizenship—occurred an average of five times every day per student.[13]

Psychologists often describe the effect of those microag-

---

* A twentieth-century federal practice used to discriminate in housing or insurance.

gressions as "death by a thousand paper cuts."[14] The messages they send daily to millions of young Black children is that they don't belong; that they are a threat. Probably all of us have been guilty of such infractions against African Americans or other marginalized groups at some point in our lives. While most of us are well intentioned, the everyday slights and invalidations should not be overlooked in the big picture. Racism hurts its victims. It is traumatic. It is sometimes deadly and it can be a permanent stain on the next generation.

Black Lives Matter cofounder Patrisse Khan-Cullors explains it this way in her bestselling memoir, *When They Call You a Terrorist*:

> The fact that more white people have always used and sold drugs than Black and Brown people and yet when we close our eyes and think of a drug seller or user the face most of us see is Black or Brown tells you what you need to know if you cannot readily imagine how someone can be doing no harm yet be harassed by police. Literally breathing while Black became cause for arrest—or worse.[15]

Racism makes the vulnerable and our society less well, physically and mentally. Living in communities with high levels of racial prejudice is associated with an elevated risk of disease and death, and not just from the police.[16]

After several years in which the United States saw a decline in school-based bullying and harassment,[17] the political environment Gen Z is growing up in today is different and more challenging to navigate. This is why local officials are moving to action—and why Moses, Makayla, and so many others I met are moving to find their voices and confront bias and racism when they see it.

In the modern era, the illiberal views propagated by a relatively small number from the far-right grassroots had not, prior to the Trump presidency, been intermingled with a top-down political strategy of a mainstream political party in the United States. Former Trump advisor and right-hand man to Steve Bannon, then-twenty-nine-year-old Andy Surabian was unapologetic when speaking with *The New York Times* about his party's fear-based, anti-immigrant platform of 2018:

> It's an issue folks are emotionally attached to, I know that upsets some people in the donor class, but it's the reality of where the party is.[18]

Trump aide Corey Lewandowski was equally defiant when he outlined what would end up being a failed Republican strategy during the 2018 midterm elections:

> If you want to get people motivated, you've got to give them a reason to vote. Saying, "Build the wall and stop illegals from coming in and killing American citizens" gives them an important issue.[19]

In other words, what Trump apologists often contended were just harmless slips of the tongue—"Trump being Trump"—or misquotes from the "fake" news media, were actually part of a deliberate campaign strategy to foster resentment and galvanize aggrieved, mostly older, white voters. While this strategy would backfire for Republicans who lost control of the House in 2018 and important off-year elections in 2019, it succeeded in unmasking unknown numbers of otherwise closeted racists and exposed impressionable young Zoomers to some of humanity's worst.

Ironically, this race-based strategy to divide Americans would be a central driver of record-setting youth participation at the polls in 2020.

With a president determined to fire up a disgruntled slice of American voters by using race as a wedge issue, and most every community upended by the botched response to the coronavirus—by Memorial Day 2020 we were a country on the edge.

As dusk was approaching on May 25, a teenage girl left her friends at a bonfire in Minneapolis because she had promised her younger cousin that she would pick her up something to eat. What she could not know was that her life was about to change forever. As would ours. Darnella Frazier, a then-seventeen-year-old varsity basketball and volleyball player with social anxiety,[20] who loves singing, fashion, and debate, would soon prompt a movement even larger and more consequential than Occupy, the ones that followed Trump's inauguration, and the Parkland massacre.

Darnella, with unthinkable courage that would later earn her a Pulitzer Prize,[21] held her iPhone out to record veteran police officer Derek Chauvin take nine minutes and twenty-nine seconds to choke the life out of George Floyd with his knee, while three other Minneapolis police officers threatened her, her cousin, and other bystanders, abetting their colleague instead of helping their fellow man.

According to crowd-counting experts, the range of protestors taking to the streets after George Floyd's murder is as low as 12 million and as high as 26 million Americans. It is marked as the largest protest in our nation's history. Nothing stands close.[22] The estimated crowd at Martin Luther King, Jr.'s March on Washington in 1963 was 250,000.

Walking through her Powderhorn Park neighborhood not long after 8 P.M., approaching Cup Foods on the corner of East Thirty-Eighth Street and Chicago Avenue, a few miles south of downtown, Darnella walked headlong into what she now calls her "first close-up death." Sadly, her cousin would also be a witness, seeing a murder before she'd celebrate her tenth birthday.[23]

Five hours later, her body still trembling, but safe back home, Darnella would search for community on social media, like the Parkland students before her. Streaming on Facebook Live, blue lights filling the black sky in her neighborhood, Darnella told the story the rest of America—white America—now seemed ready to begin reckoning with.

"They really killed somebody at Cup," she called out incredulously, yet still somehow steadily staring out her bedroom window, her iPhone trained above the tree line toward the flashing lights at the murder scene. For five minutes, she shared her testimony. She began:

> This dude at Cup, the police killed him, bro, right in front of everybody. . . . I have a ten-minute-long video. They killed this man, bro.
>
> He was crying, telling them like he couldn't breathe and everything. They didn't care. They killed this man. This was my first real close-up death, witnessing it. . . . Straight killed him. I have a whole video about it. . . .
>
> When I walked up, he was already on the ground, or whatever. The cops, their knees, they were pinning him down on his neck and he was crying, saying he couldn't breathe, and they weren't taking him serious. Like five or six minutes later, he's sitting there, dead as fuck. . . .

He was Black, he was a Black man, an older guy. . . . The cop who killed him was white. . . . They really killed him. He was crying, he like, "Mom, please bro. Somebody help me!"[24]

In the same arresting detail that she would later share in front of a jury, Darnella recalled the final moments of Floyd's life, punctuating every few sentences with "he's dead," as if to convince herself that the nightmare she was posting to Facebook was true.

Not much more than fifteen minutes after buying a pack of cigarettes with what the store clerks thought might be a counterfeit twenty-dollar bill, George Floyd was lying face-down, pressed to the pavement, knee on his neck, nose bleeding, hands tied behind his back, dead. Good Samaritans, including an off-duty firefighter who pushed forward to intervene, were held back by the police "putting their hands on Mace and guns." Floyd's death at forty-six years old, officially recorded an hour and a half after walking out of Cup, might well have been like that of the other nine men killed at the hands of Minnesota law enforcement in 2020; or the fourteen the year before; or the thirteen the year before that.[25] Forgotten, if ever recognized at all.

Judeah Reynolds, the then-nine-year-old witness to it all, thinks her cousin Darnella saved lives. "If we didn't go that day, they would keep killing us," she said.[26]

Darnella wasn't looking to be harassed by social-media trolls, nor was she looking to be a hero that night.[27] In a district courthouse less than a year later for the murder trial of Derek Chauvin, she said that when she saw George Floyd, she recognized her dad, her brothers, cousins, uncles, and friends who are Black.[28] Through watching George Floyd's fight for his life, she suffered all of their sadness and pain.

Barely more than a year later, tragedy struck Darnella and her family again. "I honestly can't believe I'm making this post right now," she wrote on Facebook two days after Independence Day 2021.[29] "Another black man lost his life in the hands of the police!" According to news reports, Darnella's uncle, Leneal Lamont Frazier, was killed when he was caught up in a violent crash involving Minneapolis police who were pursuing a robbery suspect in a high-speed chase through city streets. Mr. Frazier, who died soon after his car was struck by the Minneapolis police cruiser, was not involved in the robbery or the chase.[30] "I was hoping it was a dream," Darnella said, "but it's not and this is reality."

A year after Floyd's murder, I was conducting a focus group with residents of Houston on the state of their public schools, when I was forced to take a pause because the subject of race was too much for a young white energy-industry executive and part-time artist to bear. Choking back tears, before he could no longer hold on, Dave said:

> John, I mean George Floyd's from Houston. We'll just say that. I mean, he's from where I work. He grew up in the Third Ward; we know a lot of the same people. I work a lot in hip-hop, so a lot of times I'm the only white dude at the party. I just feel the pain for any young Black, Hispanic, just any kid, man, that gets shot by some fucking bigot cop. I mean, I'm tired of that shit. I feel that. It's fucking sad, man.

The sentiments felt by Darnella that brought her the courage to act are felt every day, by many more people than she may realize.

"Without Darnella's presence of mind and readiness to risk her own safety and wellbeing, we may never have known the truth about George Floyd's murder," Suzanne Nossel said before presenting her with the 2020 PEN/Benenson Courage Award.[31] And we almost certainly would not have witnessed the justice that was delivered the following year by a jury of Derek Chauvin's peers followed by Judge Peter Cahill's sentence of more than twenty-two years in prison.

Not long after the verdict was announced, Darnella again took to social media. This time, though, aided by the emphasis of all caps and multiple emojis, she documented her tears of *joy* for a country in her debt.

> I just cried so hard This last hour my heart was beating so fast, I was so anxious, anxiety bussing through the roof. But to know GUILTY ON ALL 3 CHARGES !!! THANK YOU GOD THANK YOU THANK YOU THANK YOU THANK YOU George Floyd we did it!! justice has been served[32]

This quintessential Generation Z habit of hers, live-streaming her life, turned out to be the first step in a painful but necessary national discussion and reckoning on race. Gen Zers were forcing uncomfortable conversations with their parents and grandparents about what generations of conscious and unconscious bigotry, racism, and oppression had wrought for Black Americans. The bullying, the bias, the systemic oppression—it was all adding up to more poverty, debt, and prison time; less education, wealth, and health care.[33] All of it leading to a lower life expectancy than whites have.[34]

Within hours of Floyd's death, a righteous movement led by Generation Z for civil rights, equality, and justice was reenergized. Within weeks, at least twelve million Americans[35]—more than half of which were under thirty years old[36]—took to the streets and attended over forty-seven hundred demonstrations covering almost half of the counties in the United States.[37]

Researchers found that the critical attention related to the history of race relations in America that followed was also influencing public opinion in near real time. Seven in ten American adults reported having conversations with family or friends about race, of which half that number posted racial equality content on social media.[38] And it was noted that after the Floyd murder, a majority of southerners (like Americans from other regions of the country) admitted to pollsters that the Confederate flag was more a symbol of racism than southern pride, although deep divisions based on age still existed.[39]

Contrary to many deceptive narratives, the overwhelming number of protests were peaceful. Ninety-six percent of events involved no property damage, and in 98 percent of protests, no injuries were reported among participants, bystanders, or police. Police were reported injured in only 1 percent of the protests, according to analysis directed by Erica Chenoweth, a Harvard professor who oversees the Nonviolent Action Lab at the Carr Center for Human Rights Policy.[40]

Douglas McAdam of Stanford University, who studies social movements, said, "Without gainsaying the reality and significance of generalized white support for the movement in the early 1960s, the number of whites who were active in a sustained way in the struggle were comparatively few, and certainly nothing like the percentages we have seen taking part in recent weeks."[41]

Half of the adults who protested after the Floyd murder were white; overall, as many were residents of the suburbs as urban areas. Democrats outnumbered Republicans by a margin of four to one.[42]

At 71 percent, white Democrats were about twice as likely as white Republicans (37 percent) to have taken the time to learn more about the history of racial inequality in the United States in the summer of 2020. In a hopeful sign, a majority of younger, white Gen Z and millennial Republicans say they sought more information, a far higher rate than their elders. More than four in five of their young Democratic counterparts did the same.[43]

Much like the growing acceptance of same-sex marriage (support increased by 26 points between 2001 and 2019[44]) and the LGBTQIA+ community more broadly (support increased by 21 points between 2002 and 2020[45]), as well as the severing of ties with religious institutions (religiously unaffiliated Americans increased by 9 points between 2009 and 2019[46])—these attitudes on race are the embodiment of how the values of society are influenced by younger generations. Attuned and empathetic to the injustice caused by systemic racism, as white Gen Zers age, public opinion, and in turn policy, will evolve, as it has in the past on other once culturally charged issues.

Despite the lack of leadership from the whole of Congress, the work of largely Zoomer-led protestors has already resulted in small but meaningful and highly tangible victories. California, Colorado, Connecticut, Iowa, Minnesota, New York, along with several other city and county officials from across the nation, banned choke holds by police. Berkeley, Philadelphia, San Francisco, Seattle, and Washington, DC, curbed the use of tear gas. Mandates from Seattle, Denver, Houston, and Connecticut now require the use of body cameras by police; and Georgia, Massachusetts, and the Minneapolis City Council have approved steps to rethink modern policing.[47]

So why now? More than one thousand Americans are

killed at the hands of police every year, a disproportionate number of them Black and Latino.[48] Why didn't all this real change in attitudes and legislation happen after Tamir Rice, Eric Garner, Breonna Taylor, and so many others?

The answer? Generation Z made it so.

Everything had been there for people to see, but no one wanted to look. Avoid the neighborhood, turn the channel, change the conversation. Repeat. With wall-to-wall coverage of an unarmed man dying, even the willfully ignorant couldn't *not* look—and they couldn't then look away. Less than two months after the murder, in addition to network and cable television, twelve million viewers watched Floyd die on the *New York Times* YouTube channel, while seven million streamed on *CBS Evening News* YouTube, two million on ABC News YouTube, and eight hundred thousand tuned in on the Fox News YouTube channel, where they saw Trey Gowdy, a former South Carolina congressman and pro-Trump pit bull, call the death of George Floyd "murder."[49]

Generation Z knows that police brutality and institutional racism existed well before the day of George Floyd's murder. His death is what sparked the protests. What gave the protests oxygen, though, was what Darnella's video represented. It was proof that Thomas Jefferson's great promise about pursuing happiness was still not available to all Americans. For large swaths of good and decent people, the government was not upholding its end of our social contract. Generations of us—especially Black and brown Americans— played by the rules, respected and obeyed the state, even when the stability and security promised in exchange never materialized. Justice, a quality education, health care, access to employment opportunities, credit, safe streets, housing, clean air and water—these very basic needs were unattainable for far too many under the current application of modern capitalism and democracy in America.

With a highly charged, impassioned, unscripted video-lecture delivered in the midst of boarded-up buildings at the heart of the summer 2020 protests, Atlanta author Kimberly Jones broke it all down and explained as well as anyone how we got to this point.

You broke the contract when you killed us in the streets!

You broke the contract for four hundred years!

We played your game and built your wealth.

You broke the contract when we built our wealth again on our own, by our bootstraps in Tulsa, and you dropped bombs on us! When we built it in Rosewood, and you came in and you slaughtered us.

You broke the contract![50]

The combination of renewed intergenerational family time during the COVID-19 lockdown, social media, and the ubiquity of news and information created meaningful opportunities to discuss these issues during the summer of 2020. Millions of Americans returned home from college sharing stories of the people they know—the Moseses and the Makaylas—to parents who had been turning a blind eye within the comfort of their daily routine for years. Americans of all stripes were now being forced to confront the heavy toll that discrimination, bigotry, and systemic racism are having on our society in deeply personal and moving ways.

The current that swept Darnella Frazier's iPhone video from Facebook to the national news media, resulting in a sea of local protests, was strikingly similar to events in 1965 that marked a turning point in the civil rights era. While reporters from multiple outlets recorded the gruesome images at the Edmund Pettus Bridge of police using fire hoses to disperse then-twenty-five-year-old John Lewis and hundreds of young, peaceful activists, it was one crew of enterprising ABC News producers who, like Darnella, captivated the nation's attention.

While others waited to share the story of "Bloody Sunday" until the following evening's newscast, ABC News was able to jet the film from Selma to New York within hours. As millions of American families were settling in to watch *Judgment at Nuremberg*, a film about the Nazi war-crimes trial, anchor Frank Reynolds interrupted the broadcast with images of militarized police siccing dogs on people singing hymns, and cracking the skulls of African Americans trying to register to vote. "The juxtaposition struck like psychological lightning in American homes," recalled Gene Roberts and Hank Klibanoff in *The Race Beat*.[51]

Like the summer of 2020, the confluence of events that evening—multiple generations collectively watching extreme police brutality—created a national reckoning and a near real-time illustration of what was happening in George Wallace's America—our America. Within days, demonstrations in support of John Lewis and the Selma marchers occurred in dozens of cities across the country.

Recognizing the long arc of history and that other generations have also fought for and sacrificed for civil rights, Ginny Hogan, a writer and comic based in Los Angeles, said Zoomers think "they're the only activists on the planet. This is not true. They're just the most effective activists on the planet."[52]

5

BACKLASH

This story so far has been about how the universe has generated more stress and fear for Zoomers at an earlier age than their immediate predecessors experienced and how they have responded to it. An escalation of fear in society also creates opportunity for ideologues, extremists, and run-of-the-mill troublemakers to recruit and create alternative communities of conspiracy, intolerance, hate, and violence. About every fifty years since the Civil War, it's been a burden that America's politics and people have had to confront.

In the decade and a half leading up to the Great Depression, backlash against America's rapidly evolving industrialized society helped the Ku Klux Klan (KKK) recruit millions of new members. The parallels between today's political and cultural environment and the early twentieth-century rise of the white supremacist and nativist movements are striking.

Vestiges of the KKK remain today. An unknown number of Klansmen work inside the Florida Department of Corrections, where they wield power over prisoners.[1] A sixteen-year-old *American Idol* finalist was dropped in May 2021 after a four-year-old Snapchat video surfaced of him seated next to someone in a KKK-style hood.[2] The next month, flyers promoting the KKK were littered across communities in Northern Virginia,[3] and a police chief from a Northern Ohio town was fired after being caught on a surveillance camera printing a note that read "Ku Klux Klan" and placing it on the raincoat of a Black officer.[4] While whited-robed, hooded Klansmen may not burn crosses on lawns, the same toxic message is amplified in town after town, on social media, and other digital-age delivery systems of hate—and are packaged and left on the "doorsteps" of Generation Z. The victims aren't only the recipients of this filth, either. Neither the Klan's message nor its motivations have changed in a century. The difference today is that the Klan has competition. Hundreds of organizations, large and small, compete for Zoomers whose coronavirus-forced social isolation, years of anxiety, and despair often lead to curious and dark pathways in search of community.

Policy makers, advocates—all of us—must work to understand and immediately confront the imminent danger posed to Gen Z by a complex generational mental health crisis leaving millions seeking belonging and community; a rising number of sophisticated and networked hate and domestic-terror groups preying on the young and vulnerable; and political, technological, and media environments that knowingly offer them oxygen in exchange for ad revenue, cable ratings, and chits in a culture war.

If David Hogg, Darnella Frazier, and the many others who fight for a more just and inclusive society represent the promise of Generation Z and America's future, young Thomas Ryan Rousseau and Bruno Joseph Cua represent the virulent backlash that such progress too often precipitates.

Raised by a single mother and older sisters in a once-reliably Republican Dallas suburb,[5] Thomas Rousseau recognized as a teenager he had "somewhat of a talent" for composition and he imagined a career as a writer. He was the staff cartoonist, wrote opinion pieces, and covered current events for the Coppell High School newspaper, *The Sidekick*. He published a portfolio with his academic and extracurricular achievements and won awards for his art. Thomas did not play varsity team sports, but physical fitness was an important part of his identity. He would regularly count calories and boast that he avoids unhealthy food and substances. He rarely missed daily sixty- to eighty-minute workouts at the gym.[6]

In what would be an ironic turn, Thomas wrote a *Sidekick* feature in January 2016 touting the benefits of his school's newly chartered Diversity Club.[7] Later that spring, he pivoted to political commentary. But it soon became clear that his own views harkened back to an earlier Texas. Thomas argued for the controversial "campus carry" law in Texas,[8] and the since partially repealed "bathroom bill" law in North Carolina,[9] which prohibited transgender people who have not taken surgical and legal steps to change the gender noted on their birth certificates from using public restrooms of the gender with which they identify.

More comfortable expressing his emerging worldview as the election drew near, Thomas was known to favor a MAGA cap and tote a Trump lunch box around a diverse school of more than thirty-five hundred mostly middle-class students, where whites like Thomas were the minority.[10]

As the election of 2016 drew closer, his views sharpened. The writing grew angrier. His rhetoric resembled that of Steve Bannon and Stephen Miller—Trump advisors known to promote theory and literature favored by the alt-right.[11] Enamored with Trump's "man against the establishment" paradigm, in his final piece before the election Thomas began publicly blending classic authoritarian rhetoric with enough xenophobic and antisemitic cues to spark a connection with the alt-right readers he seemingly sought to develop.

> The GOP has lost touch with the public and Trump has broken that stereotype, much to its dismay. While Texas Senator and former Presidential candidate Ted Cruz and others like him said, "I'm fighting for the Constitution," repeatedly, Trump says, "I'm fighting for you." That is what the American people needed so desperately to hear.
>
> Democratic nominee Hillary Clinton is being advised on foreign policy by George Soros. Soros is an international billionaire who has made his billions manipulating currency and destabilizing nations. Clinton is the visible tip of the large, corrupt iceberg that promotes globalism and the self interests of the international elite such as Soros.

Thomas closed his essay with an ominous vow that Trump's election would "deliver the American people justice." Presaging what was to come, he framed the election, the future—and the next stage of his life, at least—as a choice between "a corrupt establishment with wishes to usurp democracy" and the American people.[12]

Two weeks later, in a postelection analysis published on his school's website, Thomas wrote:

> Democratic nominee Hillary Clinton's concession speech also focused largely on reassuring her large voting coalition of minorities that there is still hope in the future for electing another president who openly celebrates America's growing lack of a white majority. . . .

The forgotten majority of the American electorate has shown that, much to the dismay of the globalist agenda, that (sic) they have not yet been replaced by the tens of millions of blue-voting immigrants from abroad. That they can still hold up some semblance of a resistance against the decay of their nation.[13]

With the election over and Trumpism taking hold in Washington, Thomas's metamorphosis from an Eagle Scout with a merit badge in "Indian Lore" into a foot soldier for the alt-right was rapidly progressing. By the following spring, he was a subject of FBI monitoring.[14] A few months later, he traveled twelve hundred miles each way to lead several dozen members of a group calling itself Vanguard America at Charlottesville's Unite the Right rally.[15] Thomas wore a prep-school-style uniform of khakis, a black baseball hat, aviator sunglasses, and a white polo shirt with a fasces-carrying eagle emblazoned over his heart. His group rode along with hate groups shouting in unison from a playlist that included "Jews will not replace us!" "Hail Trump!" "White lives matter!" and "We will be back!"[16]

Several photographs from the weekend in Charlottesville captured Thomas in the foreground with fellow Vanguard America member James Alex Fields, Jr.[17] The avowed neo-Nazi would later be convicted of the murder of thirty-two-year-old Heather Heyer.[18]

As extremists and the media were clearing out of Virginia, Thomas sought to distance himself from James Fields and his heinous crime. His answer to what he considered the "PR nightmare" embroiling Vanguard America was to rebrand the organization. Soon, Patriot Front was born—a Gen Z hate group cloaked in the US flag with a mission of reaching out to a new generation of mainstream Americans. Working out of his father's three-bedroom house not far from an elementary school in Grapevine, Texas, Thomas crafted an online identity he hoped would catch the eye of other lonely, curious, dejected, resentful members of his generation.

Designed perhaps to both intimidate and motivate, the Patriot Front website was framed in red, white, and blue with out-of-context quotes from America's forefathers, including Alexander Hamilton and "Samuel Adam" (*sic*). Its promotional video is a medley of jacked-up young white men marching and shouting in empty streets; Nazi-like symbolism; ISIS-inspired training sequences—all of which are fused with house music.[19]

In a discursive manifesto that misappropriated JFK to claim that the (tiki) "torch is now passed to our generation," Thomas set the markers of his movement's success far into the future:

> The patriots of today may not see the culmination of their grand vision, but rather in their lifetime set the nation and its people upon this task with the multi-generational spirit to stand the test of time.[20]

Undersized, with long hair, a man bun, a cowboy hat, and a megaphone, Thomas was savvy enough to avoid publicly condoning violence for fear of federal prosecution. Leaked files from Patriot Front servers offer a clear view of the danger he and his mostly Gen Z followers pose to local communities and those who engage. According to Unicorn Riot, a nonprofit media group known for reporting on far-right organizations, a number of Rousseau's fellow Patriot Front members

- obsess over firearms—and a desire to take action in "the real world";

- believe raping women is acceptable, "as long as you're raping, like, people in your own race";

- envision an ideal society where "'ethnostate rape gangs' would be allowed to freely target unmarried white women who did not adhere to 'traditional values.'"[21]

Entering its fourth year in operation, the Patriot Front organization claims a few hundred official members and several thousand followers across alt-right social media platforms, such as Gab, Telegram, BitChute, and Mind. Patriot Front is among the most active extremist groups in the nation.[22] From Massachusetts to Montana, often on or near high school and college campuses, there were nearly six thousand Patriot Front incidents listed in an extremist database from 2017 through the end of 2020. They include flash-mob-style harassment, spreading white supremacist or antisemitic propaganda, and hosting white supremacists' events.[23]

Thomas is one of few activist white racists who does not cover his face during public events. But he encourages others to do so, stating "The enemy cannot attack you if they do not know who you are."[24] Using the psychology of terror that shook so many Americans when they boarded flights after 9/11, a Patriot Front member from New York characterized how they view success:

We can make them feel as if there are thousands of us when it's only a few hundred, and we could be anyone and no one.

Next time they are at the CVS and see a white kid with a neat haircut, it could be us. Fear of the unknown is the greatest fear of all.[25]

University of Massachusetts–Amherst professor emeritus Ervin Staub says that Thomas Rousseau and his followers seek associations with extremist groups because they don't fit in anywhere else. "Why would people join groups like that?" Staub wrote. "It usually involves them finding no other socially acceptable and meaningful ways to fulfill important needs—the need for identity; the need for a feeling of effectiveness; the need for a feeling of connection.

"Often, these are people who don't feel like they've succeeded or had a chance to succeed across normal channels of success in society," Dr. Staub added. "They may come from families that are problematic or families where they're exposed to this kind of extreme views of white superiority and nationalism. If you don't feel you have much influence and power in the world, you get a sense of power from being part of a community and especially a rather militant community."[26]

The youngest of the more than five hundred insurrectionists[27] to face federal charges after the breach of the US Capitol on January 6, 2021, Bruno Joseph Cua road-tripped to Washington, DC, with his parents from Milton, Georgia—a suburb of Atlanta and one of the state's wealthiest communities. Bruno fits neatly into Dr. Staub's paradigm of a child who is raised in a family that espouses extreme views. Both parents believed that the 2020 election was stolen from Donald Trump. Their trip to the nation's capital from their nearly 5,000-square-foot country estate,[28] they believed, was to "Stop the Steal."[29]

The eldest of three children from what neighbors describe as a "deeply religious family," Bruno is known to local law enforcement as the one who would intentionally spew black exhaust fumes from his bulked-up, oversized Toyota pickup truck while harassing and intimidating those showing support for liberal causes. In court testimony, Bruno's father recalled "half a dozen times, at least" when local police were called to the family home. Bolstered by others in a caravan, Bruno and his crew would roll up to unsuspecting Biden-supporting motorists howling "faggots" or "baby killers" out the window.[30] In December 2020, he earned a visit from local authorities after blasting his air horn and driving recklessly with his giant Trump flag on his truck through an elementary school parking lot with children present. Upon receiving his citation, Bruno reportedly told police that he "had to pick up some speed" to get his flag to flap in the wind.[31]

Bruno's dad, Joseph, holds an Ivy League master's degree and until 2020[32] was an executive in charge of lifestyle brands for Wyndham Hotels.[33] Alise, his mom, is a professional photographer[34] and former veterinarian who stopped working to homeschool her son and his two younger siblings.[35] Both parents blend their professional and political lives: Joseph expressing frustration with pandemic lockdown rules and, later, the Washington "swamp," on LinkedIn; Alise using her business profile on Twitter to foment election fraud[36] and COVID-19 conspiracy theories,[37] while also re-tweeting images of Black teenage girls on the Fourth of July with a message claiming that "these ingrates will always hate America."[38]

As a self-styled foot soldier in Donald Trump's army, Bruno employed the weaponry his generation is most familiar with—social media. He turned to Instagram, posting multiple stylized photos—often with rifles in hand, tagged with #everydaycarry, #sniper, and #molonlabe (a phrase from Greek antiquity adopted by gun-rights activists). Parler, the social network favored by supporters of Donald Trump after he was censured by and then banned from Twitter, was his choice for the business of promoting the insurrection. Here is one of many similarly themed posts Bruno (@PatriotBruno) shared with his more than twenty-six hundred followers:

President Trump is calling us to FIGHT! #DOJ #SCOTUS #FBI, His own cabinet, everyone has betrayed him. It's Trump & #WeThePeople VS the #deepstate and the #CCP. He knows this is the only way to save our great country, show up on #January6th. It's time to take our freedom back the old fashioned way. #Thisisour1776.[39]

On January 6, 2021, armed with a baton, Bruno fought his way in and made it to the well of the US Senate, all the while making sure to record plenty of evidence for future investigators on his cell phone. Before 5 P.M. that fateful day, he posted this to his Instagram account (@brunocua_1776):

Yes, for everyone asking I stormed the capital (*sic*) with hundreds of thousands of patriots. I'll do a whole video explaining what happened, this is history. What happened was unbelievable. Yes, we physically fought our way in.[40]

Buoyed by his success, Bruno returned to social media in the days after the insurrection was quelled. According to court reports from *HuffPost,* the following day he took to Parler, where his violent rhetoric became even more inflamed: "The tree of liberty often has to be watered from the blood of tyrants. And the tree is thirsty. WE THE PEOPLE have a right to rise up and overthrow a tyrannical government."[41]

He wrote in another post that there "will be no 'warning shot'" the next time the people rise up.

And on January 8, he wrote that everyone in Congress "is a traitor to the people and deserves a public execution."

One month later, Bruno was in prison. Arrested in his Milton, Georgia, home and charged by the United States of America on twelve criminal counts:

1. civil disorder;
2. obstruction of an official proceeding and aiding and abetting;
3. assaulting, resisting, or impeding certain officers;
4. entering and remaining in a restricted building or grounds with a deadly or dangerous weapon;
5. disorderly and disruptive conduct in a restricted building;
6. engaging in physical violence in a restricted building or grounds;
7. entering and remaining on the floor of Congress;
8. entering and remaining in the gallery of Congress;
9. entering and remaining in certain rooms in the Capitol building;
10. disorderly conduct in a Capitol building;
11. act of physical violence in the Capitol grounds or buildings;
12. parading, demonstrating, or picketing in a Capitol building.[42]

In a mid-February hearing, Bruno's father tried to take the blame for how his then-eighteen-year-old son had turned out: "I feel responsible for bringing him up into that environment," he told a federal court. "I feel embarrassed that we drank in a lot of this rhetoric from so-called leaders that never materialized. I feel I should have known a little bit better at my age."[43]

The judge, who was aware that in late 2020 young Bruno tried to purchase an automatic rifle "under the table,"[44] was not having it. Bond was denied. The judge also commented that Joseph and Alise, who were aware of their son's intentions and the weapon he carried inside the Capitol, were unsuitable guardians.

A month later, Bruno's mother, Alise, begged for her son's pretrial release to a federal judge in Washington, DC: "I am asking for just mercy and forgiveness," she told the court, adding that she now felt "ridiculous" believing the former president's lies about voter fraud.[45]

For previous generations, it was not uncommon for gang leaders and pedophiles to prey on the vulnerable by hanging around schools and playgrounds, seeking out the unattended and lonely. Today, playgrounds are replaced by TikTok, Reddit, 4chan, video-game chats, and countless other forums where malleable, isolated, and often depressed children and teens search for answers and meaning in a world they find increasingly friendless, complex, and hostile.

While Facebook, Twitter, and Google continue to crack down on accounts and language that propagate violent and seditious acts, the short-term effect will be that extremists and conspiracy theorists will be driven further underground and onto dark platforms where they will be able to work without as much scrutiny.

In 2019, a Jewish mother of two teenagers wrote an essay for *Washingtonian* magazine[46] about how her then-thirteen-year-old son became entangled in a sort of alt-right cult after his public school failed him and he had difficulty socializing in a new private school. Within a matter of months, the writer's son, who she called "Sam" to protect his identity, embodied truly vile parts of the alt-right ideology. He became a vocal advocate for "men's rights," a Subreddit moderator of hate speech, and coached his parents on the best approach to handling the FBI if they ever appeared at their front door.

"These sort of recruiting tactics aren't just common, but systematically enforced. Recruiters are actively looking for these kinds of broken individuals who they can promise acceptance, who they can promise identity to," said Christian Picciolini,[47] a former neo-Nazi and now author and peace activist. "The ideology and the dogma are not what drive people to this extremism, it's in fact, I think, a broken search for that acceptance and that purpose and community," he continued.

After emerging from the experience with some understanding of how he was manipulated, Sam explained the lure of his alt-right handlers:

> I liked them because they were adults and they thought I was an adult. I was one of them. I was participating in a conversation. They took me seriously. No one ever took me seriously—not you, not my teachers, no one. If I expressed an opinion, you thought I was just a dumbass kid trying to find my voice.[48]

What is frightening is that, collectively, we have all been culpable in creating a highly recruitable environment for extremist and insurrectionist groups to prosper. We have produced a generation of targets more than willing to wade into social media in search of answers and escape from what seems to them an increasingly dystopic present and perilous future.

Generation Z is asking us every day to have the honest and difficult conversations about politics, race, culture, our history, and future that too many parents and school juris-dictions are unwilling to tackle. "Right now, our fear about addressing race causes us to leave kids guessing," says Shelly Tochluk, a professor of education at Mount Saint Mary's University, Los Angeles, and author of *Witnessing Whiteness: The Need to Talk About Race and How to Do It*. "They fill in the blanks with whatever they see online, and this includes hor-rifically twisted messages from white nationalists."[49]

Nigel Bromage, another former neo-Nazi turned activist, like Picciolini, told Great Britain's Sky News in late 2020 that "the far-right in Britain today is actually at its most danger-ous it's ever been," citing video games and extremist content on social media as primary methods to recruit children, in some cases as young as nine years of age.

"These video games are just like many others with re-gards to chasing and shooting people. But when you look at the sort of content of the game, what you will see is that the people who are being chased are from different ethnic communities, different religions. And because there are great graphics and there's good music, young people embrace that on every level. Unfortunately, it's a really great recruitment tool for the far-right."[50]

A British teenager, who has since escaped the grip of the far-right, explained the allure:

> Initially the main attraction was how patriotic they were. A lot of the people in the far-right said they were standing up for the soldiers in the UK, which is something that I've always felt very passionate about.
>
> I guess you could say I had started being radical-ized at that point. I thought I was standing up for my country, standing up for Britain.

The enemy in our minds was Islam, [it] was the
Muslim people, [it] was almost the police as well as
the government, and journalists as well.
We sort of stood up against authority.[51]

Isolation, questioning culture and authority, the appeal
of community—regardless of where it is found—are among
the battles every generation has faced since the recording of
history. To confront these challenges, we must all be conscious of the social, psychological, and economic circum-
stances that leave our youths searching.

In 2020, there was some interest from lawmakers on
Capitol Hill to address the anti-American and violent activities of white supremacists and other extremist groups; but
even on this topic, partisan divides still exist. The Democratic House held fourteen hearings on this topic, while the
Republican Senate held only one.[52]

One overarching lesson in all this is that fighting the extremists within our borders will take the same fortitude and
ingenuity used against al-Qaeda and ISIS in the 2000s and
2010s. Without the nation's best efforts, full commitment
of resources, and awareness within our schools, churches,
and communities, interventions cannot be advanced—and
the promise of Generation Z and America cannot be secured.

6

TIP OF THE SPEAR

Millennials, mostly now in their thirties, are a Gen Z prototype in many ways. Members of both groups have grown up with a sense of duty and service to others. Both have been let down by government and most other institutions. Both have been disparaged and ridiculed by the older, mostly white establishment: millennials, the "spoiled, lazy narcissists,"[1] and Zoomers, the "sanctimonious, sensitive, supercilious snowflakes."[2] Both share a core set of values and commitment to fairness and justice. Millennials are the tip of the spear. They have introduced America to a new, more progressive vision. Generation Z has adopted this outlook, expanded it, and is now swiftly beginning to fulfill it. To grasp this vision and understand what's ahead, it's critical we know and understand the events that shaped and influenced millennials, the next generation of leaders.

> Doesn't our generation understand that if we continue to volunteer through community service *and vote* in local and national elections, we can have a much greater impact on the issues we care about?

This is how my first conversation with a millennial voter started in 1999. It was with Western Virginia native Erin Ashwell, a first-year student at Harvard College.

Erin was particularly concerned about a divide she spotted on our campus and at many of the other colleges her friends and peers were attending across the country. Anecdotally, at least, it seemed hers was a generation committed to volunteerism and community service, but far less interested in voting, volunteering on political campaigns, serving in government, or one day entering the arena to run for office. She told me that only about one-third of young Americans (Generation X) voted in the 1996 election for president, while many more than that seemed to be engaged in community service.

With this thesis, she, along with her classmate Trevor Dryer, former Institute of Politics executive director Cathy McLaughlin, Kennedy School professor David C. King, and I set about sketching a study-group plan that we couldn't have known would continue to this day, bringing me in contact with hundreds of idealistic young people, many of whom are now shaping politics and policy from the national stage. US Transportation Secretary Pete Buttigieg and Elise Stefanik, the third-ranking Republican member of the US House, both served on the polling project's student committee when they were undergraduates in 2004.

Beginning with two focus groups with millennials representing the diverse student bodies of the Boston-area colleges and universities, twelve Harvard students and I crafted a telephone survey and interviewed eight hundred college students from dozens of institutions across the country. We sought to quantify interest and engagement in community service and more traditional political participation, the attitudes behind each, and potential avenues to make the latter more attractive.

The conclusion we issued at the end of the spring 2000 semester still holds true:

> Today's college students are not an apathetic generation. They are engaged in their communities and are interested in serving the public. As evidenced by their high degree of involvement in community service activities, college students are interested in making positive change. However, today's students do not see the political process as an agent of change. They believe community service is a more effective way to improve their communities and their country.[3]

Our students and I suggested four remedies to bridge the community and political service divide. They are as relevant today as they were when we wrote them more than two decades ago.

First, demystify the process. Our initial youth survey found that a full 92 percent of respondents believed that an effective way to motivate a greater number of students to public service and politics would be "if the process of registering and voting by absentee ballot were made easier so that students can vote from college."[4]

Second, show students how politics is an effective way to make concrete change. Nearly 90 percent of students believe greater awareness of real-life examples showing how students have made a difference would be an effective way to motivate students to engage in politics and public service.

Third, provide incentives. Creating partnerships between state or local governments and universities that enable students to participate in public service activities for academic credit (95 percent effectiveness rating) and forgiving loans or providing signing bonuses to graduates who commit to

government work (88 percent effective) both receive significant support from survey respondents.

Fourth, meet the candidates. Eighty-seven percent believe
a presidential debate that deals primarily with issues students
care about would be an effective way to get more of their
peers involved.

Entering young adulthood as independent-minded, caring,
and empathetic people, based in no small part on their
experiences serving their communities while in high school,
millennials' most formative political and cultural experiences
were the terrorist attacks of September 11, 2001, followed seven
years later by the collapse of the US real estate market and
global recession. Welcomed into adulthood by two national crises that shook everything they thought they knew about themselves and the world, at one of the most critical times in their
psychological development, millennials also witnessed

- a lonely march through an endless war in Iraq in
  search of WMDs that did not exist;

- the near loss of an American city after Hurricane
  Katrina;

- a new era of global connectedness with the launches
  of Facebook, Twitter, YouTube, and the iPhone.

Unlike their baby boomer parents, whose threat of nuclear annihilation was real but distant and unseen, the existential threats millennials feared were tangible. They were
the smoldering World Trade Center towers at Ground Zero

and the loss of a parent or loved one's job, savings, or home during the Great Recession.

These characteristics and events, in tandem with the spawning of social media, were fundamental in shaping young American minds, which neuroscience tells us are not fully developed until age twenty-five. From 9/11 onward, America's largest generation learned that security, whether physical or financial, is no longer guaranteed. It is this notion, as much as any other, that has shaped their lives and relationships.

This is why many millennials search for work that comes with an added benefit of making an impact and doing something good for people—something, they tell me, that their parents can be proud of. This upbringing also explains why millennials prize flexibility, a key component of how they define the American Dream. They understand from growing up that permanence is an illusion. It is why, similar to Gen Z, the embodiments of their "best lives" are more modest, less focused on tangibles, and more Zen-like than what we heard from previous generations. Ask your millennial child what success looks like, and this is what you will likely hear:

a happy family, a well-paid job, a house with small garden—that's everything

to have a job constantly, with a partner who loves me

to have a good house paid off, and no car loan

to be happy for what you have

doing everything you want without regrets; loving without regrets

* * *

Twelve days after the September 11 attacks, President George W. Bush's approval reached the historic high of 90 percent (outpacing his father by 1 percent) in Gallup tracking of American adults, an increase of 39 points in less than two weeks.[5]

By December, 70 percent of Americans were "satisfied with the way things were going in the United States," a number greater than double the level of satisfaction that Americans have felt in all but one quarter that Gallup has measured since 2006.[6]

Patriotism was not partisan. As members of both major political parties literally joined hands the day after 9/11 and sang "God Bless America" on the steps of the US Capitol, Americans in red communities and blue flew American flags on their front porches across every corner of the country—something unheard of in our current political climate.

In a Kaiser Family Foundation/Harvard University/ *Washington Post* poll conducted nearly a year after the attacks, 73 percent of adults, including 81 percent of Republicans, 68 percent of Democrats, and 69 percent of Independents, considered themselves either "extremely" or "very" patriotic.[7]

Young Americans reconsidered the importance of government service and political participation. "When I'm seventy, and look back at my life, I want to know that I did something for my country," Carlos Madden, fresh out of the US Army Reserve and two tours in the Middle East, relayed to me in 2010 when I asked him his motivation for joining the army at seventeen.

Studies showed Carlos was not alone. We saw a momentary boost of interest in military service, especially among higher-income, better-qualified, and educated millennials.[8] At the IOP, our students and I found dramatic improvements in how college students across America viewed the efficacy of politics and government, before and after the terrorist attacks.

In 2002, we reported that compared to the days before 9/11, college students were less likely to believe that elected officials were motivated by selfish reasons and were more likely to trust the federal government. In the emotion of the moment, a belief emerged among Americans just coming of age that political involvement can yield tangible results. Although the drawn-out wars in Iraq and Afghanistan would erode the optimism, what remained with the new generation was a belief in political engagement. This belief laid the groundwork for some enterprising political candidates to invest in organizing younger voters through the power of social networking both offline and on. This demystification of politics was fueled by movement-style campaigns, such as Howard Dean's for president in 2004, Deval Patrick's for governor of Massachusetts in 2006, and Ned Lamont's 2006 bid for the US Senate in Connecticut. It would culminate in Barack Obama's run for president in 2008, which showed a pathway to change and heralded increasing levels of youth turnout for state and national elections from 2002 through 2008.

While some like Carlos served in the military, many more members of his generation began engaging in civic life through political discourse and voting. *Bowling Alone* author and Harvard professor Robert D. Putnam and his colleague Thomas H. Sander noted that "the years since 9/11 have brought an unmistakable expansion of youth interest in politics and public affairs. For example, young collegians' interest in politics has rapidly increased in the last eight years, an increase all the more remarkable given its arrival on the heels of thirty years of steady decline."[9]

"From 1967 to 2000," Putnam and Sander wrote, "the share of college freshmen who said that they had 'discussed politics' in the previous twelve months dropped from 27 percent to 16 percent; since 2001, it has more than doubled and is now [2008] at an all-time high of 36 percent."

Energized by a growing opposition to the Iraq and Afghanistan Wars and the newfound organizing power of the internet, millennials comprised the unexpected but ultimate driving force behind Howard Dean's insurgent "netroots" campaign, which shook the political establishment in 2003 and 2004. Reflecting back on the vital role millennials played with CBS's Brian Goldsmith, Dean campaign manager Joe Trippi said:

> The biggest thing the Dean campaign did—we trusted young people. We said, we trust you to organize your own Meetup or your own Generation Dean meeting on campus. Or it was the young people in the campaign that came up with the Dean Corps. Which is, the kids would get together and go clean up a river or something wearing their Dean t-shirts.
>
> I got to be honest with you, I was sitting at headquarters going, okay, even I don't understand how that gets us votes. But then we'd get the local Davenport paper and it'd have the picture of the Dean kids in their Dean shirts bending over pulling garbage out of a river.
>
> And there'd be a story about it. And there was nothing overtly political, we're doing this to get votes. It was so authentic and real that these kids really cared about it. That I think it did help us. So, I think, basically, the biggest thing is trust.[10]

Although the number of first-time caucus-goers (of all ages) in Iowa nearly doubled from 9 percent in 2000 to 17 percent in 2004, concern over the economy and health care eventually eclipsed the war in Iraq, Governor Dean's signature issue, as most important for young caucus-goers in 2004.[11] While the Vermont doctor was the preferred choice for young Iowans who made up their mind at least a month before voting began, for those who decided later in the process, polls indicated that Senators John Kerry and John Edwards won a greater share of their vote.

Four years later, the failure of Hillary Clinton's first presidential campaign to recognize the importance of young voters and their desire for generational change was a considerable piece of why she came up just short in the 2008 primary season against Obama. Rather than carefully reviewing the data from the previous political cycle, analyzing public opinion, and seeing that Governor Dean would not have had much of a campaign without the energy and passion of young voters, the Clinton forces seemed to conclude that since Dean faded, the youth vote must be fickle, unreliable, and not worth the attention of a well-funded Democratic campaign for president.

"Did they sleep through the 2003–4 election cycle?" Trippi later wondered.[12]

In a strategy memo written to Senator Clinton on March 19, 2007, by campaign chief Mark Penn, it was noted that "there are three demographic variables that explain almost all of the votes in the primary—gender, party, and income." A fateful fourth variable—generation—went unmentioned until the last page of an eight-page memo in which Penn casually suggested the campaign should "organize a chapter of Dems for HRC on 1000 colleges." While they were at it, they could also "quickly organize 25,000 college students." This idea segued into a suggestion of finding more "elites to travel with her more and introduce her—Madeline (sic) Albright types."[13]

Less than two weeks later, senior Clinton advisor Harold Ickes emailed the campaign leadership a list of "Key Assumptions," with an assertion that the putative nominee would be chosen by Super Tuesday, February 5, 2008, one month after voting would begin.[14] Once again, there was no reference or plan (offensive or defensive) for an expanded electorate or the youth vote in the Ickes email, which was based on lengthy conversations with veteran staffers. Unlike their opponent, Clinton and her top advisors suffered from a lack of millennial perspective and strategists at the table.

Meanwhile, Obama's campaign manager David Plouffe, who was also part of the team behind Deval Patrick's 2006 expansive primary and general-election victories in Massachusetts, was overseeing an operation that dispatched staffers to Iowa to work every conceivable community and demographic group, including African Americans, Latinos, Republicans, and even high school students.[15]

The way the millennial vote later played out in that cycle came as no surprise, especially after meetings I had in the spring of 2007 with representatives from many of the Democratic and Republican campaigns for president. Armed with data and insights derived from a dozen polls and countless focus groups since 2000, then IOP director (and current US senator) Jeanne Shaheen, whose husband, Billy, chaired the Clinton efforts in New Hampshire, invited each of the presidential campaigns to take part in a briefing by our staff and students on the youth vote.

IOP Fellow and advisor to John McCain Mark McKinnon pushed us for deeper analysis of climate change and youth perceptions related to America's role in the world. Representatives from the teams of Massachusetts governor Mitt Romney and of former Wisconsin governor and HHS secretary Tommy Thompson joined us in Cambridge during the initial phases of their campaigns, as well. Others participated via conference calls and less formal meetups.

It was the interactions we had with the Clinton and Obama campaigns, though, that proved most provident. Both of our Democratic briefings took place within a few weeks of each other, as classes were wrapping up for the 2006–2007 academic year, not long after the Penn and Ickes memos were circulated to the Clinton orbit.

On the thirty-minute teleconference with the Obama campaign, several top staff members from Chicago dialed in, as well as organizers from the six states holding their caucuses or primaries before Super Tuesday. All parties were curious and well prepared, and questions were incoming from multiple disciplines within the organization. I left knowing that young people would be given significant responsibility on that campaign. Trippi's takeaway from 2004, that trust is everything, was not only heeded by the Obama team from its earliest days but invested in through talent and technology.

Paul Tewes, the Iowa state director for Obama, preached a governing philosophy for his mostly millennial staff: "Respect, Empower, Include." The campaign sought the "nicest, most attentive and most creative staff in the field," campaign manager David Plouffe would say. These millennials, new to politics, would be empowered from the top and have the freedom necessary to make their own ways as long as they delivered on the plan. They might not have had years of experience, like their Clinton counterparts, but they were "top-shelf talent," and that was not lost on anyone, including the candidate himself. "Our people knew they would not be field scum, as I was called when I started out," Plouffe would later say. "In many ways, they were the embodiment of our campaign."[16]

Obama's was a better integrated and more central effort

than the 1.0 version the Dean campaign created in the previous cycle. That's the way smart campaigns are run. They optimize the best from previous campaigns. They recognize the spirit and outlook of the moment, while utilizing tactics and tools that harness the latest data, technology, and communications opportunities available at that time. They expand the electorate, so it aligns as closely as possible with their unique visions and worldviews.

A few weeks later, when it came time for the Clinton campaign briefing, we had the attention of . . . one intern.

Don't get me wrong: Emily was smart, curious, and personable, with previous experience interning at a left-leaning Washington, DC, think tank. She was just not someone with influence over campaign strategy. Nonetheless, we imparted the same information to her that we had to the Obama leadership team. In a twenty-minute presentation we highlighted the emerging power of the millennial vote, documented the dramatic 31 percent increase in under-thirty voting turnout from 2000 to 2004, and showed how it had propelled Democratic candidates Jon Tester of Montana and Virginia's Jim Webb into the US Senate in 2006.

We made sure to tell both campaigns about the hundreds of youth-inspired grassroots social groups flourishing across the country, in support of candidates and issues. We continued with detailed analyses of the mood of the youth electorate and their most important concerns, with comparisons with older Americans where we could. Of particular note was the schism we identified between younger and older voters when it came to foreign policy and the role of the United Nations. Eighty-four percent of young Democrats in our survey, 81 percent of Independents, and nearly three in five Republicans were in favor of the UN solving international crises in conflicts, rather than the United States going it alone.[17] This interest in diplomacy, engagement, and collaboration with other nations became one of the defining issues for millennials.

In each of our campaign briefings, we also noted that after stabilizing Iraq, dealing with the genocide in Darfur was the second-most pressing foreign policy issue in first-time voters' minds. This humanitarian crisis was viewed as nearly three times more important for millennials at that time than fighting the war on terror, dealing with China as a superpower, North Korea's weapons program, Iran's nuclear ambitions, or peace between Israel and its neighbors.

These were the unique insights we offered to every interested campaign. Our goal was to help operatives and candidates from both parties better understand and hopefully create bonds with first-time voters in search of their political identities.

With little back-and-forth during our call with Emily and ahead of schedule for our allotted thirty minutes, I asked if she had any questions. "Only one," she said, as she signaled agreement with our takeaways and their implications for 2008: "How do I convince our leadership and the senator to take your poll and young people seriously?"

Somewhat bewildered because my IOP colleague Laura Simolaris and I just spent twenty minutes trying to answer that very question, Laura motioned that we should review the first slide of data again, "Turnout by Age in the 2000 and 2004 Presidential Elections." That was the page that illustrated that the 2004 increase in voter participation for Americans under the age of twenty-five was far greater than all other age groups. We felt this trend would continue, and young people would be a crucial force of energy both in the primary and the general-election campaign. Perhaps this would break the Clinton campaign out of its bubble in which they assumed, despite all data to the contrary, that new voters didn't count.

It soon became clear that Emily was not successful at persuading her bosses about the importance of the youth vote. In a June 2008 profile of the Clinton campaign, *Vanity Fair*'s Gail Sheehy reported:

> Clinton's people had no idea how excited a whole new cohort of voters would become by a youthful figure who tapped into their vital hunger for change from the ground up. Obama started cultivating these new voters at low-cost events. The turnout amazed even his own team. What began as I.M.'s and campus meet-ups developed into a genuine social movement.
>
> Such was the hubris of Hillary's team that they discounted Obama as a passing pop star to nonvoters. Politico.com reported that at a November 2007 Jefferson-Jackson dinner in Iowa, where 9,000 people showed up, 3,000 were already for Obama. "Our people look like caucus-goers," Mandy Grunwald sniffed, "and his [Obama's] people look like they are 18. Penn said they look like Facebook."[18]

Well, the people who "look like Facebook" would soon cost Hillary Clinton the 2008 Democratic presidential nomination. According to analysis by Emily Hoban Kirby, Peter Levine, and Karlo Barrios Marcelo of CIRCLE (the Center for Information and Research on Civic Learning and Engagement), the share of turnout for seventeen- to twenty-nine-year-olds in the Democratic caucus in Iowa increased by 25 percent since the previous contests four years prior.[19] David Plouffe marveled that "young voters would indeed turn out for Barack Obama. In Iowa, defying all history, voters under thirty turned out at the same rate as those over sixty-five."[20]

With George W. Bush finishing his second term in the White House—and the third of three Bush terms in twenty years—similar energy could also be found among Republicans. Iowa caucus entrance polls indicated that Arkansas governor Mike Huckabee won every age group that evening on the way to a 6-point victory over former Massachusetts governor Mitt Romney. No margin by demographic group, however, was greater than the 18-point advantage (40 percent to 22 percent) Huckabee held over Romney among millennials under thirty.[21]

To the detriment of the Clinton campaign, not only did "Facebook" show up to caucus on January 3, 2008, but an overwhelming number of young Iowans, whom the campaign described as not looking like "they could vote in any state,"[22] voted for Barack Obama. According to entrance polls, among voters between ages seventeen and twenty-four, Obama bested his seven opponents by at least 43 percentage points: Barack Obama 57 percent, John Edwards 14 percent, Hillary Clinton and Bill Richardson, 10 percent each. For those between twenty-five and twenty-nine years old, Obama held his 57 percent share, while Hillary Clinton finished second with 15 percent, followed by John Edwards at 12 percent.[23]

It was the combination of the increased share of young voters, plus the 43-point margin, that fueled Obama's victory on that first night of voting in 2008. If the election were held only among Iowans aged thirty and older, the then-forty-six-year-old first-term senator would have lost to Hillary Clinton. With New Hampshire voting less than a week later, his campaign might never have made it to Valentine's Day.

But Obama's strategy of expanding the electorate worked.

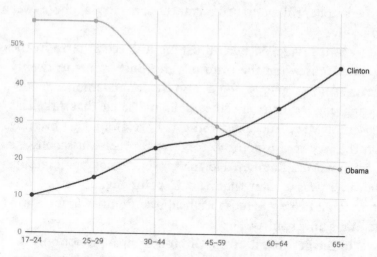

Figure 6.1. 2008 Iowa Democratic Caucus preferences by age (Obama and Clinton only).

Source: ABC News (Entrance poll conducted by Edison/Mitofsky for National Election Pool)

By empowering high schoolers, as well as Independents and Republicans who changed their party registrations for the evening, Obama won 38 percent of all votes in Iowa; John Edwards and Hillary Clinton trailed by 8 points, separated by 0.2 percent at second and third place respectively.

When Senator Clinton's plane was greeted on the frozen Nashua, New Hampshire, tarmac by longtime ally and political advisor Chuck Campion early the following morning, his next task came directly from the candidate herself. Knowing all too well that it would be difficult to lose both Iowa and New Hampshire and carry on, Clinton directed Campion with four simple words: "Find me young people." With less than a week before voting, the campaign furiously worked to establish a rapport with a demographic group they had not only ignored but disrespected for much of the last year.

Hours later, in her first public remarks after Iowa, the

New York senator spoke directly to "young people." Drawing a contrast with her challenger, she attempted to educate them on the difference between "calling for" and "producing" change in our political system:

> This is especially about all of the young people in New Hampshire who need a president who won't just call for change, or a president who won't just demand change, but a president who will produce change, just like I've been doing for thirty-five years.[24]

It worked. Hillary Clinton's eventual improvement with young voters (largely on the backs of the second-tier candidates), along with her display of what *The New Yorker*'s Hendrik Hertzberg artfully referred to as "human ordinariness" while meeting with female voters at a diner,[25] paired with Obama underperforming with Independent voters, was enough to seal a 2-point victory in the nation's first primary. Obama's momentum from the week prior was curbed, and North Carolina senator John Edwards, who polled at a distant third in the Granite State, would drop out of the race by the end of January.

The lesson of New Hampshire was that Hillary Clinton could stand to lose the millennial vote because of her strength with older and working-class members of the primary electorate, but she needed to be at least reasonably competitive with young voters.

If not for a failure to compete for millennials in the Hawkeye State, Clinton would have won the Iowa caucus and parlayed that momentum to an even more comfortable victory in New Hampshire—all of it leading to a legitimate shot at the "Super Tuesday knockout strategy" Mark Penn and Harold Ickes had been expecting for a year.[26]

Millennials tasted real political power during the 2008 primary season and could attest to the difference their engagement can make. Young voters across America would go on to play a critical role in the general election, as well. Winning two-thirds of the youth vote in the general election, Barack Obama improved significantly on John Kerry's 55 percent to 45 percent margin from 2004 when he faced George W. Bush. Indiana, North Carolina, and Virginia, three states that voted red in 2004, turned blue in 2008 because of the clout of the youth vote.[27]

Not only did Obama increase the margin with the youngest cohort of voters, but his campaign helped boost overall Democratic turnout, as well, especially in battleground states. Young voters increased their turnout percentages significantly in the two post-9/11 elections, while also increasing their share of the electorate.

To the delight of Erin and Trevor, in 2008, voters under thirty increased their turnout rate by nearly 40 percent compared to when the first millennial was eligible to vote in 2000. Their generation, it seemed, would not accept the false choice of volunteerism or voting. They would do both, as the Obama campaign turned a community-conscious generation into a full-fledged political army.

In an interview published less than a month after Obama was elected, Peter Hart, the veteran NBC News and *Wall Street Journal* pollster, told *Rolling Stone* publisher Jann Wenner:

It [youth vote] made a huge difference. Remember: When we talk about the youth vote, we're talking about all 50 states. It's not like the evangelical vote or an ethnic group that is located in one particular area. Youth voters—coast to coast, border to border—

turned to Obama in numbers that are just hard to fathom. They were drawn to him from day one, and it was a connection that was as psychological as it was issue-driven. This is somebody who spoke their language, who understood the times and who provided a direction that they wanted to see the country go in. Gore carried young voters by two points. Kerry carried them by about nine points. Obama carried them by 34 points.[28]

Mostly in their thirties now, millennials have held on to the ethic of volunteerism and community service that caught Erin and Trevor's eye two decades ago. Millennials' part in boosting Barack Obama in 2008 and their support for today's Democratic Party are fundamental elements of the party's current success—and its future. In the 2018 midterm election, the thirty- to forty-four-year-old cohort of mostly millennials supported Democrats by a substantial 19 points; in 2020, this group, along with Gen Zers, were the only age cohorts to support Biden in his victory over Trump.[29]

But, so far, the generation's influence in the corridors of Washington, DC, has been less remarkable. After Obama's reelection, Ron Fournier for *The Atlantic* suggested that "the best and brightest are rejecting public service as a career path. Just as Baby Boomers are retiring from government and politics, Washington faces a rising-generation 'brain drain.'"[30] A decade later, Fournier proved clairvoyant. "The only way Millennials might engage Washington is if they first radically change it," he said.

Relative to baby boomers when they were the same age, millennials account for a much smaller share of Congress. Over the course of their lifetimes, they've watched the average

age of a member of the House increase by nearly a decade—from forty-nine to fifty-eight—with the age of new members entering the chamber on a similar trajectory.

In the 117th Congress, which opened in January 2021, the seventh session in which millennials were eligible to serve, they accounted for just 6 percent—thirty-one members of the House, and one member of the Senate.[31] In 1985's 90th session, at a similar time in the life trajectory of boomers, they had twice the impact by share and counted sixty-three members.

In January 2021, Georgia's Jon Ossoff became the first millennial elected to the US Senate, an institution in which the median age is sixty-five and not getting younger.[32]

This disparity in representation cannot be accounted for simply by attributing a lack of interest in public service to millennials. Much like the barriers designed to disenfranchise nonlandowners, women, Black people, and college students over our history, the federal campaign-finance system, which has virtually no limit on corporate contributions, has driven the cost of winning a congressional campaign from about $800,000 in the mid-1980s (in today's dollars) to more than $1.5 million today.[33]

To succeed in this system as a young person often requires vast amounts of personal wealth, a moneyed network, or institutional support, making the success of working-class heroes like Alexandria Ocasio-Cortez, with a net worth of $7,000 at the time of her election,[34] even more exceptional.

Coming of age with a commitment to volunteerism and feeling burned by Republicans' handling of the economy and the Global War on Terror, millennials have already made their imprint on our country. They are reliably blue voters in most states in the nation. Their concerns for the working class, the climate, and social justice are aligned with the younger Generation Z, but with few exceptions, they have yet to be the dominant political force in Washington that their size and collective values might warrant. Teaming with Zoomers, and accounting for about 40 percent of all votes cast in the 2020 election, millennials are still very much ascendant and will be for years to come.

7

IMPATIENCE IS A VIRTUE

For every young millennial and Zoomer in America who's been demonstrating and rallying to reform crony capitalism, stop gun violence, address systemic racism, protect human rights, and curb climate change, millions of others overseas with progressive values are fighting for the same. In many cases, they do so at the risk of immense personal harm. The fire that President Trump and the far right's anti-science, illiberal, authoritarian agenda ignited over the last several years among American youth is burning brightly at home and is spreading across dozens of nations around the world.

Since 2017, the Carnegie Endowment for International Peace has tracked approximately 230 significant anti-government protests that have erupted worldwide. More than 110 countries have experienced protests, including in more than three-fourths of the countries led by authoritarian or authoritarian-leaning regimes.[1] It is estimated that about thirty governments or leaders have fallen as a result.[2]

Undeniably in disarray, the world in which we live is still brighter thanks to Generation Z. If not for Zoomers,

- the rights and freedoms of Hong Kong residents would be further eroded by mainland Chinese authorities;

- the president of France would not have demanded for laws to be rewritten in order to hold police accountable for their actions;

- Sudan's strongman, Omar al-Bashir, would not have been ousted, tried, and convicted for the coup that brought him to power in 1989;

- climate change would not have been one of the defining issues of the 2020 primary and general-election campaigns in the United States and would not now be a central focus of President Biden's domestic and foreign policy agendas.

Young activists played vital roles to start each of these efforts on peaceful and meaningful tracks. Jen O'Malley Dillon, who managed the Biden-Harris campaign and is serving as White House deputy chief of staff, made a point of emphasizing in a Zoom event organized by Tufts University, her alma mater, that it wasn't only young voters who moved heavily in the Democrats' direction in 2020. It was also their grandparents. Nations are transformed when the virtue and energy of youth meet the wisdom and experience of their elders—especially women, minority and indigenous groups, and working-class citizens of every age.

Ordinarily, progress in a society is gradual, slow, and steady. But not always. It took from 1776, when Abigail Adams beseeched her husband to "remember the ladies" while founding our country, until 1920 for women to even have the right to vote.

The first warnings from Quakers that William Penn's "Holy Experiment" was tainted by humans held in bondage on these shores date back even earlier, to the early 1700s.

Yet the Civil War didn't end slavery until 1865, and it took another century to secure African American voting rights—a guarantee that is incomplete and under siege in many states even to this day.

By contrast, the fight for gay marriage, led by young Gen Xers and millennials and clinched by Zoomers who didn't quite understand the nature of the controversy, happened in a historical flash. In 1973, when the University of Chicago's National Opinion Research Center first surveyed Americans about their attitudes about same-sex relationships, 73 percent of respondents described them as "always wrong," with another 7 percent saying they were "almost always wrong."[3] As recently as 2004, when Jonathan Rauch published his influential book on gay marriage, and the subject became an issue in a presidential election for the first time, the Pew Research Center found that Americans opposed same-sex marriage by a margin of two to one.[4]

With a nudge from Vice President Joe Biden, the Democratic Party officially endorsed gay marriage in the fourth year of Barack Obama's presidency. By 2015, the Supreme Court had declared it the law of the land. Public opinion polling showed conclusively that millennials, influencing their elders, led the way on this rapid social revolution.

Regardless of where they stood on the political spectrum, millennials simply didn't accept their parents' and grandparents' views on this topic. The generation that came after them took this lesson to heart, the lesson being that social change could come rapidly, but they added a new element to it: impatience. Raised by Alexa, Uber, and DoorDash, Zoomers simply aren't wired to be patient, especially when they believe human rights are at stake or basic scientific truths are on the table.

In 2006, John Mayer released a song that became the unofficial anthem of the Obama campaign the following year. It was called "Waiting on the World to Change." It was a powerful song, and it fit the moment nicely. But if there is a single difference between millennials and the next generation, it is this: Zoomers are not waiting on anything or anyone; they are going to force the issue. They will *make* the change happen—by themselves, if necessary.

When Greta Thunberg was eleven years old, one of her teachers showed her class a film depicting the effects of climate change. After seeing images of starving polar bears, extreme weather, flooding, and an island of plastic larger than Mexico floating in the South Pacific, many of her peers were able to move on. Greta, who had already been engrossed by climate science for two years by then, could not.[5]

She explained impatiently:

> I couldn't understand how that could exist, that existential threat, and yet we didn't prioritize it. I was maybe in a bit of denial, like, "That can't be happening, because if that were happening, then the politicians would be taking care of it."[6]

Making opaque politics transparent, the complicated climate science clear, and the allegedly immaterial urgent—these are Greta's superpowers. Her mom, Swedish opera singer Malena Ernman, said:

> She saw what the rest of us did not want to see. It was as if she could see our CO_2 emissions with her naked eye. The invisible, colourless, scentless, soundless abyss that our generation has chosen to ignore. She saw all of it—not literally, of course, but nonetheless

she saw the greenhouse gases streaming out of our chimneys, wafting upwards with the winds and transforming the atmosphere into a gigantic, invisible garbage dump.[7]

As Greta entered adolescence, she continued to assemble the pieces of a puzzle she knew had only one solution. Her parents became increasingly concerned and sought professional help because she appeared withdrawn, isolated, and helpless. Depressed, Greta would not eat for long periods of time, which likely stunted her growth. Today she stands at five feet tall. Barely.

Described as being born with Asperger syndrome and later diagnosed with high-functioning autism and obsessive-compulsive disorder, Greta often talks about how the world to her is a sea of "black and white." She understands that if her brain worked differently, if it were a kaleidoscope, not monochrome, she may not have the same capacity to study, prepare, and make her case so convincingly about the crisis she fears.

In 2018, three months after winning a local climate-change essay contest, and inspired by students from Parkland's Marjory Stoneman Douglas High School, Greta tried to pull a group of her peers together to join her cause after a record hot summer in Stockholm.

It started with (*sic*) a couple of youths in the United States refused to go to school because of the school shootings. And then someone I knew said, "What if children did that for the climate?" . . . And then, I thought that that was a good idea, that maybe it would make a difference. And then I tried to bring people with me, but no one was really interested, so I had to do it alone.[8]

Ably assisted in the early days by her father, Svante, an actor and descendant of 1903 Nobel Prize–winner Svante Arrhenius, a scientist who came up with a model of the greenhouse effect,[9] Greta filled her backpack with one hundred flyers, along with schoolbooks, water, lunch, a seat cushion, and an extra sweater, and rode her bicycle to the Swedish parliament. Her dad, pedaling not far behind, managed the simple three-word homemade sign (SKOLSTREJK FÖR KLIMATET) that Greta would post not far from the office of her country's prime minister.

On August 20, 2018, with two photos snapped by a passerby, Greta, who was wearing her hair in her now-trademark braids and was dressed in a blue hoodie with leopard-print pants, posted this message to Instagram (translated from Swedish to English):

> We children usually do not do as you tell us to do, we do as you do. And since you adults shit in my future, I'll do it too. I am on school strike for the climate until election day.[10]

On day two, Greta was joined by others. Students, teachers, children, and adults of all ages soon began to keep her company. Within a week, as support accelerated, ninth-grader Greta drew coverage from newspapers across her country. Delighted that she was achieving her goal, Greta's parents made clear that their preference was for her to now end the demonstration and return to school. But in true Greta fashion, she told them, "I have my books here. . . . What am I missing? What am I going to learn in school? Facts don't matter anymore, politicians aren't listening to the scientists, so why should I learn?"[11]

As she promised from the outset, her strike ended after

three weeks, but before returning to school, Greta attended and addressed a crowd of more than two thousand at the Stockholm Climate March. Her mother, Malena, recalled that this event felt different from previous climate events attended by her family. "Here, suddenly, are all conceivable kinds of people and characters," a far cry from the limited crowd of regulars, activists, and "Greenpeace volunteers in polar-bear suits"[12] they would regularly see. Suddenly, the movement looked like Sweden. All age groups and classes of people represented. Even still, few could have predicted what this moment would spawn within a matter of weeks.

Like any parent, Svante was scared "out of his wits" in the moments leading to his daughter's first public speech on this unseasonably warm Saturday in Stockholm.[13] But soon, he would witness Greta draw on the lessons of Emma González, who had addressed gun violence activists and concerned citizens just six months earlier. Calling out the "BS" in her own way, holding individuals and institutions to account, Greta empowered and then challenged her audience for more.

After initially blasting the newspapers, influencers, political parties, politicians, and everyday people who brush aside "the critical question of our time," Greta said:

> The future of all the coming generations rests on your shoulder.
>
> Those of us who are still children can't change what you do now once we're old enough to do something about it.
>
> A lot of people say that Sweden is a small country, that it doesn't matter what we do. But I think that if a few girls can get headlines all over the world just by not going to school for a few weeks, imagine what we could do together if we wanted to.

Every single person counts.

Just like every single emission counts.

Every single kilo.

Everything counts.

So please, treat the climate crisis like the acute crisis it is and give us a future.

Our lives are in your hands.[14]

Back at school, Greta would maintain a dizzying schedule. From the fall of 2018 through 2019, she continued to lead her Friday strikes while accepting invitations and reaching out to those equipped to help her cause. Traveling with her parents through Europe on weekends and holidays in an electric vehicle, Greta addressed the United Nations Climate Change Conference in Poland in December 2018, and the World Economic Forum in Switzerland in January, along with the British, French, and European parliaments in the following months. By springtime, her request for a meeting with Pope Francis was granted. The Vatican would later call Greta "a great witness to what the Church teaches on the care of the environment and the care of the person."[15]

With every tweet, post, and speech, momentum grew. Her impact was global. Public opinion among young Americans was changing in demonstrable ways. Over the last decade, increasing support for bold government solutions to curb climate change coincided with the December 2015 Paris Agreement on climate change, Trump's decision to withdraw from the accord in 2017, and then again during Greta's constant campaign and global call for action.

Captivated, politicians around the world were taking notice of Greta, our climate, and the resilience and power of Generation Z.

French president Emmanuel Macron remarked, "When

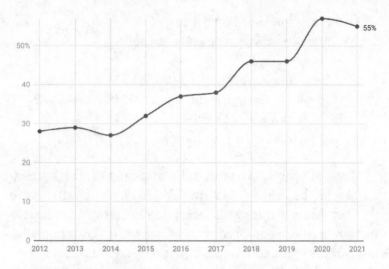

Figure 7.1. 18–29-year-olds who strongly or somewhat agree that "government should do more to curb climate change, even at the expense of economic growth."

Source: Harvard IOP Youth Poll, 2012–2021

you are a leader and every week you have young people demonstrating with such a message, you cannot remain neutral. They helped me change."[16]

After Greta addressed members of the British parliament with other school strikers in April 2019, delivering a pointed message that their behavior is irresponsible and "will no doubt be remembered in history as one of the greatest failures of humankind," Britain's then environment secretary, Michael Gove, clearly anguished, answered:

> When I listened to you, I felt great admiration, but also responsibility and guilt. I am of your parents' generation, and I recognise that we haven't done nearly enough to address climate change and the broader environmental crisis that we helped to create.

Labour politician Ed Miliband, who was responsible for introducing the UK Climate Change Act of 2008, followed:

You have woken us up. We thank you. All the young people who have gone on strike have held up a mirror to our society . . . you have taught us all a really important lesson. You have stood out from the crowd."[17]

Greta, like the Occupy- and Parkland-inspired protestors before her, was hitting the right notes. She was beginning the long journey of influencing both hearts and minds at the highest levels of government. While many Swedish, French, and British elected officials were captivated, not all of our leaders were sympathetic. Russian president Vladimir Putin, whose country and political fortunes depend on the oil and gas that accounts for about half of its federal budget revenue,[18] said Greta was likely kind but naive, and an instrument of special interests. "I may disappoint you, but I don't share the common excitement about the speech by Greta Thunberg."[19] While Putin, President Trump, Brazilian president Jair Bolsonaro, and others tried to humble Greta, she organized.

Less than two and a half years after her school strike began, nearly eighty thousand strike events have been documented in nearly eight thousand cities and more than two hundred counties. Since Greta took her message to the Swedish parliament, fourteen million other strikers have taken some action in defense of the climate, their generation, and the future.[20]

After Greta addressed a crowd the size of a papal gathering in New York City, twelve-year-old spectator Mina Garcia remarked, "She's able to do so much. It shows no matter how small you are and how little you feel, you can stand up to someone and make a difference."[21]

Greta has inspired a class of activists the world over that ensures her vision will not fade. Included in the cohort, at great personal risk, is Ou Hongyi, a then-eighteen-year-old Chinese citizen who passed on a Harvard education, at least for the moment, to remain in her country to raise awareness of China's role in the climate crisis and to pressure her government to take bolder steps to reduce emissions in the next five years.

"Everyone should realize that the climate crisis is already the biggest existential crisis facing mankind. People needed to read about the crisis, to understand it and talk to their friends and family about it. When they really read and understand it, they will know what they should do," she said to a reporter in December 2020, just a few months after she was detained and questioned for several hours by the police.[22]

In Africa, Zoomer activists like Nigeria's Adenike Oladosu, Kenya's Elizabeth Wanjiru Wathuti, and Uganda's Vanessa Nakate see the effects climate change is having in the developing world.[23] Concerned about food insecurity, displaced peoples, floods and droughts affecting crops, and clashes between farmers and herdsmen, they have joined forces with Greta, have begun striking in their hometowns, and have spearheaded demonstrations across their continent.

One of the youngest activists on the planet at age seven, Licypriya Kangujam protested in June 2019 outside the Indian parliament with a sign imploring Prime Minister Modi and members of parliament to "Pass the climate change law and save our future." Referred to, like the others, as her country's "Greta Thunberg," Licypriya has taken her message of climate justice and education to more than thirty countries. Already, she has made an impact in India as her demands for a climate curriculum were rolled out in regional school districts in 2020.[24] "The world is waking up" is what Greta

Thunberg told the United Nations General Assembly a little more than a year after she began her strike, "and change is coming whether you like it or not."[25]

Whether young people live under authoritarian regimes, full or flawed democracies, or a hybrid, Generation Z is using all peaceful means within their grasp to fight the powerful and oppose restrictions on what they consider human, political, and economic rights. Climate change, income inequality, LGBTQIA+ rights, access to quality education, reproductive choice, and police brutality are the causes that connect youth in every US state and most locales on the planet.

The point here is that the emerging generation is connected to the world through the internet, offering them a shared perspective other generations lacked. It's not American Zoomers driving this change, or Swedish, French, or Nigerian Zoomers—it's just Zoomers.

From 2011 to 2019, the number of general strikes, anti-government demonstrations, and riots around the world increased by more than 200 percent.[26] After *TIME* magazine named Greta Thunberg Person of the Year in 2019, with many dubbing it the "Year of the Protest," some inferred that the swell of demonstrations might have crested. But after a short interruption in January and February 2020 due to the COVID-19 outbreak, significant new anti-government protests roared back for the remainder of 2020 and into 2021.

Beginning in March 2020, the number of new global protests recorded exceeded the number from the same time period a year earlier.[27] The only exception was in the month of September, which had spawned an unusually high number of new protests in 2019, including one led by university students in Indonesia who successfully fought against a new criminal code that would have violated the rights of women, religious minorities, and LGBTQIA+ groups.[28]

While Joe Biden's victory may quell some of the unrest felt among young Zoomers in the United States, there are few signs globally that the demonstrations will abate anytime soon. According to the global consultancy Verisk Maplecroft, publisher of the Civil Unrest Index, seventy-five countries—more than half of which are from Europe and the Americas—will likely experience an increase in protests by late 2022.[29]

In 2020, as millions in the United States took to the streets in support of racial justice and equality, while also fighting to survive multiple waves of the coronavirus, a faltering economy, social isolation, and a remarkable presidential campaign, at least a dozen other nations saw their young citizens organize significant new protests.

Gauging the success of a protest or movement is often a subjective undertaking; most issues aren't as easy to chart as same-sex marriage. Sometimes progress can be measured when a government falls, or law is passed. Other times, success is realized over decades when awareness about an issue is raised and influences the values and politics of a generation. Through grit, persistence, and sustained civil disobedience, here are some current examples from around the world of Generation Zers creating new movements to make their countries and world a more fair and just place.

For the Climate

In January 2020, thirty thousand Australian student activists, led by Uni Students for Climate Justice and motivated by weak government policies on climate, marched across nine cities over concerns about the government response to the Australian bushfires. Prime Minister Scott Morrison soon admitted some regret over government policies, increased funding to respond to the fires that devastated the bush country, and promised that a royal commission would review the government response.[30]

For the Economy and Education

In France, 2020 was another year for protests and civil disobedience. The year began with tens of thousands of union members, public sector employees, "yellow vest" demonstrators, lawyers, rail workers, and students protesting government plans for pension reform. The protests ended in February 2020, before COVID-19 consumed Europe, when the government scrapped plans to raise the retirement age from sixty-two to sixty-four.[31] Throughout the rest of the year, the French capital saw additional uprisings ranging from fifteen thousand who gathered over concerns about racism[32] to smaller anti-mask rallies in Paris.[33]

In India, on the heels of a massive late 2019 student-led citizenship protest over rising Hindu nationalism under Prime Minister Narendra Modi, students and trade unions organized a strike to voice frustration over the government's economic policies. The objective of the protest, which took place after another gloomy economic projection, was an end to short-term labor contracts, higher pay, and a halt to the privatization of state-owned enterprises. The Modi government, which was reelected for a second term the year before but is blamed for the highest unemployment rate in forty-five years, did not respond to the protesters' demands.[34]

Beginning in the spring of 2019 in Brazil, lasting for three months, and encompassing more than one hundred thousand citizens, groups of students, teachers, and teachers' unions concerned about economic challenges and government attacks on public education protested against cuts in education spending and postgraduate scholarships. These were the first protests aimed against far-right president Jair Bolsonaro since he assumed office earlier that year.[35]

Students, unions, leftist groups, and indigenous groups began protesting in Colombia in September 2020 and have remained active through much of 2021. Motivated by the disapproval of President Iván Duque Márquez's government, rising economic inequality, corruption, police brutality, and militarized response to protests, more than one million Colombians have taken part in an ongoing fight to address rumored pension cuts, rising violence, and concerns over the country's peace deal.[36]

In Ecuador, over two weeks in May 2020, student groups, indigenous groups, transportation unions, and labor unions concerned about economic inequality and indigenous land rights protested an austerity package that would increase fuel costs and cut salaries for public sector jobs. One of the exasperated protest organizers, in Guayaquil, Ecuador's largest city, remarked, "If the coronavirus doesn't kill us, the government will." The government responded to the fuel-subsidy protests by agreeing to cancel the austerity package.[37]

For Political Transparency and Accountability

In February 2020, nearly twenty thousand Germans, led by young people, unions, and anti-fascists, took to the streets of Dresden and Erfurt to denounce state-level political co-operation with the far-right Alternative for Germany (AfD) Party. Holding placards that read NO PACT WITH FASCISTS and NO PLACE FOR NAZIS, young Germans were outraged that the business-friendly Free Democratic Party (FDP) and Angela Merkel's center-right Christian Democrats (CDU) had made a secret pact and broken the post–World War II taboo of legitimizing the far right. After the protests, Chancellor Angela Merkel's handpicked successor and ruling Christian Democratic Union's chair, Annegret Kramp-Karrenbauer, resigned, and Thomas Kemmerich, the minister president of Thuringia and member of FDP, stepped down from his position as state premier after only one month in office.[38]

For most of 2020 and into 2021, the government of Thailand has been under sustained pressure by youthful protestors demanding the resignation of Prime Minister Prayuth Chan-ocha and his cabinet, constitutional changes drafted by representatives of the people, and reform of the monarchy under the constitution. The government's failure to boost the economy during the pandemic, kidnapping of a leading political activist, and a desire to repeal Thailand's strict royal defamation law were among the specific grievances that moved more than ten thousand to the streets.[39]

Starting in Tehran, and soon spreading to a dozen other cities, more than one thousand Iranian college students angrily took to the streets in January 2020 over a lack of government transparency and accountability for the mistaken downing of a Ukrainian jetliner that killed all 176 people on board. While a top Iranian military commander made a rare public appeal for forgiveness, there was no significant policy or leadership change as a result of the student engagement.[40]

For Systemic Racism and Police Brutality

In solidarity with Black Lives Matter activists in the United States, Zoomers around the world took to the streets in their capitals to protest police brutality and systemic racism in their own lands. Thousands of students in New Zealand, along with the business community and general public, marched for a week in early June against systemic racism and police violence against indigenous people. Initially condemned by Deputy Prime Minister Winston Peters, who said they violated the country's social distancing rules and called the protesters "a small group who think they know better than everyone else," the police commissioner later announced that the New Zealand Police would do away with its armed response teams.[41]

Addressing "the myth that Portugal is not a racist country," urban young people led a demonstration of more than ten thousand against police brutality, systemic racism, and lack of government recognition of systemic racism. So far, there's not been a meaningful response recorded by the government to the protests.[42]

This global component should not come as a surprise. For one thing, although Zoomers within the United States profess less confidence than previous generations about America's singular standing in the world, those outside our borders still look to this country for cultural clues and political inspiration.[43] Moreover, the defining public policy issues for Zoomers—economic inequality, climate change, and racial inclusiveness—are transnational in scope. And COVID-19, by definition, was a global challenge.

"We don't see too many moments in history like this," Johns Hopkins University sociology professor Alexandre White told *National Geographic* magazine as the pandemic unfolded in the spring of 2020. Dr. White, who teaches a course in the history of pandemics, added, "Generation Z is going to have to find and build communities in different ways than any generation has done before."[44]

Laura Parker, the author of that *Nat Geo* article, talked to several Zoomers around the world, including Lesein Mutunkei, a then-fifteen-year-old Kenyan who was trying to negotiate the hurdle of taking online classes amid frequent power outages. An avid soccer player, Lesein was concerned about the lack of team sports, the pandemic-necessitated suspension of his tree-planting campaign, and the fate of his older sister, who was stranded in South Africa due to soaring COVID-19 infection rates.[45]

But true to the ethos of his generation, Lesein Mutunkei was also worried about everyone on the planet. "I heard the news about America," he told Parker, "and thought about our friends in America who can be sick."[46]

As the conflagration of COVID-19 swept across the globe, "We are all in this together" evolved from an aspirational theological statement of faith, to a marketing slogan, to a scientific reality. Even before the pandemic, however, it was a pretty good working definition of Zoomer philosophy. And it never did stop at lines on a map or any nation's borders.

8

ASK AND YE SHALL RECEIVE

B efore most of us heard of Wuhan or social distancing, the campaign to elect the next president of the United States was well underway, and all indications were that young voters were highly charged and motivated for 2020.

Ultimately, they would prove the difference. For the first time, most young people under thirty voted in a general election. Generation Z and young millennials outvoted their peers from the previous high-water mark of 2008. *The Washington Post* stated that 2020 marked a "big breakthrough in youth turnout," as the youth vote led as the first of five highlights from their analysis of the electorate.[1]

Once again, an early indication that enthusiasm was rising came from our own Harvard IOP spring 2019 survey. Across the demographic and political spectrum, the data showed increasing levels of interest in voting, especially compared to the previous election cycle. This attentiveness went beyond the horse race aspect of the election or even the candidates themselves, although it was apparent that the incumbent in the White House remained highly unpopular with young voters. Issues and conversations about the structural challenges our democracy was facing were resonating, as well, suggesting that to recruit Zoomers for any meaningful attachment to a political campaign meant connecting them to a cause with a higher purpose than electing a specific candidate.

Young people are almost always the lifeblood of successful political campaigns. Their influence is measured in myriad ways, and unlike other important voting cohorts, like union members, veterans, African American, Asian American, or Hispanic and Latino voters, you can find Gen Z in roughly equal proportions across all fifty states, the District of Columbia, and the US territories. Young people are just as likely to live and vote in Georgia and Pennsylvania, for example, as they are in Nevada and Michigan. And with Gen Z and millennials together accounting for nearly two in five of 2020 voters (and growing in the near future), this makes the youth vote as strategic and sturdy a base to build from as any in politics.

Heading into 2020, Barack Obama's 2008 success continued to be among the best models for integrating youth into a broad, diverse, and winning coalition. The approach draws as much on insights from psychology and sociology as political organizing. It remains a blueprint today for engaging stakeholder groups, in and outside of politics. From his earliest days as a Chicago-based community organizer, Barack Obama came to see that success with young people depended on prioritizing listening over theorizing about what matters to them. Obama would notice "how people stood up a little straighter, saw themselves differently when they learned their voices mattered."[2]

Giving power to the disenfranchised, trusting, and then challenging them to engage on their own behalves was central to how Obama modeled both campaigns and much of his presidency. It's how Joe Biden structured his successful "first 100 days" as president. In my view, it represents the best of our politics.

In late summer 2007, the Obama campaign knew that one reason he received so much attention during a critical

ABC News candidate debate was because of his appeal with younger Iowans. The first-term Illinois senator was in a virtual three-way tie for first place heading into Labor Day—and both the media and the campaign knew that young Iowans were the ballast. Among the most reliable caucus-goers—senior citizens with track records of voting—Obama consistently polled a distant third behind Hillary Clinton and John Edwards. Rather than fruitlessly trying to persuade the unpersuadable, Obama would forgo opportunities to campaign with senior citizens, even skipping a televised AARP forum for a shot at firing up a few hundred first-time voters eager to be on the ground floor of something special. Ultimately, millennials were the reason Obama won Iowa, and the day after he exited the Hawkeye State for New Hampshire with a comfortable 8-point victory, David Von Drehle wrote for *TIME*:

> Obama clearly knew something others didn't, and that zig where others zagged now appears to have been a shrewd move on the path to a dramatic achievement. Obama's youth-oriented campaign drew under-twenty-five voters to Thursday's Iowa caucuses in record numbers, and these first-time voters gave him most of his margin of victory.[3]

Reflecting on the building blocks of his meteoric rise, Obama noted that he was convinced he would win the Iowa caucus, and by extension the nomination by Thanksgiving of 2007. "Not necessarily because I was the most polished candidate, but because we had the right message for the time and had attracted young people with prodigious talent to throw themselves behind the cause." Recognizing these two forces at play is the reason why, despite the almost innumerable demands on his time, he and Michelle Obama hosted a dinner in the campaign's final weeks for the parents of the young Iowa field organizers to thank each of them for raising such "amazing sons and daughters."

"To this day," Obama wrote thirteen years later, "there's nothing I wouldn't do for those kids."[4]

To my surprise, however, similar appeals to Gen Z and young people in the 2020 Democratic primary were scarce. Most candidates did not even mention young Americans in their introductory remarks. When they did, their attempts felt forced and underwhelming.

On April 15, 2019, by contrast, when former South Bend mayor Pete Buttigieg made his candidacy official inside a steamy old Studebaker plant in South Bend, generational politics took center stage.

"I recognize the audacity of doing this as a Midwestern millennial mayor. More than a little bold—at age thirty-seven—to seek the highest office in the land," he said. "But the moment we live in compels us to act. The forces of change in our country today are tectonic. Forces that help to explain what made this current presidency even possible. That's why, this time, it's not just about winning an election—it's about winning an era."

With that, Buttigieg began his quest to win over the young voters in Iowa and nationally who were reluctant to lend their full-throated support to Bernie Sanders. Declaring to the large and boisterous hometown crowd forced inside because of weather, he reflected,

I come from the generation that grew up with school shootings as the norm, the generation that produced the bulk of the troops in the post-9/11 conflicts, the generation that is going to be on the business end of climate change for as long as we live."[5]

New York Times national political correspondent Alex Burns took note of Buttigieg's bet that there was an "intellectual and social cohesion to the population of voters under forty, and that only a person who shares their experiences and mind-set can address the problems common to this group."[6]

In the very early stages of voting, Buttigieg came close to becoming the Bernie Sanders alternative that thousands of young Democrats in most states were searching for but never found. After all, Sanders was popular, but even among Democrats, there were plenty searching for other options to run against Trump. Knowing the well-placed lack of faith his millennial generation and Zoomers have in government, Buttigieg pledged early in his campaign that the first legislation he would pursue as president would be "democratic reform. . . . Because every other issue that I care about—from gun violence to climate change—isn't going to get better" without it.[7]

Central to the Buttigieg plan was abolishing the Electoral College, a new voting-rights act, statehood for Puerto Rico and DC, and depoliticizing the Supreme Court.[8] It was as progressive a concept as any in the primary. In the end, Buttigieg strayed from his focus on youth, failed to expand his coalition to include nonwhite voters in the South and West, withdrew from the contest after the South Carolina primary, and gave Biden a boost with an endorsement soon after.

But that is hindsight. Our Spring 2019 Harvard IOP youth poll found that in a field of nineteen candidates, Bernie Sanders held the pole position, but the race for the Gen Z vote was far from decided.

Among potential Democratic caucus-goers and voters under thirty, Sanders was preferred by 29 percent. "Undecided" held second place, with a quarter telling us they were unsure who they were supporting; this was followed by Joe Biden at 18 percent, though he had not yet officially entered the fray.[9] The race among young voters was truly anyone's to win.

A harbinger of what would surface when the political calendar turned in February 2020 from the 90 percent white Iowa and New Hampshire contests to Nevada and South Carolina, we found that race and ethnicity were highly predictive and decisive factors in the Democratic primary—even among Generation Z and millennials. Deeper levels of support for Bernie Sanders among Hispanic and Latino youth, who affectionately dubbed him Tío Bernie, were obvious and outpaced his backing among young white and Black people.[10] But as popular a figure as Bernie Sanders was among young people, fewer supported him as their first choice than those who did not.

After five debates and two presidential town halls from summer through mid-October 2019, our youth polling found that the issues debated by most of the major candidates were well aligned with the goals of likely Gen Z voters. Expanding health care coverage, climate change, income inequality, and college affordability were clearly the concerns dominating our polling in 2019. However, as the caucuses and primaries drew closer, there was no such consensus on the most effective solutions or strategies for addressing these issues.

While nearly half of likely Democratic voters agreed that they "prefer big, structural policy changes that address the urgency of the problems that we are facing, even if they will not be easy to carry out"—essentially an endorsement of the Bernie Sanders and Elizabeth Warren wing of the party—nearly as many (39 percent) "prefer[red] policies that stand a good chance of being achieved as opposed to sweeping changes that will be difficult to carry out," a nod to the more moderate Biden, Buttigieg, and Klobuchar approaches.[11]

Given the dominance of Sanders against Hillary Clinton in 2016 with youth, that Gen Z and millennials were still in play in 2020 was a revelation for us. Richard Sweeney, a Harvard College junior from outside Albany, New York, and cochair of the Harvard Public Opinion Project, summarized what we learned:

> Voters under thirty are not bound by precedent or old institutional norms. Proponents of structural reforms shouldn't take young voters for granted, and those who favor a more gradual approach shouldn't write us off. Millennials and Gen Z-ers will be one-third of the eligible voting population in 2020. We're listening, and we're voting.[12]

Young voters continue to be misunderstood by people who ought to know better. I have never found the appeal of Bernie Sanders with so many young people much of a mystery. Not unlike the more moderate forty-fourth president, Obama, "Bernie's politics are 90 percent targeted to younger people." At least that was the common belief I heard when asking Zoomers why they were supporting the nearly eighty-year-old democratic socialist.

"It's all about college tuition," they said. "It's all about the wage gap. It's all about things that younger people care about. He's not arguing about 'old people' things. He's looking at the younger generation's problems, things that the younger people want done."

Elena, a then-twenty-one-year-old college student in South

Carolina, said she voted early for Sanders in her state's primary. She valued his consistency, saying "You can go through his entire political career, and his views have been the same. I respect him."

For a solid bloc of young Democrats, Bernie Sanders was more than a politician. Despite being older than their grandparents, Sanders showed young voters that he cared about them through his policies. His spirit and unflagging sense of what's right and wrong were to be admired, they thought, not belittled or dismissed.

The media was more skeptical. To his young supporters, when Sanders wasn't being ignored by journalists, he was being sold short by them. In early fall 2019, an enterprising millennial producer was compelled to gift the movement a five-minute video highlighting and then debunking some of the more irrelevant, personal, and wrongheaded pundit takes offered by invited guests on cable news outlets.[13] Among the sound bites former MTV's *The Real World* editor Matt Orfalea brought to the attention of tens of thousands of ardent Sanders supporters were the following:

It's really hard to imagine who the Bernie Sanders voter is at this point.

—Nia-Malika Henderson,
senior political reporter, CNN

The issue is, do you seem like you're in the contemporary world? He's a socialist from the 1950's, yelling at people in the same screechy voice, without smiling, without any kind of personal connection.

—Jennifer Rubin, *Washington Post* opinion columnist and political analyst, MSNBC

I don't understand young women who support him. . . .
Bernie Sanders makes my skin crawl, and I cannot even
identify what it is.

> —Mimi Rocah, legal analyst, now Westchester
> County, NY, district attorney, MSNBC

Bernie Sanders: Fall back, please get away from us.
You're disheveled, unlikable and pushy. And I don't
think you should be leading anybody.

> —Liza Treyger, stand-up comic, actress, MSNBC

Gloria Steinem has suggested that younger women
are supporting Bernie Sanders so they can meet boys.

> —Reported by Savannah Guthrie on the *Today* show

Naturally, the video went viral, and Orfalea was soon
employed directly by the campaign. His work presented Bernie at his best: forthright, but also energetic, caring, even
lighthearted at times. All of it was packaged to empower his
defenders with the goods to counter what felt like coordinated attacks from America's elite.

"The thing I like best about this ad is that it takes all of
the negativity the media hurls at him and spins it around
and hurls it right back," Jenna from North Carolina tweeted
at the time. "It puts a spotlight on everything we love about
Bernie and it does it without taking digs at any other candidate."[14]

On late-night TV appearances with Stephen Colbert,
Jimmy Fallon, and Jimmy Kimmel, and via Larry David's
reprised *Saturday Night Live* parodies, the character that was
Bernie Sanders ultimately was portrayed in a far more complimentary light. In May 2019, *The Daily Show with Trevor Noah*
featured a segment that was cut from a public-access-TV pro-

gram Sanders hosted in the mid-eighties when he was mayor of Burlington, Vermont.

"The first thing that's really apparent is how consistent Bernie has been throughout his life," Trevor Noah noted to an audience used to hypocrisy from their politicians. The piece then shifted to a younger, but still gray Mayor Sanders on a sidewalk proclaiming to the befuddled citizens of his small New England city that "We are one of two nations in the industrialized world that does not have a national health care system." On cue, the Hell's Kitchen studio audience laughed at the videoclip from a generation ago that sounded—Brooklyn accent and all—as if it were recorded that day.

One of his only significant changes in rhetoric from the time Bernie Sanders served in local government through the present has been his deepening focus on young people and the future. Sanders would spend more time addressing the concerns of Generation Z during his 2019 campaign kickoff in Brooklyn than all of his opponents combined, during their announcements.

> Today, we say to our young people that we want you to get the best education that you can, regardless of the income of your family. Good jobs require a good education. That is why we are going to make public colleges and universities tuition free, and substantially lower the outrageous level of student debt that currently exists. America once had the best educated workforce in the world, and we are going to make that happen again. . . .
>
> Instead of spending $80 billion a year on jails and incarceration, we are going to invest in jobs and education for our young people. . . .
>
> We're going to provide legal status to the 1.8 million young people eligible for the DACA program and

develop a humane border policy for those who seek asylum. . . .

We are going to bring our people together—Black, white, Latino, Native American, Asian American, gay and straight, young and old, men and women, native born and immigrant. . . .

Together, as so many of our young people have received criminal records for nonviolent offenses, we have fought to end the war on drugs, and have seen state after state decriminalize marijuana, and have seen communities expunge the criminal records of those arrested on these charges. . . .

When We are in the White House we will end the decline of rural America, reopen those rural hospitals that have been closed, and make sure that our young people have decent jobs so they do not have to leave the towns they grew up in and love.[15]

In the end, it wouldn't be enough for Bernie Sanders to buck the Democratic Party establishment he had never been a part of—at least in terms of garnering the nomination.

On the first Monday of February 2020, the eyes of the world were watching what Derek Eadon, a former Iowa Democratic Party chairman, would soon designate as a "systemwide disaster"[16] unfold. A new platform, a rushed timeline, buggy software code, and insufficient backups resulted in a delay in caucus results that indefinitely stalled the Democratic nomination process. Twenty-four hours after polling sites closed, only 62 percent of results were released to the public.[17] By every conceivable measure (except an increased youth turnout), the 2020 Democratic caucus was a comedy of errors and a disaster. Time will tell if it cost Iowa its favored status in future elections—along with tens of millions in lost advertising and tourism-related revenue. Regardless, it had an enormous and deleterious effect on the ultimate delegate winner (by the slimmest of margins), Pete Buttigieg.

According to entrance polls, 37 percent of caucus-goers were first-timers, and one-fourth of all votes cast were from Iowans under thirty.[18] This was slightly higher than the 23 percent youth share that carried Obama in 2008[19]—and it is about the same share of the electorate as for seniors.

Youth activists were ecstatic. In hindsight, the enthusiasm was premature. Stephen O'Hanlon, one of the Gen Z founders of the Sunrise Movement, told MTV News, "For young people who have a lot going on in their lives, it's a big commitment to turn out for the caucus. The fact that so many young people turned out is really notable and is a sign of what's to come in the coming months as we go through other primaries and caucuses."[20]

These youth trends, along with a two-week surge of momentum in late January,[21] suggested a strong showing for Bernie Sanders in Iowa. Four years earlier, when youth represented only 18 percent of the total vote, he walked away with 84 percent of it—on his way to a virtual tie with Hillary Clinton.[22]

The Iowa surprise in 2020, however, would not be to Sanders's benefit. In the days leading up to the caucuses, he was the odds-on favorite, but the combination of him not exceeding 50 percent of the Gen Z vote,[23] and winning only 4 percent of the senior citizen vote (Sanders won 26 percent in the 2016 caucus against Clinton and Martin O'Malley[24]), left just enough room for the well-organized and solidly funded campaign of Buttigieg to surpass Sanders by the slimmest of possible margins. Once the tallies were complete, Buttigieg received 26.2 percent of state delegate equivalents (SDE);

Sanders would follow with 26.1 percent. Massachusetts senator Elizabeth Warren (18.1 percent) took third place, a few points ahead of Biden's fourth-place finish (15.8 percent).

Buttigieg ended up taking second place to Sanders among Gen Z and millennials under thirty. In the stacked field, Sanders flipped from earning 84 percent of the youth vote in 2016 to 48 percent of the same seventeen-to-twenty-nine-year-old cohort; Buttigieg earned 19 percent, 7 points ahead of his closest rival, Elizabeth Warren. Her Iowa operation, staffed with scores of enthusiastic young campaigners, spent significant time attempting to organize Iowa's college towns and campuses, but was unable to break through.[25]

In the New Hampshire "First in the Nation" primary the following week, Bernie Sanders bested Pete Buttigieg by less than two percentage points. They each earned nine delegates to the Democratic National Convention.[26] The youth vote in

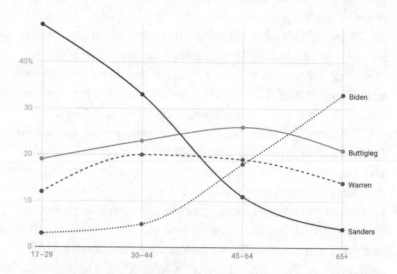

Figure 8.1. 2020 Iowa Democratic Caucus preferences by age.

Source: Entrance poll, CNN.com (first four finishers only: Buttigieg, Sanders, Warren, Biden)

New Hampshire was a near carbon copy of Iowa. Sanders again polled less than half of the Zoomer vote (47 percent), while Buttigieg held on to 20 percent.[27] Warren, Andrew Yang, and Tulsi Gabbard were separated by only 1 percentage point and were afterthoughts.[28]

Troubling, though, was that unlike in Iowa, fewer young voters turned out than in the previous primary cycle. Compared to 2016, indications were that the share of youth among all Democratic primary voters in New Hampshire dropped by more than a third, from roughly one in five votes in 2016 (19 percent) to one in eight (13 percent) in 2020. The share of young voters also decreased in Nevada and South Carolina, the next two states to hold their contests. Sanders won the youth vote in both states, but by slimmer margins than he had previously. Buttigieg was less of a factor in Nevada and South Carolina.

On his way to a decisive 29-point victory in Congressman James Clyburn's home state, Joe Biden earned a quarter of the South Carolina youth vote. Biden's victory in South Carolina effectively ended the Democratic primary. Tom Steyer withdrew the day of the vote. Pete Buttigieg did the same the following day, just two days before Super Tuesday, sending signals that the time had come for the party to begin uniting in its quest to defeat Donald Trump.

"We need leadership to heal a divided nation, not drive us further apart," Buttigieg said in his South Bend farewell, which also served as a signal of his soon-to-be-delivered support for Biden.[29]

Later that week, Amy Klobuchar, Mike Bloomberg, and Elizabeth Warren suspended their campaigns. Bernie Sanders made it official on April 8, 2020, having been unable to rally more young voters and build a reliable, diverse coalition to challenge the former vice president.

After Iowa, the youth vote in the Democratic primary

was disappointing. Turnout was uneven, leaving the Sanders operation uneasy, activists and analysts searching for answers. There is no simple explanation. "With so many candidates and so much going on, it was hard for college students to engage with the primary as a casual voter," I heard from frustrated organizers. Others felt like because they weren't following the campaign day-to-day, they didn't know enough to confidently cast their ballot.

"Candidates just haven't been reaching young people," noted youth activist Sarah Audelo, quoting her organization's poll that three in five young Democrats had not been contacted by a presidential campaign during the primaries.[30]

The best explanation is that outside of Sanders, no one committed to the big, Obama-like generational ask that's required of a campaign process designed to go from zero to sixty within weeks. Some campaigns made the calculation that with Sanders in the race, there were few persuadable young and first-time voters. This theory was flawed. It relied on data from 2016 and not from the multiple polls the Harvard IOP and others produced showing about half of Gen Z searching for an alternative voice. Some candidates were apparently concerned that appealing to young voters would require them to move further left than was comfortable, especially in largely white, rural Iowa and New Hampshire.

Others would insist that they did indeed prioritize the youth vote. They staffed up with youth organizers and digital-media specialists, campaigned on campuses, spoke about the climate, student debt, and cannabis. All of these explanations miss the lessons from history, from Obama, from Parkland, and from Bernie Sanders himself. Young voters were hurting. They were in search of personal connections with candidates who understood their struggles and stressors. They were seeking not just to be persuaded, but to be empowered.

As far as the arcane rules of the nominating process, those were a turnoff, and the meltdown in the Iowa vote-counting process hardly instilled confidence.

Ultimately, elections are about differences. Compared to the alternative living at 1600 Pennsylvania Avenue, the distinctions between the Democratic candidates were imperceptible. And unless someone other than Sanders stood up to call Generation Z to be a part of his or her campaign and movement, many Zoomers chose to stand back from the primary, saving their fight for the fall.

The latent power of Generation Z, if properly courted and harnessed, made itself clear in a statewide race in Massachusetts. The passion with which Zoomers helped rebrand and ultimately save the forty-four-year career of the dean of the Massachusetts congressional delegation was unlike anything I had witnessed in politics. In less than one year, a "benevolent goof,"[31] the "unremarkable"[32] Ed Markey went from fielding calls from friends suggesting he gracefully step aside in favor of popular millennial congressman Joe Kennedy III, to becoming guardian of Gen Z's future and progressive icon.

A year before the September 2020 Democratic primary, Markey trailed Kennedy, the grandson of Robert F. Kennedy, by nearly 20 points among Massachusetts Democratic primary voters.[33] With Generation Z and millennials, the news was worse—the then-seventy-four-year-old career politician was on the wrong end of a Hillary Clinton to Obama–like margin (five to one).[34] But as George Bachrach, Markey's first campaign manager in the 1970s, told a local reporter, "He's always been engaged in uphill fights."[35]

A consummate DC dealmaker, in his home state Markey had long been in the shadow cast by more famous names: Mike

Dukakis, Ted Kennedy, Joe Kennedy II, John Kerry, Tip O'Neill, Mitt Romney, and now Elizabeth Warren and relative newcomer Ayanna Pressley. Although it didn't happen immediately, as the early polls suggested, Markey's (re)introduction to the next generation of young Bay State voters was boosted by his prescient decision a year earlier to collaborate with Alexandria Ocasio-Cortez on the Green New Deal. A member of Congress for barely a month, she called, on February 7, 2019, for the House resolution that aimed to achieve net-zero greenhouse-gas emissions, establish millions of high-wage jobs, invest in infrastructure and industry, secure clean air and water, and promote justice and equality.

On the same day in the Senate, Ed Markey joined thirteen of his Democratic colleagues (including Bernie Sanders) to do the same. While AOC was nearly drowning in attention—from the left and the right—Markey was struggling to get his campaign off the ground.[36]

"If you're Ed Markey, you have to present a compelling reason to be returned to the Senate," pollster David Paleologos said to *The Boston Globe* a week after Labor Day 2019. If the polls were to hold up, and the primary coauthor of the Green New Deal lost a primary election the year after he introduced it, AOC and young progressives nationally knew that could undermine their movement. With AOC and grassroots groups such as the Sunrise Movement, MoveOn, Our Revolution, Indivisible, and the Progressive Change Campaign Committee in solidarity, the Democratic primary for the Senate in Massachusetts turned to a referendum on Generation Z. Markey and company ran what amounted to a national campaign for a local primary. Zoomers from Medford to Michigan felt like they held a stake in the outcome—and they worked for it.

Varshini Prakash, executive director of the Sunrise Movement, who was born and raised in Massachusetts and knew of his blue-collar roots, his similar ethic, Boston accent, and now-famous vintage Nike Air Revolutions, said:

> We can help make Ed Markey into this figure on the left, this lovable, quirky older guy who kind of has some of the similar characteristics of somebody like Bernie.[37]

Encouraged rather than deterred by naysayers, Markey's campaign strategy was straightforward and transparent. Lock down the insiders and old guard first. Before Kennedy announced his candidacy, Markey asked for and received pledges of support from dozens of elected officials, influencers, and activists throughout the commonwealth. Next, own the future. Videos of Markey standing shoulder to shoulder with Generation Z activists who organized the Boston climate strike on December 6, 2019, were hardwired into the brains and phones of young voters, who would soon tell their parents Markey was far from finished. As the coronavirus shut down much of the state, making retail politicking more difficult, Markey ramped up his presence on digital and social media.

It worked. Ancient grudges over such issues as Markey's support for the war in Iraq, the USA Patriot Act, and abandoning his working-class neighbors in Malden for tony Chevy Chase, Maryland, decades ago were overlooked. Joe Kennedy endorsed the Green New Deal in 2018 and was one of its 101 cosponsors in the House, but to no effect. To idealistic Zoomers, Markey had been transformed from the establishment Democratic pol who served with Tip O'Neill, to the Bernie-style insurgent with young ideas. Kennedy was characterized as just another white man of privilege, despite a lifetime dedicated to public service, fighting for the most vulnerable.

To Teddy Landis, a Harvard-educated youth vote activist

who moved to Wisconsin after graduation to canvas for Joe Biden,

> Markey totally embraced youth in both substantive and aesthetic ways. He had a lovable and edgy image, starting with the pic of him wearing Jordans outside his house. He came off like a lifelong rebel with a substantive agenda to back it up.

When the ballots were counted on primary night, Markey wasted no time thanking those who made his resounding 10-point victory possible. "This campaign has always been about the young people of this country," Markey said. "You are our future. And thank you for believing in me, because I believe in you."

His campaign did what few others would dare to do. From day one, he prioritized and invested in Generation Z, even in a primary in a pandemic against one of the country's leading millennial elected leaders. It was clear he was not just in sync with their issues, but in what a generation sought in elected officials and demanded from their government. In the final weeks, Markey released an ad that so fired up his youthful supporters that they were ready "to run through a brick wall,"[38] were "crying rn [right now]," and had "literal chills."[39] In a three-minute "uncannily cool" spot that ran through the highlights of a decades-long career of rendering laws rooted in the shared values of America's youth, Senator Markey played off JFK's inaugural address imploring Generation Z "to start asking what your country can do for you."[40] Whether or not it was a rebrand or reawakening, it does not much matter now. Markey's campaign from the beginning to the end listened to Generation Zers. He trusted them, and they met the challenge.

Markey's support among the political establishment and

the progressive bedroom communities surrounding Boston, matched with his unyielding pursuit of the youth vote, were the bedrocks of his primary victory. His campaign slogan, a turn of a phrase shared with a then-sixteen-year-old Google Science Fair prize—winning scientist from England who's tackling both Alzheimer's disease and breast cancer,[41] was "It's not your age—it's the age of your ideas that's important."[42]

Fourteen years earlier, Markey campaign manager John Walsh and seasoned Boston political strategist Doug Rubin had navigated Deval Patrick's improbable primary and general-election victories for governor of Massachusetts. Now Walsh had done it again, and to him, Markey's comeback win presaged the future. "We're going to find that there is a coalition for change in our country that relies on—and celebrates—a surge in young people's participation," Walsh said. Referencing one of his Gen Z volunteers, he described the principles of his organizing strategy:

> We go get the kids and then they get their parents. It's deliberate, and it's so powerful. It's not just, "Tell ya fatha, tell ya motha." It's, "Tell your teacher. Tell your neighbor."[43]

Ed Markey empowered thousands of young Massachusetts voters; he gave them a voice and brought them into the political process. For me, he also proved that Generation Z's failure to show up in force during the presidential primary season was not confirmation of the idea that Zoomers don't care and will always let you down. It showed nearly the opposite: that no one other than Bernie Sanders had really asked them to care in a way that was convincing to them. Until Ed Markey did just that, and out they came. That's the secret. Listen to them, then ask for their votes, and ye shall receive.

9

I HEAR YOU

In the summer of 2020, I took a leave from my research position at Harvard. My company was hired by the Biden campaign, where I was to lead youth polling efforts and advise on strategic communications. Well before I was affiliated with the campaign, I spoke in public settings about two youth-related strategic imperatives necessary to help the Democratic Party nominee secure an Electoral College victory in the fall.

The first piece of business was finding and then building upon the enthusiasm that fueled 2018's historic midterm turnout. Dramatically improving the level of youth participation that contributed to Clinton's 2016 loss to Trump was imperative.

Second, the nominee would have to reach a 60 percent threshold of support from the under-thirty vote. Reaching this level was not easily assured. It would mean that then-seventy-seven-year-old Joe Biden, not a natural favorite among Gen Z voters to date (he received only 17 percent of the Super Tuesday youth vote[1]), would need to match President Obama's 2012 mark, something that previous nominees Al Gore, John Kerry, and Hillary Clinton did not get close to.

I thought it was doable. My sense from watching the primaries from the sideline was that the Biden camp (and the others) never gave themselves enough credit for the potential of their appeal to a significant number of young progressive voters seeking an alternative to Bernie Sanders. If presented well, the values and personal story of Joe Biden would resonate with younger voters. Once I started talking with Zoomers in battleground states, it became clear to me that despite his many years in Washington and positive perceptions earned as Obama's vice president, Joe Biden was still not distinguishable for many first-time Gen Z voters. Those within the pool of what we believed to be eligible, persuadable voters often perceived Biden as a moderate in a progressive era, a longtime creature of Washington, and . . . old. None of which was disqualifying.

Compounding the lack of knowledge was the fact that Zoomers and millennials—especially first-time voters—had a notable and understandable lack of confidence in government more broadly. Our task, therefore, was to share Joe Biden's life story, his working-class roots, his commitment to family, experience, record, values, and vision with a new generation just tuning in to politics—while also providing concrete examples of what government can do, the difference it can make for people, when operating at its best. If we could tie both of these elements together and communicate it broadly to millions of Zoomers and millennials, I liked our chances.

On March 17, 2020, after sweeping Florida, Illinois, and Arizona and creating an insurmountable delegate lead, Biden swiftly began efforts to unite the party, starting with the new generation of Democrats. The former vice president ensured that the mistakes of 2016, the failure to unite the establishment and progressive wings of the party, and a lack of interest in the youth vote, would not be repeated. In brief televised remarks that caught the attention of Twitter influencers, Biden reached out directly to Senator Sanders's supporters, saying, "I hear you," and expressing their common vision and goals, including "affordable health care" and "tackling the existential challenge of climate change."[2]

Three weeks later, on April 8, it was Senator Sanders's turn to address the nation in a live-streamed speech. "I could not in good conscience continue to mount a campaign that cannot not (*sic*) win, and which would interfere with the important work required of all of us in this difficult hour."[3] Ten million Americans had recently lost their jobs, global coronavirus cases topped one million, and UK prime minister Boris Johnson was in intensive care.

Shortly after Sanders's remarks, Biden's campaign issued an unusually expansive statement on social media. In hindsight, this might have served as a playbook for running a youth-oriented campaign for the White House. It was a sign of respect from Biden to a colleague and rival—and sincere recognition of the millions of Zoomers and millennials who believed in a cause bigger than themselves, put in the work, and had almost twice helped the democratic socialist from Vermont to the finish line. Like Obama before him, Biden proved himself a listener. The statement was another indication that he was in closer alignment with the young, progressive side of his party than he was credited for.

> Bernie gets a lot of credit for his passionate advocacy for the issues he cares about. But he doesn't get enough credit for being a voice that forces us all to take a hard look in the mirror and ask if we've done enough.
>
> While the Sanders campaign has been suspended— its impact on this election and on elections to come is far from over. We will address the existential crisis of climate change. We will confront income inequality in our nation. We will make sure healthcare is affordable and accessible to every American. We will make

education at our public colleges and universities free. We will ease the burden of student debt. And, most important of all, we will defeat Donald Trump. . . .

And to your supporters I make the same commitment: I see you; I hear you, and I understand the urgency of what it is we have to get done in this country. I hope you will join us. You are more than welcome. You're needed.[4]

Of the statement, which takes about four minutes to read on Medium, it was noted that the most highlighted parts were the lines reprised from his March 17, St. Patrick's Day, "I hear you" remarks. Three simple words, when delivered with empathy and purpose, and followed by substance and action, can be as impactful as any in our lexicon. They are everything millions of Zoomers were waiting to hear.

The almost seven weeks between the suspension of Sanders's campaign and Memorial Day was a relatively quiet period for the Democrats on the voter engagement front. The country was rightly consumed with the growing pandemic, looming economic crisis, and a president proving he was ill-equipped to meet the moment. During this time period, the *RealClearPolitics*[5] and *FiveThirtyEight*[6] aggregators averaged Trump's approval rating to 44 percent, an ominous sign for an incumbent in a two-person election less than six months away.

The week before Memorial Day, Trump's approval slipped to 43 percent. Of the last eight US presidents who reached the same tenure in office, which dates back to the Johnson administration more than a half century ago, the only ones with lower ratings than Trump at this point in time were George H. W. Bush and Jimmy Carter—both polled at 40 percent before losing reelection.

Meanwhile, outside of public view, Biden and the team were engaged in the vice-presidential selection process, meeting regularly with public health and economic advisors, finalizing the details of major domestic policy initiatives like the Build Back Better and climate plans, and hashing out the delicate politics between his and the Sanders camp.

Then George Floyd was murdered by the police. Millions joined the Black Lives Matter protests; civil unrest gripped the nation. Meanwhile President Trump took to Twitter to fan the flames, coyly threatening violence against Black protesters. Trump's May 29 "When the looting starts, the shooting starts" tweet, which Twitter flagged with a warning for "glorifying violence," was an idiom once employed by bigoted police, segregationist sheriffs, and policy makers like Miami police chief Walter Headley, Alabama public safety commissioner Eugene "Bull" Connor, and Alabama governor and 1968 presidential candidate George Wallace.[7]

Eight days after Floyd's death, standing in front of a backdrop of American flags at Philadelphia City Hall, Joe Biden delivered one of the most somber and meaningful public addresses of his life. What Generation Z, in particular, saw that day, and in the days that followed, through a video that was produced and shared widely on social and digital media, was a leader who exuded empathy and respect, who recognized the racism that has been tearing us apart, while at the same time offering proof that government can and has done big things before.

> The history of this nation teaches us that it's in some of our darkest moments of despair that we've made some of our greatest progress. The 13th and 14th and

15th Amendments followed the Civil War. The greatest economy in the history of the world grew out of the Great Depression. The Civil Rights Act of 1964 and Voting Rights Act of 1965 came in the tracks of Bull Connor's vicious dogs. To paraphrase Reverend Barber—it's in the mourning we find hope.

It will take more than talk. We've had talk before. We've had protests before.

Let us vow to make this, at last, an era of action to reverse systemic racism with long overdue and concrete changes. That action will not be completed in the first 100 days of my Presidency—or even an entire term. It is the work of a generation.[8]

Like the Parkland students two years earlier, Biden reached tens of millions of angry, anxious, confused, embarrassed, and tired Americans, but especially Zoomers, summoning them to join his fight.

Watching that speech and witnessing the reactions from dozens of Zoomers across the many racial, ethnic, and socioeconomic divides within America, I knew the Biden campaign was on its way. The polls might not have reflected it yet—a May CNN/SSRS survey noted Biden's favorability with young voters was 33 percent, with 55 percent unfavorable[9]—but I was convinced the campaign was on the right path. Some Zoomers, especially those latched on to Bernie Sanders, assumed that Biden's long tenure in Washington, his history of shepherding a tough crime bill through Congress, and his reputation as someone once friendly with Senate segregationists meant he was a defender of the status quo. This speech, which showed his openness to change, helped turn that perception. For students who were unaware or unsure of his position on civil rights, the message was clear that he was willing to lead the necessary national effort to confront racism. And for first-time voters who already were without faith in government's capacity for good, the former vice president reminded them of how it's through the darkest of times that America shines brightest.

The more progressive and politically active young voters, already beginning to warm to him, received another boost after the Fourth of July, when the Biden-Sanders Unity Task Force on "Combating the Climate Crisis and Pursuing Environmental Justice" issued its recommendations to the soon-to-be nominee of the party. The climate task force, which counted both Biden and Sanders appointees as members, was cochaired by current climate czar John Kerry and Green New Deal author Alexandria Ocasio-Cortez. The group declared rising fossil fuel emissions a nationwide emergency and prioritized a need to address environmental justice, specifically the racial injustices that have led low-income communities to bear a disproportionate level of air and water pollution.

In a reversal of harsh criticisms leveled at Biden by the Gen Z–founded Sunshine Movement during the primary season,[10] Executive Director Varshini Prakash, who served on the committee, said that she left the process feeling "cautiously optimistic" and that she believed Biden "really does care about the issue."[11] Alexandria Ocasio-Cortez tweeted similarly positive feedback,[12] noting that the committee was a collaborative effort and resulted in a meaningful and substantial improvement of the vice president's prior positions.

Purposefully engaging on racial justice and climate change and doing so in an open and collaborative manner with the party's left flank paid dividends in the latter stages of the campaign for the youth vote. Biden's words to Sanders supporters from the spring now carried more weight moving forward. Trust was developing. Balanced always with other political and policy concerns, these political activities were important for young activists who began sending signals that Biden was someone worth investing in.

The Democrats' August nominating convention was another critical building block in securing increased participation, especially among Democrats and progressive independent voters. Attracting an average of nearly twenty-two million adult viewers nightly,[13] the Emmy-nominated broadcast of the convention was tuned in to by Zoomers because they knew the stakes of the election better than they knew Joe Biden. Before the convention, a first-time voter from Wisconsin told me, with his tongue planted firmly in his cheek, that after having a difficult time deciphering between randomized remarks by Trump and assorted twentieth-century fascists on a social media app, "It was extremely frightening to the point where I would be willing to be coughed on by a random stranger in order to go and vote."

Another Zoomer from Western Pennsylvania, a new mother not quite all in for Biden yet, echoed the sentiment of many of her peers in explaining her motivation to vote in the fall:

Because it's my responsibility . . . to do everything that I can to make the world even just a little bit better. Even if it's not the world that I would like to see, I cannot in good conscience allow the status quo to continue. He may not be my ideal candidate, but Biden is not going to maintain the current status quo.

A young man from Arizona shared the reason he will never pass on the opportunity to cast a ballot, while reminding me of the importance of strong mentors and civic education:

I'm the product of a single mom. Every November I was with her waiting in line for thirty or forty minutes. It was drilled into me to go out and vote. Until the rules change, play by the rules they give you. If it's time to vote, go vote. I can complain, too, but then I can say, "I voted."

When it mattered most, Gen Z found the attention they were seeking in the acceptance speech of the now-official Democratic nominee. Joe Biden told them that their voice was being heard—and is invaluable in pushing us all forward:

One of the most powerful voices we hear in the country today is from our young people. They're speaking to the inequity and injustice that has grown up in America. Economic injustice. Racial injustice. Environmental injustice.

I hear their voices and if you listen, you can hear them too. And whether it's the existential threat posed by climate change, the daily fear of being gunned down in school, or the inability to get started in their first job—it will be the work of the next president to restore the promise of America to everyone.[14]

In the Harvard IOP polling released after both conventions concluded (during my leave), Biden maintained a 60 percent to 28 percent advantage over Trump among voters under thirty. Coming out of the summer convention period with our margin intact, and building trust among Zoomer activists, the Biden-Harris campaign was ready to focus on a paid media strategy that would both persuade lingering voters and mobilize the others.

With otherwise stressed-out, casual Zoomer voters beginning to check in with the election in September, the campaign cut several television and digital spots that filled in the gaps of a long, but not fully appreciated, career in public service. Proving again that political science is not rocket science, the Biden media operation demonstrated that the best creativity is often rooted in the principal's own words, even unscripted, to highlight a point of human connection, whether it's struggle, pain, joy, or redemption. These ads emphasized Joe Biden's natural empathy and past tragedies in a way that drew parallels with the struggles of Zoomers today. This is what some Zoomers had to say:

> I wanted to know more about his life story. So, I think that really connects me. I really liked it, especially the one that talked about where he was from and showed his house that he grew up in. And so, being able to relate to someone who is working class or middle class, I think that that to me, is really impactful.

> I feel like all of these videos made him seem more relatable and in tune with our issues. He just seems more human, really.

> My favorite spoke to empathy and understanding where people are coming from, which I know a lot of us felt like he doesn't understand us, or relate to us, or know our struggles. And I know it was a short clip, but if you really look at some of those images . . . the way he was even just sitting, engaged with, I think it was a woman in a wheelchair, or his expressions with the children, it just said to me, someone who is actively listening to people, which is something I don't think necessarily we get to see a lot.

By late October, after two debates, CNN/SSRS released a poll showing that over the last five months, the candidate's favorability among young voters had improved by an astounding net 45 points since May—from −22 to +23. With early voting well underway, 55 percent of America's youth thought of Biden favorably, only 32 percent unfavorably.

I have a hard time envisioning a Biden presidency, a Democratic House, and Democratic Senate today without Gen Z; but politics is complex—a never-ending contest of addition and subtraction. Variables are interdependent and hard to disentangle. All I know is that Joe Biden, whether he showed it or not in the primary, first, always cared about and shared a set of values and a governing philosophy with much of Generation Z. That made most of our jobs easy. Not every candidate meets even that threshold. Second, he invested in, and empowered young people constantly, by listening, engaging, collaborating, and compromising. Third, he asked them for more—to join him and restore the soul of this nation. To make the future a safer, more just, equitable, and prosperous place for all Americans. I am proud that the Biden-Harris campaign outperformed the 2016 team across most every demographic cohort we measured; a new, strong, diverse, and broad coalition of support was created. The campaign's success with suburban voters (most youths in battleground states live in suburbs) and baby boomers, his strength with women and people of color were critical elements to the coalition.

Five battleground states flipped from red to blue, based on the turnout and preference for Biden among voters under thirty, according to analysis[15] provided by Tufts University's Kei Kawashima-Ginsberg and Abby Kiesa, the director and executive director of CIRCLE.

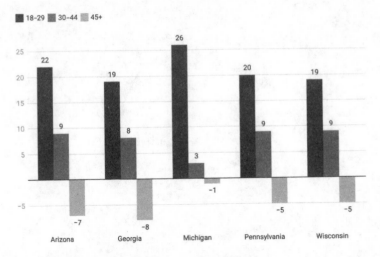

Figure 9.1. Biden advantage by age group in battleground states.

Source: AP VoteCast, *The New York Times*

TIME magazine called 2020 a breakthrough for young voters. "In the same way that Millennials were shaped by their experiences at the dawn of the 21st century, from 9/11 to the election of Obama and the economic recession, it's clear that the last five years have dramatically shaped how young voters see their role in American politics. Gen Z in particular is stepping into the political arena after being antagonized by Trump, radicalized by the reckoning over racial justice, and demoralized by a year of virtual schooling due to COVID-19," explained Charlotte Alter, national correspondent for *TIME* and author of *The Ones We've Been Waiting For.*[16]

Will these trends continue in the future? The short answer is that the Republican Party, at least as presently constituted, had better hope not. The more complete answer will be known in the fullness of time. But the long arc of American

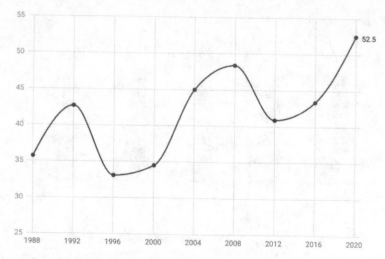

Figure 9.2. 18–29-year-old turnout in presidential elections, 1988–2020.

Source: United States Elections Project (based on U.S. Census Bureau Current Population Survey and using Census Weight for Vote Overreport Bias Correction)

history suggests that the GOP will evolve with the changing times and changing demographics of America, or ultimately be replaced.

According to Catalist, a progressive data and analytics company, Joe Biden won 60 percent of the eighteen-to-twenty-nine-year-old vote in the general election; among millennials and young Gen Xers between thirty and forty-four, he won 56 percent. These two generations account for about 40 percent of all votes cast, and they're quickly making voting a habit.

In 2024, according to demographers Rob Griffin, William H. Frey, and Ruy Teixeira, Gen Z and millennials will make up a larger share of eligible voters than baby boomers.[17] By 2028, they estimate, these two groups will be half the electorate. This is neither an academic nor long-term question for America's two dominant political parties. The reality of what this means is already here, in the persons of Jon Ossoff and Raphael Warnock. These two freshmen senators from Georgia owe their seats to young voters, specifically young Black voters. Simply put, Zoomers are why Mitch McConnell is no longer Senate majority leader.

Warnock won his January 5, 2021, runoff against incumbent Republican senator Kelly Loeffler by some 93,000 votes out of 4.5 million votes cast. Ossoff's margin was even closer, fewer than 55,000 votes. Since under-thirty Georgia voters broke for the two Democrats by margins of nearly two to one, both of these Atlanta-based Democrats—a young Jewish entrepreneur and a well-known African American pastor—were sent from the heart of the Old Confederacy to the nation's capital because young people wanted them there.[18]

In so doing, Zoomers helped Georgia come full circle. The first time the phrase the South "will rise again" was uttered publicly in this country, it was by a Georgia Democrat named Alfred Iverson. He did so in a fiery 1861 speech announcing his resignation from the US Senate to join the Southern states' rebellion.

But there are many ways to "rise," as Gen Z has shown. Propelling Democratic victories to retake the House in 2018, the presidency in 2020, and the Senate in 2021, Zoomers have only begun to fight.

10

TO THE FUTURE

If systemic racism and gun violence are to be curbed in this country; if global warming is to be addressed; if free-market capitalism, America's reputation abroad, and Western democracy are to be preserved—and these things feel like big "ifs" some days—we are obliged to take our cue from Generation Z. Their spirit, their courage, their sense of justice, and their perseverance have already made their communities and our country a better, fairer, and more just place.

Left to our own devices (I'm referring to my own Generation X and those older), it would be business as usual. The National Rifle Association would regroup and add to its clout. The White House press corps would gradually forget how President Biden's predecessor tried to delegitimize the media. Public attention would drift away from mass shootings and Earth's warming climate. Big business would drift away from social responsibility and back to maximizing short-term profits. Police unions would reassert their prerogative to protect violent cops.

Generation Z will let none of that happen. In just a handful of years, Zoomers have taken on the most imperishable and destructive forces holding our country back from meeting its undeniable promise. They do so with their voices, their homemade signs, their memes, their ballots, and their wallets. Because they have no choice. With an unparalleled knowledge of history and science for their age, they are filled with fear but using it to find the courage that propels their lives and this era in our nation forward.

The main questions remaining, therefore, are: How will Generation Z put its energy, spirit, and moral code to use? And what will America look like in three decades from now as Zoomers raise their own families, invent new industries, lead governments, and take the helm of our nation's public and private institutions?

Halfway through writing this book, I put these questions to Alex, a nonbinary Black high school student from a small industrial city in the Midwest. Having met Alex in a previous focus group, I was so taken by their wisdom that I tracked them back down to continue the conversation.

Reflecting on the future, Alex, who will be forty-five years old in the year 2050, told me:

> Where the older generations wanted to do what was best for them, leaving us in a world getting sicker and sicker, we will do what's best for both us *and* the future.

> I believe we are the most socially aware generation. We were born with technology at our fingertips. We had all the information in the world available to us, which has had a large impact on us.

> We are more empathetic, tuned in to the news, and educated.

> Many of us are also more politically aware at a younger age and have pretty much stopped the phenomenon

where you vote as your parents did with no other information. We have a lot of strengths older generations can't even dream of.

We can be extremely effective leaders, as many of us have been educating ourselves on social issues for a lot of our lives. We can also coordinate groups and rallies much easier to reach supporting members of our cause.

I think a few of the issues we would tackle that the older generations have not are racism and bigotry, the shrinking lower middle class, and environmental issues.

Americans more broadly tend to be less optimistic than Alex. In December of 2018, when researchers from the Pew American Trends Panel asked a robust sample of more than twenty-five hundred Americans their views on where we will be by 2050, their forecasts were bleak.

- Sixty percent predict that a terrorist attack on the United States as bad or worse than 9/11 will happen.

- A majority expect that the US economy will be weaker.

- More than three in five expect that the share of Americans in the lower class will increase.

- Half envisage Americans having less job security.

- Only one-fifth of Americans see the future standard of living for families getting better; most expect it to get worse.[1]

Only six days into the third decade of the twenty-first century, angry insurrectionists, stirred up by their Republican leaders, stormed the US Capitol in an orgy of anger that cost six Americans their lives. It came the summer after well-intentioned protests had turned into fiery riots in many US cities, and a global viral pandemic had induced huge swaths of Americans to deny the simple facts of science. The "Roaring Twenties" of the previous century had become something much darker: call it the "Raging Twenties."

The rise in right-wing domestic terror plots that started during Obama's second term ramped up during Trump's four years in office. In addition, between 2019 and 2020, the number of violent anarchist, anti-fascist, and other like-minded attacks and plots aimed at police, military, and government personnel and facilities in the United States more than doubled.[2]

Previously decentralized extremists are increasingly coordinating with each other, and forces overseas, in preparation for a second civil war, aimed at destroying our government in favor of a white ethno-state. These seditious plans are not being hatched in a network of caves, like their al-Qaeda cousins had done, but in front of our eyes, online, and in dozens of communities, whether they are Republican red or Democratic blue.

As noted in chapter 5, these adherents to nihilistic ideologies are alienated people of all ages, young and old alike. Their numbers will multiply in the immediate months and years ahead, recruited from the growing pool of Zoomers suffering from depression and isolation, too easily duped into joining communities that start by offering a sense of respect and belonging, before soon serving bigotry and hate.

The "Death Valley Hate Camps," with outposts in Texas, Virginia, Washington, Nevada, and elsewhere, are home to Gen Z and millennial-generation Atomwaffen Division (AWD) members who worship Adolf Hitler and Charles Manson and recently graduated a teenager filled with so much rage that he viciously murdered a former high school classmate, University of Pennsylvania student Blaze Bernstein.[3]

In Winnebago, Wisconsin, a twenty-three-year-old man known as "Commander Red" spends his time as an Antifa member hatching schemes with others to incite violence in otherwise peaceful protests. After a Black Lives United–Green Bay protest in August 2020, he was arrested for carrying a flamethrower, smoke grenades, and fireworks during a demonstration; in another similar incident, he was detained for pointing a loaded gun at a police officer, biting and kicking police.[4]

Like Thomas Rousseau and Bruno Cua, these men are not sole practitioners; they do not operate in a vacuum.

As the 2020s advance, the people holding these and similarly twisted and violent ideologies will be worthy adversaries. Hundreds, at least, have embedded themselves in institutions we were taught to trust, blindly and without judgment. They will be found in various "QAnon caucuses" in federal and state governments, reserve and active military units, law-enforcement agencies, the Secret Service, the media, and areas in which they can influence and poison otherwise unspoiled minds of our youth. At least one active-duty military officer, a US Marine Corps major, was arrested and charged with storming the Capitol on January 6, 2021, and at least fifty-four others have some current or former connection to the military.[5]

Just as the G. W. Bush and Obama administrations focused the Pentagon, three-letter agencies, and allies on dismantling the networks and threats from overseas terrorism in the first two decades of the century, President Biden and his successor will do the same in our homeland. In May 2021, the Biden administration launched the Center for Prevention Programs and Partnerships, or CP3. Its goal is to take a "whole-of-society" approach and prevent radicalization at its early stages by enlisting the help of researchers, other government agencies, and community members to find and close gateways to extremism.

It will be ugly, but extremists will be defeated. The challenges Generation Zers will face in the decade ahead of them, like the troubles from the 2010s, will fortify their values and strengthen their resolve at this critical time in their development.

They will set their differences aside and build a better, if imperfect, America.

Futurists often stand their predictions on demographic, economic, political, and technology-based trends and footings. Doing so in this moment—without ample examination and weighting of the generational morals and principles that will guide Zoomers—leaves an unfinished and possibly distorted portrait.

Fully appreciating Generation Z's America requires us to channel Zoomers' values and visions through the frame and wisdom of today's global leaders. I have long been a proponent of the "wisdom of crowds" approach when dealing with notable and complex issues. In addition to my own polling and review of other public opinion, social science, and economic forecasts, I tapped my own "smart tribe" to help me scope out 2050. As a group of about three dozen people, they leaned slightly more optimistic than pessimistic. One fittingly described how we sit on the knife's edge of history, questioning whether Generation Z has time to reverse the bleak political and climate trends ahead of Generation Alpha's* emergence:

> Depending on what happens, we will either see significant changes that enhance democracy, or we will become a de facto plutocracy under the guise of populist governance. If the former, the United States will continue to play a significant role in the world order, although American hegemony will slowly decline. If the latter, the world will grow increasingly chaotic due to an America that is at once rudderless and, with its military and nuclear weapons, an existential threat to the planet.

I asked my group of artists, farmers, laborers, lawyers, politicians, service workers, business leaders, students, academics, and entrepreneurs representing a range of locales from around the globe, from St. Louis to the Silicon Valley, from Killington to Kashmir, Riyadh, and Rwanda, to privately share their unguarded insights into the America Gen Z will create. With a focus on work, food, government, and politics—all adding up to an understanding of how we will live—here are ten things we can expect:

---

* The generation of Americans following Gen Z, born after 2010.

I. The purpose of work will change.

With increasing competition for companies and enterprises of all kinds to hire the best and brightest in an increasingly competitive world, Zoomers will apply pressure from the ground up to ensure companies serve a social purpose, aligned broadly to their values, that helps fill the time they spend outside their families and leisure activities. If necessary, they will rewrite the rules to ensure that's the case when they're in charge. The penalties—less competitive workforce and weaker brand affinity—for not doing so will be too great.

At its best, "work will be a social good," said Jill Reynolds, who helps lead the Human Services practice at Public Consulting Group, when I asked her to think about what work looks like in thirty years. John Michael Schert, an artist, coach, and social entrepreneur who currently calls Boise, Idaho, home, added, "If Daniel Pink tells us that mastery, purpose, and autonomy are the balancing forces of work, I posit we have prioritized mastery over the past four economies—and purpose is on the rise as millennials and now Zoomers enter and begin leading the workforce." Continuing, Schert said he believes that while there will not be enough work for everyone, "the role of labor organizing itself, and government as the central leviathan, will create new systems to combat inequality. They will be imperfect, but market forces will no longer run unchecked. Likely, the pendulum will then swing too far in the opposite direction and further corrections will be needed, but humans will evolve to work toward a greater shared purpose."

2. There will be plenty of jobs for Americans— who have a solid education footing.

Work-life harmony (not balance), for all Americans, measured by happiness and overall wellness, is what Generation Z will strive for in 2050. The conventional models and workplace environments that we know today will no longer exist. Much of the work in technology, professional services, and the creative classes will be decentralized, conducted virtually, including from remote, mixed-use locations. Employers will prioritize wellness, offering part-time, flexible, gig, and freelance opportunities that can evolve as life happens. "Work will be less structured and less formal; 'flexible' describes it well," said Deema Bibi, a global leader in building bridges between the social, private, and public sectors, and founder and CEO of INJAZ, a nonprofit based in Jordan that inspires and prepares youth to become productive members of society. "Flexible in terms of physical location, office hours, commitment, process, structure. These changes will be met with a more results-oriented relationship with employers, and highly dependent on advanced technologies," she said. Because technology will play a larger role and replace much of the drudgery and dangerous tasks required today, there's hope that more time will be made available for innovation and other ways of expressing creative talents.

3. A federalized job corps with basic income guarantees will support displaced industries and reward essential family and community service.

"AI will have taken over everything it can. There will be no minimum-wage jobs, which presents a great social quandary for the United States and other nations," said Rick Majzun, vice president and chief operating officer of Stanford Children's Health, the Bay Area's largest health care system exclusively dedicated to children and expectant mothers. Despite global market opportunities, there are many who will be left behind because they will lack the skills, knowledge, or training to compete with others in a hyperconnected and increasingly virtual world.

Massive investments to rethink the purpose of public education and lifelong skill-building will be required, as will universal basic-income programs, allowing government to support a growing number of workers who will serve in previously undervalued roles, such as mentoring students, assisting with public health needs, caring for the elderly, preserving the environment—among other activities that strengthen the bonds within families and communities. Improving underperforming education systems, whether in the United States or in other parts of the world, which hamper their citizens from fully engaging in the economy, will be a top priority.

4. We will see massive disruption of agriculture; Generation Z will be the first plant-forward generation.

Geopolitics, an estimated two billion more humans, a 60 percent increase in global food demand, increasing interest in health, wellness, and sustainable living, along with the massive disruption caused by climate change, means that few industries will evolve more over the next thirty years than agriculture. According to the United Nations, food production currently accounts for 40 percent of land use, 30 percent of greenhouse gas emissions, and 70 percent of freshwater consumption—all of which is unsustainable.[6] In the next decade, investments in food innovation are expected to jump fivefold and be a $700 billion market by 2030[7]—and with it will change the way most of us in the United States eat and drink. Among the most sensitive crops in the world to temperature changes are coffee and grapes (wine).

In the United States, we are now reaching "peak meat" status. The average American family consumes between seven hundred and one thousand pounds of meat annually, roughly translating to 9 billion chickens, 32 million cattle and calves, 242 million turkeys, 121 million hogs, and 2 million sheep and lambs.[8] "When the next generation realizes they have been terribly lied to by the meat (and sugar) industries through their special interest–funded research, they will gain an even deeper perspective on personal health and the role of plant protein. Habits will change," predicted Jeff C. Frazier, a North Carolina–based technology executive.

Aramark, which provides food and dining services to more than five hundred college campuses in the United States, is quickly adapting to meet the evolving preferences and tastes of Zoomers, and with that, the nation's future. Aramark's research suggests that millions of Gen Zers, primarily motivated to improve their own health, are shifting toward eating more "plant-forward foods," as 60 percent want to reduce their meat intake. More than three-quarters of Zoomers in the Aramark research indicated that going meatless one to two times per week is appealing.[9] In a Tufts University nutrition report, it was found that not only do Zoomers prefer this healthy lifestyle, but they are more willing than even millennials to pay extra for it.[10]

The plant-based meat market is projected to grow by a multiple of twenty in the next decade, reaching $85 billion in annual sales globally by 2030.[11] Lab-grown or "cultured meat," which is currently far more expensive than livestock, will find new markets within the next five years, at which point the texture of favorites like steak, burgers, chicken, and meatballs can be replicated. Consumed less frequently, animal protein will still be available to us in 2050. Its use will grow in the developing world, and it will be of higher quality everywhere. Ultimately, Gen Z's behavior changes will result in "far less animal and worker abuse," said Jennifer Hashley, director of the New Entry Sustainable Farming Project and a vegetable and livestock farmer in Lincoln, Massachusetts.

5. America will undergo a rural and urban agricultural renaissance.

While mass agricultural production will continue to be necessary, in the United States, Generation Z will eat locally and seasonally, use indoor, urban, and vertical farms, World War II–style victory gardens, and other DIY methods to make their connection and reconnection to the earth a priority for their health, for the climate, and as further means to deliver justice. Next-generation farmers will modernize and invest in family farms, therefore providing younger, diverse Americans with an opportunity to enter and reclaim their stake in US agriculture. Federal programs will improve Black and other minority farmers' access to land, most of which was lost over the last century due to racial violence and unfair lending and land-ownership policies.[12] Through the farm bill (Agriculture Improvement Act of 2018) and other federal programs, incentives to buy local will be as impactful to farmers, regional economies, and the more than twenty million low-income and low-access Americans living in food deserts—as corn and soybean subsidies are today.[13]

Nathan W. L'Etoile, regional director for the American Farmland Trust, is optimistic that by 2050, "We will have found ways to drive forward the use of the land for multiple purposes—food and fiber production combined with water cleansing, carbon sequestration, energy production, and more."

6. Generation Z will lead a resurgence of civic participation, and US citizens will be among the most active voters in the world.

Raised during one of the most politically turbulent times in history, Generation Z will continue to engage in politics through community service, as well as through the traditional means of casting a ballot, in presidential and off-year and local races, as well. By 2050, technological and security advances, such as biometric voter registration, will allow for individuals and especially those most likely to be victims of suppression to have access to the polls, whether in the church basement, on one's mobile device, or at their kitchen table. Technology will outpace the racists, and laws designed to suppress the vote of Black people, immigrants, and young Americans will be irrelevant. Over the next thirty years, with Zoomers and their children leading the way, voter turnout will increase sharply, moving the United States up the charts from its current position of twenty-eighth in the world, closer to countries with more fulsome participation, such as Sweden, Australia, Denmark, Belgium, South Korea, and Israel—all of which see more than three in four members of their voting age population vote in national elections.[14]

With this, Archon Fung, a professor of citizenship and self-government at Harvard Kennedy School, notes, "Full participation will increase political competition and compel the creation of policy proposals and relational strategies that resonate and connect with all Americans, not just half of us."[15]

7. Republican efforts to tighten voting procedures in the name of preventing voter fraud will alienate Zoomers even more.

Democrats will have a sustained advantage in national elections; Republicans will counter by either evolving or withdrawing to a handful of red states and districts. By now, we know that Generation Z has played an essential role in electing Democrats in the era of Trump. If voting were capped at age twenty-nine, meaning only Gen Z and the youngest millennials could participate, Joe Biden would have won ten times more electoral votes than Trump in 2020, according to an analysis of the available data from two exit-poll sources. Averaging the AP VoteCast and Edison Research for the National Election Pool data sets together, Biden would win the youth vote in thirty-four states. Trump would win only six states, with Indiana and Tennessee, having eleven electoral votes each, being the largest Trump states. Biden and Trump tied in two states according to the polls, and the remaining eight, plus the District of Columbia, reported no exit poll data.

As older and more conservative voters in the silent generation and baby boomer generation age out of the electorate, they will be replaced every year by more active and engaged Zoomer voters, who bring a fundamentally different perspective and set of values to politics and government, and now a record of voting for Democrats. The notable popular-vote advantage Democrats enjoy today—Biden's party won the popular vote in seven of the last eight elections, which date back to 1992—will build to a pronounced and sustained Electoral College advantage.

While the political jet streams can change, and Democrats could easily bungle this, there is virtually no scenario in which this is welcome news for the Republican Party as presently constituted. This is almost certainly why the last few guardians at the gate work so hard to impose voter suppression efforts in Washington, DC, Georgia, Florida, Texas, and in Republican-controlled state legislatures from coast to coast. As of May 2021, the Brennan Center for Justice counted more than 389 bills that were introduced by lawmakers or states with provisions that would curb the vote or restrict voting access in forty-eight states.[16]

Unless the GOP transfigures itself into a political party more aligned with its founding as an abolition party, it will be the underdog for the foreseeable future in presidential elections and will soon become a regional political party. The best they can hope for, without a dramatic repositioning toward the center-right Romney/Murkowski/Baker/Hogan wing of the party, will be a governing scenario in which Democrats dominate national elections and big-city mayorships, while Republicans maintain a diminishing but important set of state legislative houses and districts, and seats in the US Senate. Under this scenario, Bill Shaw, a patent attorney and expert in international collaboration at Tufts University, told me, "We will vote by our feet. The country will become more and more segmented, with like-minded people moving to places together."

If the Republican Party chooses to maintain this ultimately more destructive path it's on and does not evolve—instead bathes in the backlash—then-twenty-six-year-old Peter Bailey-Wells imagines a country in which in the remaining red states, "we will see an extension of the strip-mining of government, where schools, municipal services, and climate change mitigation will continue to be under-funded and undersupported. And in those places, the ripple effects of those policies will continue voter suppression, both in law and via the ongoing distrust of government to solve people's problems. I think this scenario involves continued crumbling of the American reputation and will contribute to a general faltering of democracy globally."

8. Gen Zers will ensure we have the necessary democratic reforms and sweeping civic and social infrastructure investments.

Heading toward 2050, the combination of Generation Z joining millennials as the dominant voting cohorts in the electorate, along with expected higher levels of voter participation, will amount to a sustained period of active, progressive government that builds on the infrastructure that Biden-Harris Democrats were able to put into place over a difficult and divided 2020s Congress. Middle-aged Americans will remember the fraught democracy of their youth and young adulthood and institute reforms to support and sustain healthy democracy. Generation Z will fight to ensure that campaign finance laws remove dark money from politics, that gerrymandering has limits, and that automatic voter registration at eighteen is law; abolishing the Electoral College, if not complete, will be within reach.

Viewed largely through the prism of climate change, domestic policy priorities will include: continued investment in new and renewable energy sources and public transportation, including high-speed rail, to meet the needs of growing regional economies; an expansive health care system that prioritizes wellness and mental health and invests in finding cures and treatments for the growing number of otherwise healthy people suffering from dementia, Alzheimer's, and other untreatable diseases of the brain; a federal job corps that blends universal basic income and essential-services work for millions of displaced and previously undervalued workers; and a modern public education system that provides local authorities ample resources to remove the remnants of redlining, and to extend physical and virtual school settings into 24/7, twelve-month-a-year, customized community centers where children come for friendship and social interactions, knowledge, skill-building, and mentorship.

"We will have suffered through a number of violent episodes. We will see greater expenditures on social programs, and we will take better care of each other," said Rick Majzun when I asked him to tell me how the priorities of our government might evolve in the decades ahead. Undoubtedly, these priorities and values of Generation Z will not be constrained to the United States. Leonard Mungarulire, a public policy graduate student who was studying in Boston before returning to Rwanda during COVID-19, sees that in 2050, "We will vote for leaders with hearts and minds, leaders who want to collaborate with the rest without enforcing their will on others. This pandemic and economic crisis has demonstrated that we are all inextricably linked."

9. Generation Z will ultimately face an intense, global cold war against a militantly nationalistic China intent on breaking democracy.

By 2050, most Americans believe that the United States will have ceded its global role of dominance to China, whose sphere of influence already runs outside of Asia, into the Middle East, throughout Africa, and to Latin America, where they are already the region's top trading partner.[17] In the next cold war, the United States, Europe, India, Japan, South Korea, and Pacific allies will be matched against China, Russia, Pakistan, and the Central Asian countries. The battle for the unaligned countries of Southeast Asia will be one of the final pieces to fall in the U.S.-China chessboard in the years ahead.

Beyond building economic and military muscle, under President Xi Jinping, China has embarked on a sophisticated reeducation campaign of its two hundred million Zoomer-aged citizens, unlike anything since Chairman Mao's Cultural Revolution. "We need to seize this critical period that determines and forms teenagers' values and guide them so they can do up life's first buckle," President Xi Jinping declared in 2018.[18]

The window that was once ajar, which allowed me to have a reasonably open exchange of ideas about politics with Chinese college students during my first visit to Beijing in 2008, now seems closed. Whereas not long ago, many young Chinese would admittedly be open to Western ideologies or thought, a strident nationalism now reigns. Since 2019, young Chinese nationalists have been organized against the Hong Kong protestors, with all the "tact and grace" of their young, far-right counterparts in the United States. According to Vicky Xiuzhong Xu, who writes for *Foreign Policy*, "In Toronto, young nationalists drove Ferraris draped with Chinese flags and ridiculed Hong Kongers for being 'poor cunts.' In London, a sign at a rally demanded that Hong Kongers 'lick [their] master's ass.' In several separate incidents in Australia, Chinese protesters attacked a journalist, assaulted Hong Kong sympathizers, and lambasted anyone who doesn't love China with chants of 'get the fuck out.' In response to 'Hong Kong stay strong' on one university campus, young Chinese students shouted in unison, 'Fuck your mother!'"[19]

In a world of competing priorities, engaging the youth of the developing nations today on common values and issues—like justice, climate, and liberty—is paramount, so that the world in 2050 remains safe and prosperous for the United States and its allies.

10. Success and the American Dream will be defined by the bonds you make, not the stuff you buy.

Beginning with COVID-19 changing the way in which we work and educate our children in the 2020s, the communities of 2050 will bear little resemblance to our current way of life. The multicultural large cities, the hubs of art and culture, will continue to thrive and be a magnet to those around the world with ample resources. With so much of the new economy relying on the virtual, many Zoomers will flee the traffic and expenses of big cities, choosing smaller or more rural places to build better communities, improving upon the lessons learned from the areas they once inhabited. The quest for "flexibility," an essential element of Gen Zers' American Dream, will further drive these trends.

Elected officials, at every level of government, will be judged on the soundness of their education policy. In the decades ahead, education will be to politics what climate has been in the last few election cycles. It will be table stakes for anyone running for office, anywhere. Americans will understand it's the only way to ensure a just, prosperous, and democratic union. John Michael Schert sees that school will "become more diverse, more customized to the student, as we better understand the diversity of thought and abilities latent in our youth. Almost like mutants from science fiction, we will understand the powers each individual possesses and better societally apply them."

As Generation Z breaks the twentieth-century baby

boomer traditions that defined success too often through the single lens of wealth, by the 2050s success will be measured by the amount of social wealth and capital accrued. America will see a resurgence of multigenerational families living together, whether they are defined by beliefs, blood, or belonging. Queer communities, religious communities, ethnic communities, even militia communities, and others will be welcoming for those seeking the bonds of fellowship.

Dina Sherif, a self-described entrepreneur, investor, innovator, and educator, who splits time between Boston and Cairo and leads a center for development and entrepreneurship at the Massachusetts Institute of Technology business school, told me, "If I am still alive in 2050, I hope to be living in a communal home by the beach with friends I love and hold dear to me. I suspect education by then will be fully democratized and digitized."

Large numbers of Zoomers who relied on parents' support for school, sports, after-school activities, and college will readily return the favor and include their parents in their families' lives in a more direct way moving forward. The lack of social interactions from the workplace will be replaced with more time spent in our local communities and with those we love. The bonds Americans built after World War II through bowling leagues and other associations will be renewed and strengthened. America and Americans will be well on their way to being healthier in both body and spirit.

Is all of this a lot to ask from members of a stressed-out generation that have already been working hard to clean up the mess we have left for them?

Yes, it certainly is.

The beauty of Generation Zers is that they do not yet

fully grasp the difference they've already made, or the enormity of the challenges that lie ahead.

What have they been fighting for? Who have they been fighting for? When I ask, this is what they tell me:

They are fighting for those working two jobs but still struggling with debt and unable to live a comfortable life.

They're fighting for those under attack and others simply feeling unwelcome in their own country due to their race, ethnicity, religion, or sexual identity.

They're fighting for those new to America who are afraid they will live their lives on the street, not ever able to afford a home.

They are fighting for their future children, their children's children, and everyone deserving of a clean and healthy planet.

The answer is us. They're fighting for every single one of us.

I say we help them.

I often share the anxiety of Zoomers and the fear they carry about the future. Especially about the state of our politics and our country right now. Friendships have been lost, family ties frayed, and all of it traced back to the divides the last decade has wrought. And for millions of other Americans, it's so much worse than that.

I'm fearful about the months and the years ahead. I am not sure whether we can quiet the chaos. But what keeps me hopeful? The courage and the fighting spirit of Gen Z, the next great generation of Americans.

I cannot wait for the day when I walk into a room of young people, ask them how their life and our country are going, and, rather than hearing tales of fear and despair, I'm overwhelmed with accounts of faith and progress.

I have a feeling those days might come sooner than we think.

ACKNOWLEDGMENTS

The odds were slim in the late 1980s (when I was about the age of many of the subjects in this book) that the girl who would be my summer job supervisor would earn the most prominent acknowledgment for this book—and most everything else that's good in our now-thirty-five-year ride together. That I would convince her to stick with me as I finished college and traveled the country working on political campaigns from Appomattox to Chicago, with plenty of stops in between, is the greatest accomplishment of my life. I am eternally grateful to my wife, Linda, for the personal and professional sacrifices she has made for me and our family. This book, and my journey for the two decades that led to it, would not be possible without her unconditional love and support.

This book would also not have been possible without the gift of seeing and experiencing the world through the eyes of our three Zoomer children: Andrew, the comedian and writer; Ali, the teacher, activist, and law school student; and Emma, the athlete and campaigner for good causes and healthy food. Each in their own way—through empathy, grit, and an innate sense of justice—represent the best of their generation. The optimism I hold for the future is largely due to them.

I understand how fortunate I am to have found my way to, and be represented by, the incomparable Mel Berger of WME. Mel's unflagging confidence in me, and this subject, kept me going for a good long time. Without the vision and early guidance of Stephen Power and the legendary Thomas Dunne, this book would not have taken shape. I regret that the coronavirus pandemic impacted the publishing industry so deeply, and ultimately our collaboration.

The talent and patience of my editor, Hannah O'Grady, can never be overstated. In the throes of the pandemic and in the midst of a presidential campaign I did not expect to join, she rescued me and the manuscript. Without knowing me well, Hannah had a striking ability to help me find my voice and sharpen the narrative. For Kate Davis, Chrisinda Lynch, Mark Lerner, Kathryn Hough, Mac Nicholas, and everyone associated with St. Martin's who contributed ideas, edits, and encouragement along the way, I am profoundly grateful for every insight offered and comma added.

While the book may have been written, I might not have had a business to return to if not for Jonathan Chavez. Jonathan and I have been collaborators and partners since he was recruited into my Harvard study group by then-undergraduate Peter Buttigieg in 2002. His incredible intellect is only matched by his kindness, good humor, and dedication to SocialSphere, the company we founded a decade-plus ago, and the stable of clients we are honored to serve. There were many weeks, over multiple years, that I was "off the grid" in one way or another in service of this project. Without Jonathan's sacrifices and leadership I would never have been in the position to take this on. To Richard Berkowitz, Christopher MacMaster, Julia Kennedy, Keith Gibson, Mary Schein, Lloyd Simon, Karissa Vincent, Deb Gordon, and the team who organized much of the research for this book and shouldered the additional responsibility I left behind at SocialSphere, I cannot thank you enough. I am fortunate to be surrounded by such considerate and dedicated colleagues.

Well before HGTV and Discovery+ brought America *House Hunters: Comedians on Couches,* a series in which the likes of John Mulaney, Seth Rogen, Ali Wong, and J. B. Smoove make jokes and riff over Zoom, I relied on Richard Berkowitz and his couch on

Chappaquiddick to do that with me and my manuscript. Along with Jonathan Chavez, Richard has played a central role in about every element of the focus groups and town meetings I've hosted with Zoomers, whether online or in person. No one else spent more time with me talking over the big picture and the minute details of this story. Richard's insights, along with his brilliant, and bruising, when necessary, sense of humor, made some of the loneliest days of writing brighter—and the story smarter.

I also owe a good deal of thanks and credit to my "smart tribe" of friends, colleagues, and Eisenhower Fellows from close by and around the world, whose expertise and perspective were relied on at critical junctures during this project. I will never be able to formally credit or thank everyone whose knowledge influenced me but would be remiss if I did not acknowledge His Excellency Mohammed N. Al Jasser, Irina Anghel-Enescu, Kellen Arno, Peter Bailey-Wells, Matthew Baum, Deema Bibi, David Bray, Allison Conte, Jamie Druckman, Lucinda Duncalfe, Christopher Fang, Joshua Fang, Jeff C. Frazier, Jon Green, Jennifer Hashley, Steve Johnson, Leland Kirshen, Bob Larkin, David Lazer, Eric Lesser, Nathan W. L'Etoile, Rick Majzun, Sean McNeeley, David Mooradian, Jr., Julia Mooradian, Jon Moore, Raj Narayan, Aaron Niederhelman, Mohammed Nosseir, Katherine Ognyanova, Nina Park, Roy Perlis, Brian Reich, Jill Reynolds, Doug Rubin, Mauricio Santillana, John Michael Schert, John Shattuck, Bill Shaw, Michael Sheehan, Randy Shepard, Dina Sherif, Chris Sherman, Seve Simeone, Matthew Simonson, Noah Tocci, Gail Urso, Sam Watman, Joe Welsh, and Greg Wilson.

For introducing me and then accepting me into the Eisenhower Fellowships family and continuing to show me the world, I owe so much to Tim Cahill, George de Lama, Erin Hillman, John Wolf, and the entire EF staff past and present, the board, and network.

Without the curiosity and foresight of Erin Ashwell and Trevor Dryer, two Harvard undergraduates I met in 2000, this book would never have been written. It was their idea to start a survey of young

Americans; I was the fortunate one living in Boston who could facilitate. I owe my career as a youth-oriented pollster who's carved out a place between the academy and the practical world of politics and business first and foremost to them.

Erin, Trevor, and I were only able to get this project off the ground because of the support and continued commitment of the Institute of Politics leadership and many generous Senior Advisory Committee board members, but especially Ambassador Caroline Kennedy and Heather Campion. Cathy McLaughlin, the former executive director of the IOP, who now serves in a similar capacity at the Biden School of Public Policy and Administration at the University of Delaware, pulled everything together and continues to be an unsung hero to countless young men and women who serve our nation through community and public service. The guidance and friendship of Professor David King was instrumental in my early years at Harvard, and thankfully continues to this day.

Through most of my time at the IOP, I was blessed to have the undying support and camaraderie of Amy Howell and so many generous colleagues and fellows who are dedicated to the legacy of President Kennedy and his ideals of public service. As former executive director, Amy never wavered in support of our students, young voters, or me—not for a minute. She and I were joined in our pursuit by countless, dedicated public servants, but the youth survey would not have been elevated to the heights it found if not for every one of the IOP directors I served under, especially former Secretary Dan Glickman, who was the first to see its promise, and Senator Jeanne Shaheen, who formalized the institute's research program in 2005. I am thankful for my current and former IOP colleagues, especially Anne Aaron, Stephane Alexandre, Eric Andersen, Candice Antrop, Emily Brother, Morgan Burke, Mary Cappabianca, Nanda Chitre, Kerri Collins, John Culver, Bill Delahunt, Katherine Delaney, Carrie Devine, Kelsey Donahue, Christian Flynn, Mark Gearan, Trey Grayson, Abbie James, Jim Leach, Gordon Li, John McCarthy,

Cathey Park, Esten Perez, Jennifer Phillips, Sadie Polen, Bill Purcell, Julie Schroeder, Phil Sharp, Laura Simolaris, Theresa Verbic, Andrew Vincent, Setti Warren, Rob Watson, and Maggie Williams, for their efforts to always elevate the voice of the rising generation.

Collaborating with what is now hundreds, if not thousands, of undergraduates from Harvard and other campuses to better understand the opinions, attitudes, and values that will shape our future remains one of the best jobs in America. I owe my gratitude to every study group member and student chair who served with me, and especially the most recent group of leaders who have made the Harvard Public Opinion Project (HPOP) a model program for any campus: Jing-Jing Shen, Justin Tseng, Cathy Sun, Richard Sweeney, Teddy Landis, and Eric Fliegauf, for sharing your passion and curiosity about our future with me and so many others.

This story would truly not be possible without David Hogg, whom I met a few weeks after Parkland and am honored today to call a friend and inspiration.

For the opportunity to serve on the Biden-Harris polling team, I offer my most sincere gratitude to President Biden, Dr. Jill Biden, Valerie Biden Owens, Mike Donilon, Steve Ricchetti, and Jen O'Malley Dillon. Through my collaboration with fellow Biden-Harris pollsters John Anzalone, Celinda Lake, Matt Barreto, Dr. Silas Lee, and their teams—I learned so much about our country, and how to do my job better.

For taking time during reporting of the 2020 presidential campaign to read a very early draft of the manuscript and provide feedback and support—thank you to Jackie Alemany, Mika Brzezinski, Stephanie Ruhle, and Joe Scarborough.

My collaboration with *RealClearPolitics* has allowed me to probe even deeper on the issues that matter most to America during these turbulent times. I'm grateful to Tom Bevan, John McIntyre, Erin Waters, Carl Cannon, Andrew Walworth, and Liz Martin for that opportunity.

No one can ask for a better or more loyal friend than Carl Cannon. Carl was one of the first people I called after signing the book deal. When I expressed some concern for not fully realizing what I had gotten myself into, Carl said calmly, "Don't worry, pal, we'll get it done." And *we* did. From ever-so-diplomatically telling me to trash my first draft of the first chapter in 2019, to a few late nights during March Madness 2021 and beyond, Carl's support never wavered. I am honored by his generosity of spirit and am fortunate to be the beneficiary of his talents for writing, editing, and storytelling. This book is better because of him.

John Welsh, for providing me with decades of laughs, friendship, and a most constructive review and edit of the "first pass pages," I am so very thankful.

To Doug Schoen, Mark Penn, Jack Maguire, Greg Schneiders, and Keith Frederick—thank you for opening up your worlds to me. I didn't know I wanted to be a pollster until Doug suggested it to me in 1991, back in the day of thirty-minute landline surveys.

Thanks to Paul Sternburg. Everything's just better with Paul's touch.

To my in-laws, Ovsanna and the late Mihran Mooradian, thank you for your love and support—you are the embodiment of the American Dream.

And to my mom, Diane, who gifted my sister, Kristen, and I an abundance of love and curiosity, and my dad, Jim, who never stopped showing me what's important in life, even in his final days as I worked to complete the manuscript, thank you so much. I am grateful and forever indebted.

To every young person in America and around the globe who stands up for what's right, who faces their fears, and who fights in the selfless pursuit of a better life for others, you're an inspiration— please do not ever give up this fight.

NOTES

Introduction

1. Kim Parker and Ruth Igielnik, "On the Cusp of Adulthood and Facing an Uncertain Future: What We Know About Gen Z So Far," Pew Research Center, May 14, 2020, https://www.pewsocialtrends.org/essay/on-the-cusp-of-adulthood-and-facing-an-uncertain-future-what-we-know-about-gen-z-so-far/.
2. Jeffrey M. Jones, "LGBT Identification Rises to 5.6% in Latest U.S. Estimate," Gallup, February 24, 2021, https://news.gallup.com/poll/329708/lgbt-identification-rises-latest-estimate.aspx.
3. Parker and Igielnik, "What We Know About Gen Z So Far."
4. Alex Williams, "Actually, Gen X Did Sell Out, Invent All Things Millennial, and Cause Everything Else That's Great and Awful," *New York Times*, May 14, 2019, sec. Style, https://www.nytimes.com/2019/05/14/style/gen-x-millenials.html.
5. Ibid.
6. "Election2016: Exit Polls," CNN Politics, accessed July 5, 2021, https://www.cnn.com/election/2016/results/exit-polls.
7. "Voter Turnout Demographics: Turnout Rates: Age," United States Elections Project, accessed March 29, 2021, http://www.electproject.org/home/voter-turnout/demographics.
8. "U.S. House Results—2014," CNN Politics, accessed June 22, 2019, http://www.cnn.com/election/2014/results/race/house/.
9. "Exit Polls 2018," CNN Politics, accessed June 22, 2019, https://www.cnn.com/election/2018/exit-polls.
10. "How Groups Voted in 2000," Roper Center for Public Opinion Research, accessed November 11, 2020, https://ropercenter.cornell.edu/how-groups-voted-2000.
11. "Exit Polls 2018."

12. Stephen Vaisey and Omar Lizardo, "Cultural Fragmentation or Acquired Dispositions? A New Approach to Accounting for Patterns of Cultural Change," *Socius* 2, January 1, 2016, https://doi.org/10.1177/2378023116669726.

I. United by Fear

1. Adam Serwer, "Birtherism of a Nation," *The Atlantic,* May 13, 2020, https://www.theatlantic.com/ideas/archive/2020/05/birtherism-and-trump/610978/.

2. Jean M. Twenge et al., "Age, Period, and Cohort Trends in Mood Disorder Indicators and Suicide-Related Outcomes in a Nationally Representative Dataset, 2005–2017," *Journal of Abnormal Psychology* 128, no. 3 (April 2019): 185–99, https://doi.org/10.1037/abn0000410.

3. Ellen M. Burstein and Alan Zhang, "Young Americans Are Facing a Mental Health Crisis and Need Action," *Boston Globe,* May 6, 2021, https://www.bostonglobe.com/2021/05/06/opinion/young-americans-are-facing-mental-health-crisis-need-action/.

4. "Suicide," National Institute of Mental Health, accessed July 4, 2021, https://www.nimh.nih.gov/health/statistics/suicide#part_155143.

5. Sally C. Curtin, M.A., "State Suicide Rates Among Adolescents and Young Adults Aged 10–24: United States, 2000–2018," Centers for Disease Control and Prevention, National Vital Statistics Reports 69, no. 11 (September 11, 2020): 10, https://www.cdc.gov/nchs/data/nvsr/nvsr69/nvsr-69-11-508.pdf.

6. Ibid.

7. Ibid.

8. "Harvard Youth Poll, 41st Edition, Spring 2021, Top Trends and Takeaways," Harvard Kennedy School Institute of Politics, April 2021, https://iop.harvard.edu/youth-poll/spring-2021-harvard-youth-poll.

9. "Inaugural Address: Trump's Full Speech," CNN Politics, January 20, 2017, https://www.cnn.com/2017/01/20/politics/trump-inaugural-address/index.html.

10. "Spring 2012 Survey: The 21th Biannual Youth Survey on Politics and Public Service," Harvard Kennedy School Institute of Politics, April 24, 2012, https://iop.harvard.edu/survey/details/spring-2012-survey.

11. Jeffrey M. Jones, "Biden Begins Term With 57% Job Approval," Gallup, February 4, 2021, https://news.gallup.com/poll/329348/biden-begins-term-job-approval.aspx.

12. Erica Chenoweth et al., "Analysis: The Trump Years Launched the Biggest Sustained Protest Movement in U.S. History. It's Not Over.," *Washington Post,* February 8, 2021, https://www.washingtonpost

.com/politics/2021/02/08/trump-years-launched-biggest-sustained
-protest-movement-us-history-its-not-over/.

13. Glenn Kessler, "Spicer Earns Four Pinocchios for False Claims on Inauguration Crowd Size," *Washington Post,* January 22, 2017, https://www.washingtonpost.com/news/fact-checker/wp/2017/01/22/spicer-earns-four-pinocchios-for-a-series-of-false-claims-on-inauguration-crowd-size/.

14. Glenn Thrush and Dave Itzkoff, "Sean Spicer Says He Regrets Berating Reporters Over Inauguration Crowds," *New York Times,* September 18, 2017, sec. Arts, https://www.nytimes.com/2017/09/18/arts/television/sean-spicer-emmys.html.

15. Ryan Teague Beckwith, "Read Steve Bannon and Reince Priebus' Interview at CPAC," *Time,* February 23, 2017, https://time.com/4681094/reince-priebus-steve-bannon-cpac-interview-transcript/.

16. "Trump's Muslim Ban," C-SPAN, December 7, 2015, https://www.c-span.org/video/?c4737466/user-nclip-trumps-muslim-ban.

17. "Harvard IOP Spring 17 Poll," Harvard Kennedy School Institute of Politics, April 25, 2017, https://iop.harvard.edu/youth-poll/harvard-iop-spring-17-poll.

18. Elle Hunt, "Where Next for the US and the Paris Deal?," *The Guardian,* June 2, 2017, sec. Environment, https://www.theguardian.com/environment/live/2017/jun/01/donald-trump-paris-climate-agreement-live-news.

19. "2016 Pennsylvania Presidential Election Results," *Politico,* accessed July 4, 2021, https://www.politico.com/2016-election/results/map/president/pennsylvania/.

20. "Joe Biden Won in Pennsylvania, Flipping a State Donald Trump Won in 2016.," *Politico,* January 6, 2021, https://www.politico.com/2020-election/results/pennsylvania/.

21. Scott Clement and Brady Dennis, "Post-ABC Poll: Nearly 6 in 10 Oppose Trump Scrapping Paris Agreement," *Washington Post,* June 5, 2017, https://www.washingtonpost.com/news/energy-environment/wp/2017/06/05/post-abc-poll-nearly-6-in-10-oppose-trump-scrapping-paris-agreement/.

22. Jared Keller, "Research Suggests Trump's Election Has Been Detrimental to Many Americans' Mental Health," *Pacific Standard,* January 15, 2019, https://psmag.com/news/research-suggests-trumps-election-has-been-detrimental-to-many-americans-mental-health.

23. David R. Williams and Morgan Medlock, "Health Effects of Dramatic Societal Events—Ramifications of the Recent Presidential Election," *New England Journal of Medicine,* June 8, 2017, https://www.nejm.org/doi/full/10.1056/NEJMms1702111.

24. Eric W. Dolan, "Study: Anti-Trump Young Adults Faced Spike in Stress Hormone Cortisol After Election Day in 2016," *PsyPost,* April 14, 2018,

https://www.psypost.org/2018/04/study-anti-trump-young-adults
-faced-spike-stress-hormone-cortisol-election-day-2016-51036.

25. Ibid.

2. Just a Student

1. Katherine Schaeffer, "6 Facts about Economic Inequality in the U.S.," Pew Research Center, February 7, 2020, https://www.pewresearch .org/fact-tank/2020/02/07/6-facts-about-economic-inequality-in -the-u-s/.

2. Arne Kalleberg and Till von Wachter, "The U.S. Labor Market During and After the Great Recession: Continuities and Transformations," *Russell Sage Foundation Journal of the Social Sciences* 3, no. 3 (April 2017): 1–19, https://doi.org/10.7758/rsf.2017.3.3.01.

3. Tommy Andres, "Divided Decade: How the Financial Crisis Changed Housing," *Marketplace,* December 17, 2018, https://www.marketplace .org/2018/12/17/what-we-learned-housing/.

4. William Schneider, Jane Waldfogel, and Jeanne Brooks-Gunn, "The Great Recession and Behavior Problems in 9-Year-Old Children," *Developmental Psychology* 51, no. 11 (November 2015): 1615–29, https:// doi.org/10.1037/dev0000038.

5. Romeo Vitelli, PhD, "How Have Children Been Affected by the Great Recession?," *Psychology Today,* September 14, 2015, https://www .psychologytoday.com/blog/media-spotlight/201509/how-have -children-been-affected-the-great-recession.

6. Schneider, Waldfogel, and Brooks-Gunn, "The Great Recession and Behavior Problems in 9-Year-Old Children."

7. "The American Dream Persists but Faces Threats: Poll," *Morning Joe,* MSNBC March 6, 2019, https://www.msnbc.com/morning-joe/watch /the-american-dream-persists-but-faces-threats-poll-1452912707673.

8. Julianne Pepitone, "Hundreds of Protesters Descend to 'Occupy Wall Street,'" CNNMoney, September 17, 2011, money.cnn.com/2011/09 /17/technology/occupy_wall_street/index.htm.

9. Heather Gautney, "What Is Occupy Wall Street? The History of Leaderless Movements," *Washington Post,* October 10, 2011, sec. On Leadership, https://www.washingtonpost.com/national/on-leadership/what -is-occupy-wall-street-the-history-of-leaderless-movements/2011/10 /10/gIQAwkFjaL_story.html.

10. "Op-Ed: Occupy Wall Street Protesters' Goals," *Talk of the Nation,* NPR, October 17, 2011, https://www.npr.org/2011/10/17/141427331 /op-ed-occupy-wall-street-protesters-goals.

11. Micah White and Kalle Lasn, "The Call to Occupy Wall Street Resonates Around the World," *The Guardian,* September 19, 2011, http://

www.theguardian.com/commentisfree/cifamerica/2011/sep/19/occupy-wall-street-financial-system.

12. NR Interview, "DeMint Weighs In," *National Review*, January 19, 2012, https://www.nationalreview.com/2012/01/demint-weighs-interview/.

13. Kayleigh McEnany, "Occupy Wall Street: The Naïve Child of Greece," *Daily Caller*, October 19, 2011, https://dailycaller.com/2011/10/19/occupy-wall-street-the-naive-child-of-greece/.

14. Sam Sanders, "The Surprising Legacy of Occupy Wall Street In 2020," *All Things Considered*, NPR, January 23, 2020, https://www.npr.org/2020/01/23/799004281/the-surprising-legacy-of-occupy-wall-street-in-2020.

15. Peter Dreier, "Americans Have Been in the Streets for Almost Ten Years," Public Seminar, June 11, 2020, http://publicseminar.org.dream.website/essays/americans-have-been-in-the-streets-for-almost-ten-years-george-floyd/.

16. Kalle Lasn and Adbusters, eds., *Meme Wars: The Creative Destruction of Neoclassical Economics*, illustrated ed. (New York: Seven Stories Press, 2012).

17. "United States Youth Unemployment Rate | 1948–2021 Data | 2022–2023 Forecast," accessed March 13, 2021, https://tradingeconomics.com/united-states/youth-unemployment-rate.

18. "Student Debt and the Class of 2019," The Institute for College Access & Success, October 2020, https://ticas.org/wp-content/uploads/2020/10/classof2019.pdf.

19. Richard Fry, Jeffrey S. Passel, and D'Vera Cohn, "A Majority of Young Adults in the U.S. Live with Their Parents for the First Time Since the Great Depression," Pew Research Center, September 4, 2020, https://www.pewresearch.org/fact-tank/2020/09/04/a-majority-of-young-adults-in-the-u-s-live-with-their-parents-for-the-first-time-since-the-great-depression/.

20. "Availability of Credit to Small Businesses, September 2012," Board of Governors of the Federal Reserve System, https://www.federalreserve.gov/publications/other-reports/availability-of-credit/September-2012-Executive-Summary.htm

21. Kate Rabinowitz and Youjin Shin, "The Great Recession's Great Hangover," *Washington Post*, September 7, 2018, https://www.washingtonpost.com/graphics/2018/business/great-recession-10-years-out/.

22. Joe Weisenthal, "No Rhyme or Reason," Business Insider, July 30, 2009, https://www.businessinsider.com/no-rhyme-or-reason-2009-7.

23. Andrew M. Cuomo, "No Rhyme or Reason: The 'Heads I Win, Tails You Lose' Bank Bonus Culture," Andrew Cuomo Bonus Report, July 2009,

https://www.scribd.com/document/17850928/Andrew-Cuomo-Bonus-Report.

24. "Share of Total Net Worth Held by the Top 1% (99th to 100th Wealth Percentiles)," Federal Reserve Bank of St. Louis, https://fred.stlouisfed.org/series/WFRBST01134.

25. "Fall 2011 Survey," Harvard Kennedy School Institute of Politics, December 15, 2011, https://iop.harvard.edu/survey/details/fall-2011-survey

26. Jon Meacham, "Show Them the Money," *Time,* October 12, 2011, https://ideas.time.com/2011/10/12/show-them-the-money/.

27. John Harwood, "10 Questions with Bernie Sanders," CNBC, May 26, 2015, https://www.cnbc.com/2015/05/26/10-questions-with-bernie-sanders.html.

28. Eric J. Lyman, "Bernie Sanders Attacks Capitalism Abuses During Trip to Vatican," *USA Today,* April 15, 2016, https://www.usatoday.com/story/news/world/2016/04/15/bernie-sanders-vatican-capitalism/83082802/.

29. The Institute of Politics, Harvard Kennedy School, *Campaign for President: The Managers Look at 2016* (Lanham, MD: Rowman & Littlefield, 2017).

30. Aaron Zitner, Dante Chinni, and Brian McGill, "How Clinton Won: How Hillary Clinton Overcame the Challenge from Sen. Bernie Sanders," *Wall Street Journal,* June 7, 2016, http://graphics.wsj.com/elections/2016/how-clinton-won/.

31. Annie Lowrey, "Why the Phrase 'Late Capitalism' Is Suddenly Everywhere," *The Atlantic,* May 1, 2017, https://www.theatlantic.com/business/archive/2017/05/late-capitalism/524943/.

32. Lydia Saad, "Socialism as Popular as Capitalism Among Young Adults in U.S.," Gallup, November 25, 2019, https://news.gallup.com/poll/268766/socialism-popular-capitalism-among-young-adults.aspx.

33. Jarrett Moreno, "How Much You Need to Work to Cover Tuition in 1978 vs. 2014," ATTN:, October 27, 2014, https://archive.attn.com/stories/197/how-much-you-need-work-cover-tuition-1978-vs-2014.

34. Steven Pearlstein, *Can American Capitalism Survive?,* 1st ed. (New York: St. Martin's Press, 2018).

35. Neil Bhutta, Andrew C. Chang, Lisa J. Dettling, and Joanne W. Hsu, "Disparities in Wealth by Race and Ethnicity in the 2019 Survey of Consumer Finances," Board of Governors of the Federal Reserve System, September 28, 2020, https://doi.org/10.17016/2380-7172.2797.

36. Ibid.

37. "15 Things You Can Buy with That $600 Stimulus Check," *KOLR-OzarksFirst.com,* December 30, 2020, https://www.ozarksfirst.com/local-news/local-news-local-news/heres-a-list-of-15-things-you-can-buy-with-that-600-stimulus-check/.

38. "Fall 2018 National Youth Poll," Harvard Kennedy School Institute of Politics, October 2018, https://iop.harvard.edu/fall-2018-national-youth-poll.

39. "From the Archives: President Teddy Roosevelt's New Nationalism Speech," The White House, December 6, 2011, https://obamawhitehouse.archives.gov/blog/2011/12/06/archives-president-teddy-roosevelts-new-nationalism-speech.

40. "Franklin D. Roosevelt First Inaugural Speech," The History Place: Great Speeches Collection, accessed July 28, 2020, https://www.historyplace.com/speeches/fdr-first-inaug.htm.

41. William R. Emmons, Ana H. Kent, and Lowell R. Ricketts, "The Demographics of Wealth: How Education, Race and Birth Year Shape Financial Outcomes," 2018 Series, May 15, 2018, https://www.stlouisfed.org/~/media/Files/PDFs/HFS/essays/HFS_essay_2_2018.pdf?la=en.

42. Michael Gerson, "Despite What Trump and Sanders Say, the American Dream Has Not Been Stolen," *Washington Post,* February 1, 2016, sec. Opinion, https://www.washingtonpost.com/opinions/despite-what-trump-and-sanders-say-the-american-dream-has-not-been-stolen/2016/02/01/20919c2e-c90a-11e5-88ff-e2d1b4289c2f_story.html.

43. Raj Shetty et al., "The Fading American Dream: Trends in Absolute Income Mobility Since 1940," The National Bureau of Economic Research, Issue Date: December 2016, Revision Date: March 2017, https://www.nber.org/papers/w22910.

44. "The Great Gatsby Curve," Bloomberg, October 6, 2013, https://www.bloomberg.com/graphics/infographics/the-great-gatsby-curve-explained.html.

45. Ibid.

46. "Americans' Views of Government: Low Trust, but Some Positive Performance Ratings," Pew Research Center, September 14, 2020, https://www.pewresearch.org/politics/2020/09/14/americans-views-of-government-low-trust-but-some-positive-performance-ratings/.

47. "Harvard Youth Poll, 39th Edition, Spring 2020," Harvard Kennedy School Institute of Politics, April 2019, https://iop.harvard.edu/youth-poll/spring-2020-poll.

48. Ibid.

49. C. Haerpfer et al., "World Values Survey Wave 7 (2017–2020)," World Values Survey, https://www.worldvaluessurvey.org/WVSDocumentation WV7.jsp.

50. Rod Dreher, "Woke Capitalism Is Our Enemy," *American Conservative,* April 22, 2019, https://www.theamericanconservative.com/dreher/woke-capitalism-is-our-enemy/.

51. Lawrence Glickman, "The American Tradition of Consumer Politics," The American Historian, Organization of American Historians, accessed September 12, 2020, https://www.oah.org/tah/issues/2017 /may/the-american-tradition-of-consumer-politics/.

52. Carl Cannon, "'Woke' Capitalism and the 2020 Election," *RealClear-Politics*, February 27, 2020, https://www.realclearpolitics.com/articles /2020/02/27/woke_capitalism_and_the_2020_election_142501.html.

53. Sarah Nassauer, "How Dick's Sporting Goods Decided to Change Its Gun Policy," *Wall Street Journal*, December 4, 2018, sec. Business, https://www.wsj.com/articles/how-dicks-sporting-goods-decided-to -change-its-gun-policy-1543955262.

54. Nathan Bomey, "Walmart Bans Gun Sales to Anyone Under 21 After Parkland, Florida School Shooting," *USA Today*, February 28, 2018, https://www.usatoday.com/story/money/2018/02/28/walmart-bans -gun-sales-anyone-under-21-after-parkland-florida-school-shooting /383487002/.

55. Cannon, "'Woke' Capitalism and the 2020 Election."

56. Abha Bhattarai, "'The Status Quo Is Unacceptable': Walmart Will Stop Selling Some Ammunition and Exit the Handgun Market," *Washington Post*, September 3, 2019, https://www.washingtonpost.com/business /2019/09/03/status-quo-is-unacceptable-walmart-will-stop-selling -some-ammunition-exit-handgun-market/.

57. Nathan Bomey, "NRA Fallout: See the List of Companies That Cut Discounts for NRA Members after Parkland, Florida School Shooting," *USA Today*, February 26, 2018, https://www.usatoday.com/story/money /2018/02/26/nra-companies-parkland-school-shooting/372271002/.

58. Ree Hines, "Dixie Chicks Open Up About Controversy That Changed Their Careers 17 Years Ago," *Today*, March 6, 2020, https://www.today .com/popculture/dixie-chicks-controversy-changed-their-careers-17 -years-ago-t175454.

59. Bethany Biron, "Hobby Lobby Reportedly Leaving Stores Open Based on a Message from God," Business Insider, March 22, 2020, https:// www.businessinsider.com/hobby-lobby-reportedly-leaving-stores -open-message-from-god-2020-3.

60. Tory Newmyer, "The Finance 202: Trump's Call for Goodyear Boycott Joins Long History of Bullying Companies That Cross Him," *Washington Post*, August 20, 2020, https://www.washingtonpost.com/politics/2020 /08/20/finance-202-trump-call-goodyear-boycott-joins-long-history -bullying-companies-that-cross-him/.

61. Reuters Staff, "Trumps Tweet Support for Goya Foods amid Boycott Campaign," Reuters, July 15, 2020, https://www.reuters.com/article /us-goya-boycott-ivanka-trump/trumps-tweet-support-for-goya-foods -amid-boycott-campaign-idUSKCN24G0L6.

62. Mark Muro et al., "Biden-Voting Counties Equal 70% of America's Economy. What Does This Mean for the Nation's Political-Economic Divide?", Brookings, November 9, 2020, https://www.brookings.edu /blog/the-avenue/2020/11/09/biden-voting-counties-equal-70-of- americas-economy-what-does-this-mean-for-the-nations-political- economic-divide/.

63. "Joint Statement on Protecting Voting Access," Civic Alliance, April 2, 2021, https://www.civicalliance.com/votingaccess/

64. David Gelles, "Corporate America Flexes Its Political Muscle," *New York Times,* January 16, 2021, sec. Business, https://www.nytimes.com /2021/01/16/business/dealbook/ceos-politics-trump.html.

65. "How a 'Youth Boom' Could Shake Up Spending Trends," Morgan Stanley, August 16, 2019, https://www.morganstanley.com/ideas/gen -z-millennials-set-for-consumer-spending-increases.

66. "General Motors 2019 Sustainability Report," General Motors, accessed September 16, 2020, https://www.gmsustainability.com/.

67. Alex Abad-Santos, "Nike's Colin Kaepernick Ad Sparked a Boycott— and Earned $6 Billion for Nike," *Vox,* September 24, 2018, https:// www.vox.com/2018/9/24/17895704/nike-colin-kaepernick-boycott-6 -billion.

68. "Business Roundtable Redefines the Purpose of a Corporation to Pro- mote 'An Economy That Serves All Americans,'" Business Roundta- ble, August 19, 2019, https://www.businessroundtable.org/business -roundtable-redefines-the-purpose-of-a-corporation-to-promote-an -economy-that-serves-all-americans.

3. Six Minutes in Parkland

1. Carey Codd, "Uber Driver: Cruz Said He Was Headed to Music Class Prior to Shooting," CBS Miami, February 27, 2018, https://miami.cbslocal .com/2018/02/27/uber-driver-cruz-school-shooting/.

2. "Initial Report: Submitted to the Governor, Speaker of the House of Rep- resentatives and Senate President," Marjory Stoneman Douglas High School Public Safety Commission, January 1, 2019, http://www.fdle .state.fl.us/MSDHS/Meetings/2018/December-Meeting-Documents /Marjory-Stoneman-Douglas-High-School-Public-Draft1.aspx.

3. Codd, "Uber Driver: Cruz Said He Was Headed to Music Class."

4. "Initial Report: Submitted to the Governor, Speaker of the House of Representatives and Senate President."

5. Ibid.

6. David Hogg and Lauren Hogg, *#NeverAgain: A New Generation Draws the Line,* 1st ed. (New York: Random House, 2018).

7. Ibid.

8. Eric Levenson and Joe Sterling, "These Are the Victims of the Florida School Shooting," CNN, February 21, 2018, https://www.cnn.com/2018/02/15/us/florida-shooting-victims-school/index.html.

9. David Fleshler et al., "Captain in Parkland School Shooting Was Brought onto Force by Sheriff Israel," *South Florida Sun Sentinel,* March 2, 2018, https://www.sun-sentinel.com/local/broward/parkland/florida-school-shooting/fl-florida-shooting-bso-perimeter-20180302-story.html.

10. Patricia Mazzei, "After 2 Apparent Student Suicides, Parkland Grieves Again," *New York Times,* March 24, 2019, https://www.nytimes.com/2019/03/24/us/parkland-suicide-marjory-stoneman-douglas.html.

11. Julia Jacobo, Joshua Hoyos, and Rachel Katz, "16-Year-Old Calvin Desir Identified as 2nd Stoneman Douglas Teen Dead from Apparent Suicide," ABC News, March 26, 2019, https://abcnews.go.com/US/parkland-teen-dies-apparent-suicide-week-authorities/story?id=61907802.

12. "Initial Report."

13. Associated Press, "3 Years Later, Parkland School Shooting Trial Still in Limbo," WGN-TV, February 11, 2021, https://wgntv.com/news/3-years-later-parkland-school-shooting-trial-still-in-limbo/.

14. Hogg and Hogg, *#NeverAgain.*

15. Ibid.

16. Ibid.

17. Dakin Androne, "Student Journalist Interviewed Classmates as Shooter Walked Parkland School Halls," CNN, February 18, 2018, https://www.cnn.com/2018/02/17/us/david-hogg-profile-florida-shooting.

18. "Student Says Heroic Janitor Saved Many Lives During Shooting," Fox News, February 14, 2018, https://www.foxnews.com/transcript/student-says-heroic-janitor-saved-many-lives-during-shooting.

19. Ibid.

20. Charlotte Alter, "The School Shooting Generation Has Had Enough," *Time,* March 22, 2018, https://time.com/longform/never-again-movement/.

21. Dave Cullen, *Parkland: Birth of a Movement,* 1st ed. (New York: HarperCollins, 2019).

22. Ibid.

23. Ibid.

24. CNN Staff, "Florida Student Emma Gonzalez to Lawmakers and Gun Advocates: 'We Call BS,'" CNN, February 17, 2018, https://www.cnn.com/2018/02/17/us/florida-student-emma-gonzalez-speech/index.html.

25. Ibid.

26. Tyler Kingkade, "Active Shooter Drills Are Meant to Prepare Students. But Research Finds 'Severe' Side Effects.," NBC News, September 3,

2020, https://www.nbcnews.com/news/us-news/active-shooter-drills-are-meant-prepare-students-research-finds-severe-n1239103.

27. Alter, "The School Shooting Generation Has Had Enough."

28. Michael Tackett and Rachel Shorey, "Young People Keep Marching After Parkland, This Time to Register to Vote," *New York Times*, May 20, 2018, sec. Politics, https://www.nytimes.com/2018/05/20/us/politics/young-voters-registration-parkland.html.

29. "The 12th Biannual Youth Survey on Politics and Public Service," Harvard Kennedy School Institute of Politics, April 2007, https://iop.harvard.edu/sites/default/files_new/survey_s2007_topline.pdf.

30. "Institute of Politics Spring 2013 Poll," Harvard Kennedy School Institute of Politics, April 30, 2013, https://iop.harvard.edu/survey/details/institute-politics-spring-2013-poll.

31. German Lopez and Kavya Sukumar, "After Sandy Hook, We Said Never Again. And Then We Let 2,654 Mass Shootings Happen," *Vox*, updated July 21, 2020, https://www.vox.com/a/mass-shootings-america-sandy-hook-gun-violence.

32. "Gunfire on School Grounds in the United States," Everytown Research & Policy, accessed March 19, 2021, https://everytownresearch.org/maps/gunfire-on-school-grounds/.

33. Debbie Lord, "Florida's Gun Laws: How Have They Changed After the Parkland Shooting?," *Atlanta Journal-Constitution*, June 13, 2018, https://www.ajc.com/news/national/florida-gun-laws-how-have-they-changed-after-the-parkland-shooting/BIhOP1bppQJjV7Nl1F7ZXI/.

34. Matt Vasilogambros, "After Parkland, States Pass 50 New Gun-Control Laws," Stateline, August 2, 2018, https://pew.org/2MaUDLp.

35. Hogg and Hogg, *#NeverAgain*.

36. Paula McMahon and Brittany Wallman, "How the FBI Botched Tips About the Parkland School Shooter," *South Florida Sun Sentinel*, August 29, 2018, https://www.sun-sentinel.com/local/broward/parkland/florida-school-shooting/fl-florida-school-shooting-fbi-tips-problems-20180828-story.html.

37. "Stress in America™: Generation Z," American Psychological Association, October 2018, https://www.apa.org/news/press/releases/stress/2018/stress-gen-z.pdf.

38. Jason Johnson, "Yes, the March for Our Lives Was About Black People, Too—and It's About Time," *The Root*, March 26, 2018, https://www.theroot.com/yes-the-march-for-our-lives-was-about-black-people-too-1824082682.

39. Emma González, "A Young Activist's Advice: Vote, Shave Your Head and Cry Whenever You Need To," *New York Times*, October 5, 2018, sec. Opinion, https://www.nytimes.com/2018/10/05/opinion/sunday/emma-gonzalez-parkland.html.

40. Nate Silver, "Trump's Base Isn't Enough," *FiveThirtyEight*, November 20, 2018, https://fivethirtyeight.com/features/trumps-base-isnt -enough/.

4. Right in Front of Everybody

1. "In Depth: Race Relations," Gallup, accessed June 28, 2021, https:// news.gallup.com/poll/1687/Race-Relations.aspx.
2. Ibid.
3. Michael C. Dawson and Lawrence D. Bobo, "One Year Later and the Myth of a Post-Racial Society," *Du Bois Review: Social Science Research on Race* 6, no. 2 (2009): 247–49, http://nrs.harvard.edu/urn-3:HUL .InstRepos:10347165.
4. Daniel Villarreal, "Hate Crimes Under Trump Surged Nearly 20 Percent Says FBI Report," *Newsweek*, November 16, 2020, https://www .newsweek.com/hate-crimes-under-trump-surged-nearly-20-percent -says-fbi-report-1547870.
5. Tim Arango, "Hate Crimes in U.S. Rose to Highest Level in More Than a Decade in 2019," *New York Times*, November 16, 2020, sec. U.S., https://www.nytimes.com/2020/11/16/us/hate-crime-rate.html.
6. Griffin Sims Edwards and Stephen Rushin, "The Effect of President Trump's Election on Hate Crimes," SSRN Electronic Journal, January 4, 2018, https://doi.org/10.2139/ssrn.3102652.
7. Ibid.
8. Rosemary K. M. Sword and Philip Zimbardo, PhD, "The Trump Effect: An Update," *Psychology Today*, January 30, 2018, https://www.psychology today.com/blog/the-time-cure/201801/the-trump-effect-update.
9. Francis L. Huang and Dewey G. Cornell, "School Teasing and Bullying After the Presidential Election," *Educational Researcher* 48, no. 2 (March 1, 2019): 69–83, https://doi.org/10.3102/0013189X18820291.
10. Valerie Strauss, "Study: Bullying Rates at Virginia Middle Schools Were Higher in Trump Country after His Election," *Washington Post*, January 10, 2019, https://www.washingtonpost.com/education/2019/01 /10/study-bullying-rates-virginia-middle-schools-were-higher-trump -country-after-his-election/.
11. "State Superintendent Tony Thurmond Launches New 'Education to End Hate' Initiative to Combat Bias, Bigotry, and Racism," California Department of Education, news release, September 21, 2020, https:// www.cde.ca.gov/nr/ne/yr20/yr20rel77.asp.
12. James W. Loewen, *Sundown Towns: A Hidden Dimension of American Racism* (The New Press: 2018).
13. Devin English et al., "Daily Multidimensional Racial Discrimination Among Black U.S. American Adolescents," *Journal of Applied Develop-*

mental Psychology 66 (January 1, 2020): 101068, https://doi.org/10
.1016/j.appdev.2019.101068.

14. Derald Wing Sue, "Microaggressions: Death by a Thousand Cuts," *Scientific American*, March 30, 2021, https://www.scientificamerican.com
/article/microaggressions-death-by-a-thousand-cuts/.

15. Patrisse Khan-Cullors and asha bandele, *When They Call You a Terrorist*, 1st ed. (New York: St. Martin's Press, 2018).

16. David R. Williams and Morgan M. Medlock, "Health Effects of Dramatic Societal Events—Ramifications of the Recent Presidential Election," *New England Journal of Medicine*, June 8, 2017, https://www.nejm
.org/doi/full/10.1056/NEJMms1702111.

17. Lauren Musu-Gillette, Rachel Hansen, Kathryn Chandler, and Tom Snyder, "Measuring Student Safety: Bullying Rates at School," National Center for Education Statistics, May 1, 2015, https://nces.ed.gov/blogs
/nces/post/measuring-student-safety-bullying-rates-at-school.

18. Jonathan Martin and Maggie Haberman, "Forget Tax Cuts. Trump Wants to Rally the G.O.P. Base Over Immigration.," *New York Times*, June 18, 2018, sec. U.S., https://www.nytimes.com/2018/06/18/us
/politics/trump-immigration-midterms.html.

19. Ibid.

20. Skyler Romero, "Teen Who Filmed George Floyd Killing Harassed Online," *Parentology*, June 1, 2020, https://parentology.com/teen-who
-filmed-george-floyd-killing-harassed-online/.

21. Larry Buchanan, Quoctrung Bui, and Jugal K. Patel, "Black Lives Matter May Be the Largest Movement in U.S. History," *New York Times*, July 3, 2020, sec. U.S., https://www.nytimes.com/interactive/2020/07
/03/us/george-floyd-protests-crowd-size.html.

22. Adrienne Broaddus, "A Walk to the Store: 9-Year-Old Who Witnessed Floyd Death Writing Book," KARE-TV, Minneapolis–St. Paul, June 30, 2020, https://www.kare11.com/article/news/local/breaking-the
-news/a-walk-to-the-store-9-year-old-who-witnessed-floyd-death
-writing-book/89-b6bfa25d-1607–4aab-9bfe-e6a87e2dcbb2.

23. "Special Citations and Awards," The Pulitzer Prizes, accessed July 4, 2021, https://www.pulitzer.org/prize-winners-by-category/260.

24. Darnella Frazier, "They really killed than man bro ♥," Facebook, accessed on July 4, 2021, https://www.facebook.com/darnellareallpretty-
marie/videos/1425381660996269.

25. Jeff Hargarten et al., "Every Police-Involved Death in Minnesota since 2000," *Star Tribune*, accessed March 21, 2021, https://www
.startribune.com/every-police-involved-death-in-minnesota-since
-2000/502088871/.

26. Broaddus, "A Walk to the Store."

27. Paul Walsh, "Teen Who Recorded George Floyd Video Wasn't Looking to Be a Hero, Her Lawyer Says," *Star Tribune,* June 11, 2020, https://www.startribune.com/teen-who-shot-video-of-george-floyd-wasn-t-looking-to-be-a-hero-her-lawyer-says/571192352/.

28. Yamiche Alcindor and Sam Lane, "'He Was Terrified:' Witnesses Offer Emotional Testimony About Floyd Death in Chauvin Case," *PBS News Hour,* March 30, 2021, https://www.pbs.org/newshour/show/he-was-terrified-witnesses-offer-emotional-testimony-about-floyd-death-in-chauvin-case.

29. Darnella Frazier, "I honestly can't believe I'm making this post right now . . . I'm so hurt . . . nothing feels real . . . ," Facebook, accessed July 7, 2021, https://www.facebook.com/darnellareallprettymarie/posts/1759633094237789.

30. Tim Harlow, Paul Walsh, and Alex Chhith, "Darnella Frazier Identifies Innocent Man Killed During Minneapolis Police Pursuit as Her Uncle," *Star Tribune,* July 6, 2021, https://www.startribune.com/darnella-frazier-identifies-innocent-man-killed-during-police-pursuit-as-her-uncle/600075380/.

31. "PEN America to Honor Darnella Frazier, Young Woman Who Documented George Floyd's Murder," PEN America, October 27, 2020, https://pen.org/press-release/pen-america-to-honor-darnella-frazier-young-woman-who-documented-george-floyds-murder/.

32. Darnella Frazier, "I just cried so hard. . . ." Facebook, accessed May 10, 2021, https://www.facebook.com/darnellareallprettymarie/posts/1700867960114303.

33. Shayanne Gal, Andy Kiersz, Michelle Mark, Ruobing Su, and Marguerite Ward, "26 Simple Charts to Show Friends and Family Who Aren't Convinced Racism Is Still a Problem in America," Business Insider, Flipboard, accessed July 8, 2020, https://www.businessinsider.com/us-systemic-racism-in-charts-graphs-data-2020-6.

34. Elizabeth Arias, PhD, and Jiaquan Xu, MD, United States Life Tables, 2017. National Vital Statistics Reports; vol 68 no 7. Hyattsville, MD: National Center for Health Statistics. 2019, https://www.cdc.gov/nchs/data/nvsr/nvsr68/nvsr68_07-508.pdf.

35. Amanda Barroso and Rachel Minkin, "Recent Protest Attendees Are More Racially and Ethnically Diverse, Younger than Americans Overall," Pew Research Center, June 24, 2020, https://www.pewresearch.org/fact-tank/2020/06/24/recent-protest-attendees-are-more-racially-and-ethnically-diverse-younger-than-americans-overall/.

36. Lara Putnam, Jeremy Pressman, and Erica Chenoweth, "Analysis: Black Lives Matter Beyond America's Big Cities," *Washington Post,* July 8, 2020, https://www.washingtonpost.com/politics/2020/07/08/black-lives-matter-beyond-americas-big-cities/.

37. Buchanan, Bui, and Patel, "Black Lives Matter May Be the Largest Movement in U.S. History."

38. Kim Parker, Juliana Menasce Horowitz, and Monica Anderson, "Amid Protests, Majorities Across Racial and Ethnic Groups Express Support for the Black Lives Matter Movement," Pew Research Center, June 12, 2020, https://www.pewsocialtrends.org/2020/06/12/amid-protests -majorities-across-racial-and-ethnic-groups-express-support-for-the -black-lives-matter-movement/.

39. Nate Silver, @natesilver, Tweet: "Obviously the presidential toplines are what's going to get attention here, but this poll shows a majority of Southerns now think of the Confederate flag as a symbol of racism rather than 'Southern pride'. Rapid shifts in opinion on these issues.," Twitter, July 15, 2020, https://twitter.com/NateSilver538/status /1283487757860560903.

40. Erica Chenoweth and Jeremy Pressman, "Analysis: This Summer's Black Lives Matter Protesters Were Overwhelmingly Peaceful, Our Research Finds," *Washington Post,* October 16, 2020, https://www .washingtonpost.com/politics/2020/10/16/this-summers-black -lives-matter-protesters-were-overwhelming-peaceful-our-research -finds/.

41. Buchanan, Bui, and Patel, "Black Lives Matter May Be the Largest Movement in U.S. History."

42. Barroso and Minkin, "Recent Protest Attendees Are More Racially and Ethnically Diverse."

43. Juliana Menasce Horowitz et al., "Amid National Reckoning, Americans Divided on Whether Increased Focus on Race Will Lead to Major Policy Change," Pew Research Center, October 6, 2020, https://www .pewresearch.org/social-trends/2020/10/06/amid-national-reckoning -americans-divided-on-whether-increased-focus-on-race-will-lead-to -major-policy-change/.

44. "Changing Attitudes on Same-Sex Marriage," Pew Research Center, May 14, 2019, https://www.pewforum.org/fact-sheet/changing -attitudes-on-gay-marriage/.

45. Jacob Poushter and Nicholas Kent, "The Global Divide on Homosexuality Persists," Pew Research Center, June 25, 2020, https://www.pewresearch .org/global/2020/06/25/global-divide-on-homosexuality-persists/.

46. "In U.S., Decline of Christianity Continues at Rapid Pace," Pew Research Center, October 17, 2019, https://www.pewforum.org/2019/10 /17/in-u-s-decline-of-christianity-continues-at-rapid-pace/.

47. Orion Rummler, "The Major Police Reforms Enacted Since George Floyd's Death," Axios, accessed July 7, 2020, https://www.axios.com/police -reform-george-floyd-protest-2150b2dd-a6dc-4a0c-a1fb-62c2e999a03a .html.

48. "Fatal Force: Police Shootings Database," *Washington Post,* accessed July 16, 2020, https://www.washingtonpost.com/graphics/investigations/police -shootings-database/.

49. Spencer Neale, "'This Is Murder': Trey Gowdy Says He 'Doesn't Need to Wait for the Feds' to Judge George Floyd Death," *Washington Examiner,* May 28, 2020, sec. News, https://www.washingtonexaminer.com /news/this-is-murder-trey-gowdy-says-he-doesnt-need-to-wait-for-the -feds-to-judge-george-floyd-death.

50. "How Can We Win Kimberly Jones Video Full Length David Jones Media Clean Edit #BLM 2020 What Can I Do," June 9, 2020, https://www .youtube.com/watch?v=llci8MVh8J4.

51. Gene Roberts and Hank Klibanoff, *The Race Beat: The Press, the Civil Rights Struggle, and the Awakening of a Nation* (New York: Vintage, 2007).

52. Ginny Hogan, "What Millennials Want to Cancel About Gen Z," Medium, February 22, 2021, https://thebolditalic.com/what-millennials -want-to-cancel-about-gen-z-378a5f6ab731.

5. Backlash

1. Jason Dearen, "Inside a KKK Murder Plot: Grab Him up, Take Him to the River," Associated Press, July 27, 2021, https://apnews.com/article /government-and-politics-business-race-and-ethnicity-racial-injustice -only-on-ap-2b4106de3ebcbfae85948439a7056031.

2. Jaclyn Peiser, "'American Idol' Boots Finalist Caleb Kennedy over Video Featuring a KKK-Style Hood," *Washington Post,* May 13, 2021, https:// www.washingtonpost.com/nation/2021/05/13/caleb-kennedy -american-idol-kkk/.

3. Justin Wm. Moyer, "KKK Fliers Found in Northern Virginia, Authorities Say," *Washington Post,* June 24, 2021, https://www.washingtonpost.com /local/public-safety/kkk-fliers-found-in-northern-virginia-authorities -say/2021/06/24/588e0944-d527-11eb-baed-4abcfa380a17_story.html.

4. Nicole Acevedo, "Ohio Police Chief out after Leaving 'Ku Klux Klan' Note on Black Officer's Coat," NBC News, July 3, 2021, https://www .nbcnews.com/news/us-news/ohio-police-chief-out-after-leaving-ku -klux-klan-note-n1273049.

5. Alex Daugherty, "Some Texas Suburbs Shift from Republican Territory to Democrats' Best Hope," *Fort Worth Star-Telegram,* February 6, 2017, https://www.star-telegram.com/news/politics-government/state -politics/article131126489.html.

6. "Thomas Rousseau's Portfolio," accessed March 24, 2021, https:// thomasrousseauportfolio.wordpress.com/.

7. Thomas Rousseau, "Diversity Club Brings Friendly Atmosphere to Students of Varied Backgrounds," *Coppell Student Media,* January 28, 2016,

https://coppellstudentmedia.com/62416/news/diversity-club-brings
-friendly-atmosphere-to-students-of-varied-backgrounds/.

8. Thomas Rousseau, "Controversy on Texas Campuses as 'Campus Carry' Legalized," *Coppell Student Media,* March 31, 2016, https://coppellstudentmedia.com/65095/opinions/controversy-on-texas-campuses-as-campus-carry-legalized/.

9. Thomas Rousseau, "Corporations Preach from Unfounded Moral High Ground, Spout Hypocrisy," *Coppell Student Media,* May 12, 2016, https://coppellstudentmedia.com/66310/opinions/corporations-preach-from-unfounded-moral-high-ground-spout-hypocrisy/.

10. "Coppell High School: Demographics / Overview," accessed July 4, 2021, https://www.coppellisd.com/domain/180

11. Simon Clark, "How White Supremacy Returned to Mainstream Politics," Center for American Progress, July 1, 2020, https://www.americanprogress.org/issues/security/reports/2020/07/01/482414/white-supremacy-returned-mainstream-politics/.

12. Thomas Rousseau, "Making America Great Again, One Vote at a Time," *Coppell Student Media,* October 26, 2016, https://coppellstudentmedia.com/68178/opinions/making-america-great-again-one-vote-at-a-time/.

13. Thomas Rousseau, "Trump: The Silent Majority No Longer Silent," *Coppell Student Media,* November 14, 2016, https://web.archive.org/web/20161203120836/https:/coppellstudentmedia.com/68851/opinions/trump-the-silent-majority-no-longer-silent/.

14. "Thomas Rousseau," Southern Poverty Law Center, accessed March 24, 2021, https://www.splcenter.org/fighting-hate/extremist-files/individual/thomas-rousseau.

15. "Vanguard America," Anti-Defamation League, accessed March 26, 2021, https://www.adl.org/resources/backgrounders/vanguard-america.

16. David Neiwert, "When White Nationalists Chant Their Weird Slogans, What Do They Mean?," Southern Poverty Law Center, October 10, 2017, https://www.splcenter.org/hatewatch/2017/10/10/when-white-nationalists-chant-their-weird-slogans-what-do-they-mean.

17. texasantifa, "Inside Patriot Front Headquarters: Neo-Nazis Hiding in Plain Sight," Texas Against Fascism (blog), accessed March 26, 2021, https://texasantifa.noblogs.org/inside-patriot-front-thomas-rousseau-grapevine-texas/.

18. "Thomas Rousseau."

19. "Reclaim America," Patriot Front, accessed March 27, 2021, http://patriotfront.us/.

20. "Life, Liberty, Victory," Patriot Front, Manifesto, accessed December 29, 2020, https://patriotfront.us/manifesto/.

21. Chris Schiano, "'We're Americans, And We're Fascists': Inside Patriot Front," Unicorn Riot (blog), March 5, 2018, https://unicornriot.ninja/2018/americans-fascists-inside-patriot-front/.

22. Carol Schaeffer and Fritz Zimmermann, "They Are Racist; Some of Them Have Guns. Inside the White Supremacist Group Hiding in Plain Sight.," ProPublica, November 8, 2019, https://www.propublica.org/article/they-are-racist-some-of-them-have-guns-inside-the-white-supremacist-group-hiding-in-plain-sight?token=-LWC0UDWQ7X23i LEOqYYQFkDs9mlu7vg.

23. "ADL H.E.A.T. Map," Anti-Defamation League, accessed March 26, 2021, https://www.adl.org/education-and-resources/resource-knowledge-base/adl-heat-map.

24. Schaeffer and Zimmermann, "They Are Racist."

25. Ibid.

26. Sharon Jayson and Kaiser Health News, "What Makes People Join Hate Groups?," *U.S. News & World Report,* August 23, 2017, https://www.usnews.com/news/national-news/articles/2017-08-23/what-makes-people-join-hate-groups-studies-say-childhood-torment-social-isolation.

27. Clare Hymes, Cassidy McDonald, and Eleanor Watson, "500 Arrested so Far in Capitol Riot Case, Including 100 Charged with Assaulting Federal Officers," CBS News, accessed June 30, 2021, https://www.cbsnews.com/news/capitol-riot-arrests-latest-2021-06-30/.

28. "14745 Wood Rd, Milton, GA," Trulia Real Estate Search, accessed July 2, 2021, https://www.trulia.com/p/ga/milton/14745-wood-rd-milton-ga-30004--2029219742.

29. Rowan Scarborough, "Joseph and Alise Cua, Parents of Capitol Rioter Bruno Cua, Renounce Trump's 'Stop the Steal,'" *Washington Times,* April 14, 2021, sec. National, https://www.washingtontimes.com/news/2021/apr/14/joseph-and-alise-cua-parents-capitol-rioter-bruno-/.

30. Otis Taylor, Jr., "He Heeded Trump's Call to Fight. Now a Milton Teen Awaits the Consequences.," *Atlanta Journal-Constitution,* April 3, 2021, https://www.ajc.com/news/he-heeded-trumps-call-to-fight-now-a-milton-teen-awaits-the-consequences/HBIEZ7C2SRHTDAPGGW52DKJLTY/.

31. Shaddi Abusaid, "Metro Atlanta Teen Charged in U.S. Capitol Attack," *Atlanta Journal-Constitution,* February 6, 2021, https://www.ajc.com/news/metro-atlanta-teen-charged-in-us-capitol-attack/U7EPRZANXVBFPB7KRW7EQ3VRIE/.

32. Taylor, Jr., "He Heeded Trump's Call to Fight. Now a Milton Teen Awaits the Consequences."

33. Joseph Cua, LinkedIn, accessed March 26, 2021, https://www.linkedin.com/in/joseph-cua-42349035/.

34. "Alise Cua Photographer-4 Recommendations-Alpharetta, GA," Next-door, accessed July 2, 2021, https://nextdoor.com/pages/alise-cua -photographer-alpharetta-ga/.

35. Taylor, Jr., "He Heeded Trump's Call to Fight. Now a Milton Teen Awaits the Consequences."

36. Alise Cua, @AliseCuaPhoto, Tweet: "NO WAY ! And If You Are OK with the Attempted COUP, You Are OK with Doing What Is Needed to STOP It!," Twitter, December 7, 2020, https://twitter.com/AliseCuaPhoto /status/1335956756657278977.

37. Alise Cua, @AliseCuaPhoto, Re-Tweet: Candace Owens, @RealCandaceO, Tweet: "Serious Question. What Do You Guys Think the REAL #corona-virus Death Toll Is? Under 10k? Please Make This Video Viral: 'It Means Technically Even If You Died of a Clear Alternate Cause, but You Had COVID at the Same Time, It's Still Listed as a COVID Death," Twitter, May 10, 2020, https://T.Co/2fiqCX3QAx.

38. Alise Cua, @AliseCuaPhoto, Re-Tweet: Michelle Malkin, @michelle-malkin, Tweet: "Newsflash: No matter how many times you talk about HBCUs, Juneteenth, 'school choice' & the low black unemployment rate, these ingrates will always hate America.," Twitter, July 4, 2020, https://twitter.com/michellemalkin/status/1279519138797326336.

39. United States District Court for the District of Columbia, "United States of America v. Bruno Joseph Cua, Criminal Complaint and State-ment of Facts," January 29, 2021, https://www.justice.gov/usao-dc /case-multi-defendant/file/1365571/download.

40. Ibid.

41. Ryan Reilly, "MAGA Mom Whose Son Stormed Capitol Feels 'Stu-pid' For Buying Trump's Voter Fraud Lies," *HuffPost*, March 4, 2021, https://www.huffpost.com/entry/bruno-cua-trump-capitol-attack_n _603fb5f8c5b6d7794ae37145.

42. United States District Court for the District of Columbia, "United States of America v. Bruno Joseph Cua, Indictment," filed April 9, 2021, https:// www.justice.gov/usao-dc/case-multi-defendant/file/1386276/download.

43. Pilar Melendez, "'Embarrassed' Dad of Teen Insurrectionist: I Regret Taking My Son to Capitol," The Daily Beast, February 12, 2021, sec. U.S. News, https://www.thedailybeast.com/embarrassed-dad-of-teen -insurrectionist-says-he-regrets-taking-son-to-capitol.

44. Dina Temple-Raston, "A Tale of 2 Radicalizations," *Morning Edition*, NPR, March 15, 2021, https://www.npr.org/2021/03/15/972498203/a -tale-of-2-radicalizations.

45. Reilly, "MAGA Mom Whose Son Stormed Capitol Feels 'Stupid' for Buying Trump's Voter Fraud Lies."

46. Anonymous, "What Happened After My 13-Year-Old Son Joined the Alt-Right," *Washingtonian*, May 5, 2019, https://www.washingtonian

.com/2019/05/05/what-happened-after-my-13-year-old-son-joined-the
-alt-right/.

47. Paris Martineau, "The Alt-Right Is Recruiting Depressed People," *The
Outline*, February 26, 2018, https://theoutline.com/post/3537/alt-right
-recruiters-have-infiltrated-the-online-depression-community.

48. Anonymous, "What Happened."

49. Joanna Schroeder, "Racists Are Recruiting. Watch Your White Sons.,"
New York Times, October 12, 2019, sec. Opinion, https://www.nytimes
.com/2019/10/12/opinion/sunday/white-supremacist-recruitment
.html.

50. Mark White, "Right-Wing Extremism Is UK's Fastest Growing Threat,
Says Top Counter-Terror Cop," Sky News, November 18, 2020, https://
news.sky.com/story/right-wing-extremism-fastest-growing-threat
-says-uks-top-cop-in-counter-terrorism-12135071.

51. Katerina Vittozzi, "'The Enemy in Our Minds Was Islam': Why Boy, 14,
Joined the Far-Right—and How He Escaped," Sky News, November 18,
2020, https://news.sky.com/story/the-enemy-in-our-minds-was-islam
-why-boy-14-joined-the-far-right-and-how-he-escaped-12133887.

52. Simon Clark et al., "4 First Steps for Congress to Address White Supremacist Terrorism," Center for American Progress, October 30, 2020, https://
www.americanprogress.org/issues/security/reports/2020/10/30/492095
/4-first-steps-congress-address-White-supremacist-terrorism/.

6. Tip of the Spear

1. Stef W. Kight, "Poll: People View Millennials as 'Spoiled' and 'Lazy,'"
Axios, March 10, 2018, https://www.axios.com/millennials-a-tale-of
-two-generations-ff2a6de5-cfde-42c5-ab38-ec0908fbfcc9.html.

2. "Attorney General Jeff Sessions Delivers Remarks to Turning Point USA's
High School Leadership Summit," US Department of Justice, July 24,
2018, https://www.justice.gov/opa/speech/attorney-general-jeff-sessions
-delivers-remarks-turning-point-usas-high-school-leadership.

3. "Spring 2000 Youth Survey - Summary of Results," Harvard Kennedy
School Institute of Politics, April 2000, https://iop.harvard.edu/survey
/details/spring-2000-youth-survey-summary-results.

4. "Spring 2000 Youth Survey - Summary of Results."

5. "Presidential Approval Ratings—George W. Bush," Gallup, accessed July
10, 2019, https://news.gallup.com/poll/116500/Presidential-Approval
-Ratings-George-Bush.aspx.

6. "Satisfaction with the United States," Gallup, accessed July 6, 2021,
https://news.gallup.com/poll/1669/General-Mood-Country.aspx.

7. "A Generational Look at the Public: Politics and Policy," *Washington
Post*/Kaiser Family Foundation/Harvard University, October 2002,

https://www.kff.org/wp-content/uploads/2002/10/wph015-older
-voters_-web-version-final.pdf.

8. James Dao, "The 9/11 Decade: They Signed Up to Fight," *New York Times,* September 6, 2011, sec. U.S., https://www.nytimes.com/2011 /09/06/us/sept-11-reckoning/troops.html.

9. Thomas H. Sander and Robert D. Putnam, "Democracy's Past and Future: Still Bowling Alone?: The Post-9/11 Split," *Journal of Democracy* 21, no. 1 (January 2010): 9–16, https://doi.org/10.1353/jod.0.0153.

10. Brian Goldsmith, "A Conversation with Joe Trippi," CBS News, March 15, 2007, https://www.cbsnews.com/news/a-conversation-with-joe-trippi/.

11. Katharine Q. Seelye and Marjorie Connelly, "THE 2004 CAMPAIGN: IOWA; Dean's New-Voter Strategy Seemed to Work, for Others," *New York Times,* January 21, 2004, sec. U.S., https://www.nytimes.com /2004/01/21/us/the-2004-campaign-iowa-dean-s-new-voter-strategy -seemed-to-work-for-others.html.

12. Gail Sheehy, "Hillaryland at War," *Vanity Fair,* June 30, 2008, https:// www.vanityfair.com/news/2008/08/clinton200808.

13. Joshua Green, "Penn Strategy Memo, March 19, 2007," *The Atlantic,* August 11, 2008, https://www.theatlantic.com/politics/archive/2008 /08/penn-strategy-memo-march-19-2008/37952/.

14. Joshua Green, "Harold Ickes Lists the Campaign's 'Key Assumptions,' March 29, 2007," *The Atlantic,* August 11, 2008, https://www .theatlantic.com/politics/archive/2008/08/harold-ickes-lists-the -campaigns-key-assumptions-march-29-2007/37955/.

15. David Plouffe, *The Audacity to Win* (New York: Viking, 2009).

16. Ibid.

17. "The 12th Biannual Youth Survey on Politics and Public Service," Harvard Kennedy School Institute of Politics, April 2007, https://iop.harvard .edu/sites/default/files_new/survey_s2007_topline.pdf.

18. Sheehy, "Hillaryland at War."

19. Emily Hoban Kirby, Peter Levine, and Karlo Barrios Marcelo, "The Youth Vote in the 2008 Iowa Caucus," CIRCLE (The Center for Information & Research on Civic Learning and Engagement), January 7, 2008, http:// archive.civicyouth.org/PopUps/FactSheets/FS08_iowacaucus.pdf.

20. Plouffe, *The Audacity to Win.*

21. "Profile of the Iowa Caucusgoers," *New York Times,* December 6, 2016, sec. Election 2008, https://www.nytimes.com/elections/2008/primaries /results/vote-polls/IA.html.

22. Samuel L. Popkin, *The Candidate: What It Takes to Win—and Hold—the White House* (Oxford University Press, 2012).

23. "ABC News 2008 Democratic Primary Exit Poll Results—Key Groups," ABC News, https://abcnews.go.com/images/PollingUnit/08DemPrimary KeyGroups.pdf.

24. Marc Santora, Kate Phillips, and Adam Nagourney, "Race Upended, Candidates Sprint Toward Tuesday Vote," *New York Times,* January 4, 2008, sec. Politics, https://www.nytimes.com/2008/01/04/us/politics /04cnd-elect.html.

25. Hendrik Hertzberg, "Second Those Emotions," *New Yorker,* January 13, 2008, https://www.newyorker.com/magazine/2008/01/21/second -those-emotions.

26. Dick Morris, "Who's to Blame? It Was Mark Penn," *RealClearPolitics,* June 11, 2008, https://www.realclearpolitics.com/articles/2008/06 /whos_to_blame_it_was_mark_penn.html.

27. "Election Results 2008: National Exit Polls Table," *New York Times,* November 5, 2008, accessed January 2, 2020, https://www.nytimes .com/elections/2008/results/president/national-exit-polls.html.

28. Jann S. Wenner, "How Obama Won," *Rolling Stone,* November 27, 2008, https://www.rollingstone.com/politics/politics-news/how-obama-won -42930/.

29. "National Results 2020 President Exit Polls," CNN Politics, accessed July 6, 2021, https://www.cnn.com/election/2020/exit-polls /president/national-results.

30. Ron Fournier, "The Outsiders: How Can Millennials Change Washington If They Hate It?," *The Atlantic,* August 26, 2013, https://www .theatlantic.com/politics/archive/2013/08/the-outsiders-how-can -millennials-change-washington-if-they-hate-it/278920/.

31. Carrie Blazina and Drew Desilver, "Boomers, Silents Still Have Most Seats in Congress, Though Number of Millennials, Gen Xers Is Up Slightly," Pew Research Center, February 12, 2021, https://www.pewresearch .org/fact-tank/2021/02/12/boomers-silents-still-have-most-seats-in -congress-though-number-of-millennials-gen-xers-is-up-slightly/.

32. Ibid.

33. "Vital Statistics on Congress: Data on the U.S. Congress, Updated February 2021" Brookings, February 8, 2021, https://www.brookings.edu /multi-chapter-report/vital-statistics-on-congress/.

34. Emily Stewart, "Alexandria Ocasio-Cortez Isn't Rich. There's No Reason to Talk About It.," *Vox,* November 20, 2018, https://www.vox.com /policy-and-politics/2018/11/20/18105305/alexandria-ocasio-cortez -net-worth-clothes.

7. Impatience Is a Virtue

1. "Global Protest Tracker," Carnegie Endowment for International Peace, accessed January 1, 2021, https://carnegieendowment.org /publications/interactive/protest-tracker.

2. Deidre McPhillips and Lydia Chebbine, "Tracking Anti-Government Protests Worldwide," *U.S. News & World Report,* July 21, 2020, https://

www.usnews.com/news/best-countries/articles/2020-07-21/tracking
-anti-government-protests-worldwide.

3. Karlyn Bowman and Bryan O'Keefe, "AEI Studies in Public Opinion: Attitudes About Homosexuality & Gay Marriage," American Enterprise Institute, December 31, 2004, https://web.archive.org/web/20050517
033538/http:/www.aei.org/docLib/20050121_HOMOSEXUALITY
.pdf.

4. "Changing Attitudes on Same-Sex Marriage," Pew Research Center, May 14, 2019, https://www.pewforum.org/fact-sheet/changing
-attitudes-on-gay-marriage/.

5. Amy Goodman, "School Strike for Climate: Meet 15-Year-Old Activist Greta Thunberg, Who Inspired a Global Movement," Democracy Now!, December 11, 2018, https://www.democracynow.org/2018/12
/11/meet_the_15_year_old_swedish.

6. Charlotte Alter, Suyin Haynes, and Justin Worland, "TIME 2019 Person of the Year: Greta Thunberg," *Time*, December 23, 2019, https://
time.com/person-of-the-year-2019-greta-thunberg/.

7. Malena Ernman, "Malena Ernman on Daughter Greta Thunberg: 'She Was Slowly Disappearing into Some Kind of Darkness,'" *The Guardian*, February 23, 2020, sec. Environment, https://www.theguardian
.com/environment/2020/feb/23/great-thunberg-malena-ernman-our
-house-is-on-fire-memoir-extract.

8. Goodman, "School Strike for Climate."

9. "Greta Thunberg: Who Is the Climate Campaigner and What Are Her Aims?," BBC News, July 28, 2021, sec. Science & Environment, https://
www.bbc.com/news/world-europe-49918719.

10. Greta Thunberg, @gretathunberg, "Vi barn gör ju oftast inte som ni säger åt oss att göra, vi gör som ni gör. Och eftersom ni vuxna skiter i min framtid, så gör jag det med. Jag skolstrejkar för klimatet fram till valdagen," Instagram, August 20, 2018, https://www.instagram.com
/p/BmsTxPPlOqW/.

11. David Crouch, "The Swedish 15-Year-Old Who's Cutting Class to Fight the Climate Crisis," *The Guardian*, September 1, 2018, sec. Science, http://www.theguardian.com/science/2018/sep/01/swedish-15-year
-old-cutting-class-to-fight-the-climate-crisis.

12. Malena Ernman, "Malena Ernman on Daughter."

13. "September 2018 Weather in Stockholm—Graph," timeanddate.com, accessed January 14, 2021, https://www.timeanddate.com/weather
/sweden/stockholm/historic?month=9&year=2018.

14. Greta Thunberg, *No One Is Too Small to Make a Difference* (New York: Penguin Books, 2019).

15. Elise Harris, "Vatican Calls Greta Thunberg 'Great Witness' of Church's Environmental Teaching," *Crux*, December 12, 2019, https://

cruxnow.com/vatican/2019/12/vatican-calls-greta-thunberg-great -witness-of-churchs-environmental-teaching/.

16. Alter, Haynes, and Worland, "TIME 2019 Person of the Year: Greta Thunberg."

17. Jonathan Watts, "The Greta Thunberg Effect: At Last, MPs Focus on Climate Change," *The Guardian,* April 23, 2019, sec. Environment, https:// www.theguardian.com/environment/2019/apr/23/greta-thunberg.

18. "Claim in 2018: 'Russia Relies Heavily on Energy Exports for Close to Three-Quarters of Its Export Earnings and Over Half of Its Budget,'" Russia Matters, accessed February 14, 2021, https://www.russiamatters .org/node/11300.

19. Vladimir Soldatkin and Dmitry Zhdannikov, "Putin: I Don't Share Excitement About Greta Thunberg's U.N. Speech," Reuters, October 2, 2019, sec. Europe News, https://www.reuters.com/article/us-russia -putin-thunberg-idUSKBN1WH1FM.

20. "Strike Statistics," Fridays for Future, accessed January 14, 2021, https://fridaysforfuture.org/what-we-do/strike-statistics/.

21. Anne Barnard and James Barron, "Climate Strike N.Y.C.: Young Crowds Demand Action, Welcome Greta Thunberg," *New York Times,* September 20, 2019, sec. New York, https://www.nytimes.com/2019 /09/20/nyregion/climate-strike-nyc.html.

22. Steven Lee Myers, "Ignored and Ridiculed, She Wages a Lonesome Climate Crusade," *New York Times,* December 4, 2020, sec. World, https://www.nytimes.com/2020/12/04/world/asia/ou-hongyi-china -climate.html.

23. Emma Marris, "Why Young Climate Activists Have Captured the World's Attention," *Nature* 573 (September 18, 2019): 471–72, https:// www.nature.com/articles/d41586-019-02696-0.

24. Catherine Caruso, "Meet the 8-Year-Old Climate Activist Cleaning Up India," Global Citizen, April 30, 2020, https://www.globalcitizen.org /en/content/youth-climate-activist-cleaning-up-india/.

25. Thunberg, *No One Is Too Small to Make A Difference.*

26. "Global Peace Index 2020: Measuring Peace in a Complex World," Institute for Economics & Peace, June 2020, https://www.visionofhumanity .org/wp-content/uploads/2020/10/GPI_2020_web.pdf.

27. Benjamin Press and Thomas Carothers, "Worldwide Protests in 2020: A Year in Review," Carnegie Endowment for International Peace, December 21, 2020, https://carnegieendowment.org/2020/12/21 /worldwide-protests-in-2020-year-in-review-pub-83445.

28. Ibid.

29. Tim Campbell and Miha Hribernik, "A Dangerous New Era of Civil Unrest Is Dawning in the United States and Around the World," Verisk Maplecroft, December 10, 2020, https://www.maplecroft.com

/insights/analysis/a-dangerous-new-era-of-civil-unrest-is-dawning
-in-the-united-states-and-around-the-world/.

30. Helen Regan and Jessie Yeung, "Tens of Thousands Protest Australian PM's Climate Policies amid Bushfire Crisis," CNN, January 10, 2020, https://www.cnn.com/2020/01/10/australia/australia-fires-climate -protest-morrison-intl-hnk/index.html.

31. Adam Nossiter, "Macron Scraps Proposal to Raise Retirement Age in France," *New York Times,* January 11, 2020, sec. World, https://www .nytimes.com/2020/01/11/world/europe/france-pension-protests.html.

32. "French Police Clash with Anti-Racism Activists in Paris," BBC News, June 13, 2020, sec. Europe, https://www.bbc.com/news/world-europe -53036388.

33. Nicole Trian, "2020: A Year of Protests and Civil Disobedience," France 24, December 28, 2020, https://www.france24.com/en/europe /20201228-2020-a-year-of-dissent-and-civil-disobedience.

34. Amrit Dhillon and Luke Harding, "Indian Towns and Cities Grind to Halt as Workers Stage 24-Hour Strike," *The Guardian,* January 8, 2020, http://www.theguardian.com/world/2020/jan/08/india-towns-and -cities-grind-to-halt-as-workers-stage-24-hour-strike.

35. Diane Jeantet and Marcelo Silva De Souza, "Crowds Protest Cuts in Federal Funding for Brazil Schools," ABC News, May 15, 2019, https:// abcnews.go.com/International/wireStory/crowds-protest-cuts-federal -funding-brazil-schools-63063780.

36. Ana Vanessa Herrero, "Protests Have Spread Across Colombia. Here's Why.," *Washington Post,* May 7, 2021, https://www.washingtonpost .com/world/2021/05/07/colombia-protests-duque-faq/.

37. "Coronavirus: Ecuador Protests Against Cuts amid Pandemic," BBC News, May 26, 2020, https://www.bbc.com/news/world-latin-america -52803400.

38. Katrin Bennhold, "Germans Unnerved by Political Turmoil That Echoes Nazi Era," *New York Times,* February 7, 2020, sec. World, https://www.nytimes.com/2020/02/07/world/europe/germany -thuringia-afd.html.

39. Nikkei Staff Writers, "Thailand Latest: Government Bans Protests after COVID Uptick," Nikkei Asia, accessed December 31, 2020, https://asia.nikkei.com/Politics/Turbulent-Thailand/Thailand-latest -Government-bans-protests-after-COVID-uptick.

40. Farnaz Fassihi and David D. Kirkpatrick, "Iran Cracks Down as Protests Over Downing of Airliner Grow," *New York Times,* January 14, 2020, sec. World, https://www.nytimes.com/2020/01/12/world /middleeast/iran-plane-protests.html.

41. Billy Perrigo, "Crowds Protest in New Zealand Against George Floyd's Death and Police Brutality Against Indigenous Communities,"

Time, June 1, 2020, https://time.com/5845981/new-zealand-george
-floyd/.

42. Anthony Deutsch and Ingrid Melander, "Protests over George Floyd's
    Death Expose Raw Race Relations Worldwide," Reuters, June 2, 2020,
    https://www.reuters.com/article/us-minneapolis-police-protests
    -global-idUSKBN2392PE.

43. Hannah Hartig and Hannah Gilberstadt, "Younger Americans More
    Likely Than Older Adults to Say There Are Other Countries That Are
    Better Than the U.S.," Pew Research Center, January 8, 2020, https://
    www.pewresearch.org/fact-tank/2020/01/08/younger-americans
    -more-likely-than-older-adults-to-say-there-are-other-countries-that
    -are-better-than-the-u-s/.

44. Laura Parker, "For Young People, Two Defining Events: COVID-19 and
    Climate Change," *National Geographic,* April 28, 2020, https://www
    .nationalgeographic.com/science/article/gen-z-pandemic-will-define
    -formative-years-coronavirus-climate-change.

45. Ibid.

46. Ibid.

8. Ask and Ye Shall Receive

1. Scott Clement and Daniela Santamariña, "What We Know About the
   High, Broad Turnout in the 2020 Election," *Washington Post,* May 13,
   2021, sec. Politics, https://www.washingtonpost.com/politics/2021
   /05/13/what-we-know-about-high-broad-turnout-2020-election/.

2. Barack Obama, *A Promised Land* (New York: Crown, 2020).

3. David Von Drehle, "Obama's Youth Vote Triumph," *TIME,* January 4, 2008, http://content.time.com/time/politics/article
   /0,8599,1700525,00.html.

4. Obama, *A Promised Land.*

5. Alexander Burns, "Pete Buttigieg's Campaign Kickoff: Full Speech,
   Annotated," *New York Times,* April 15, 2019, sec. U.S., https://www
   .nytimes.com/2019/04/15/us/politics/pete-buttigieg-speech.html.

6. Ibid.

7. Michael Burke, "Buttigieg Says His First Legislative Pursuit Would Be
   'Democratic Reform,'" The Hill, March 3, 2019, https://thehill.com
   /homenews/campaign/432390-buttigieg-says-his-first-legislative
   -pursuit-would-be-democratic-reform.

8. "Pete Primer," The Pete Channel, accessed February 25, 2021, https://
   thepetechannel.com/pete-primer.

9. "Harvard Youth Poll, 39th Edition, Spring 2020," Harvard Kennedy
   School Institute of Politics, April 2020, https://iop.harvard.edu/youth
   -poll/spring-2020-poll.

10. Ibid.
11. Ibid.
12. Josh Carter, "Polls Finds Young Voters Divided on Change Needed for Nation," *Harvard Gazette,* November 18, 2019, https://news.harvard.edu/gazette/story/2019/11/polls-finds-young-voters-divided-on-change-needed-for-nation/.
13. Matt Orfalea, "Rising Up: Bernie 2020," October 3, 2019, https://www.youtube.com/watch?v=3ZhkKATtqtU&feature=emb_logo.
14. Jenna, @BoomBoomMeow __, Tweet: "The thing I like best about this ad is that it takes all of the negativity the media hurls at him and spins it around and hurls it right back. It puts a spotlight on everything we love about Bernie and it does it without taking digs at any other candidate.," Twitter, October 4, 2019, accessed February 11, 2021, https://twitter.com/BoomBoomMeow__/status/1180125904657358848.
15. "Full Text: Sen. Bernie Sanders' 2020 Presidential Campaign Kickoff Speech," VTDigger, March 2, 2019, https://vtdigger.org/2019/03/02/full-text-sen-bernie-sanders-2020-presidential-campaign-kickoff-speech/.
16. Shane Goldmacher and Nick Corasaniti, "'A Systemwide Disaster': How the Iowa Caucuses Melted Down," *New York Times,* February 4, 2020, sec. U.S., https://www.nytimes.com/2020/02/04/us/politics/what-happened-iowa-caucuses.html.
17. Domenico Montanaro, "3 Big Questions After the Iowa Results Meltdown," NPR, February 4, 2020, https://www.npr.org/2020/02/04/802681380/what-the-iowa-meltdown-means-and-where-we-go-from-here.
18. "2020 Primaries and Caucuses Exit and Entrance Polls," CNN Politics, accessed February 13, 2021, https://www.cnn.com/election/2020/entrance-and-exit-polls.
19. "Iowa Dem Caucus Exit Poll," ABC News, January 3, 2008, https://abcnews.go.com/images/PollingUnit/IADemHorizontal.pdf.
20. Ella Ceron, "Young People Made Themselves Heard In Iowa: 'Our Generation Knows What's At Stake,'" *MTV News,* February 5, 2020, http://www.mtv.com/news/3155194/iowa-caucus-2020-young-voters/.
21. "Election 2020: Iowa Democratic Presidential Caucus," *RealClearPolitics,* accessed February 13, 2021, https://www.realclearpolitics.com/epolls/2020/president/ia/iowa_democratic_presidential_caucus-6731.html.
22. "Election 2016: Iowa Entrance Polls," CNN Politics, accessed February 25, 2021, https://www.cnn.com/election/2016/primaries/polls/ia/dem.
23. "2020 Primaries and Caucuses Exit and Entrance Polls."
24. "Election 2016: Iowa Entrance Polls."
25. Mallory Tope, "Elizabeth Warren to Return to Iowa State," *Iowa State Daily,* January 29, 2020, https://www.iowastatedaily.com/news

/elizabeth-warren-iowa-state-university-iowa-caucus-ames-democ
ratic-presidential-candidate-2020-election/article_066c9446-42e3
-11ea-80d1-f7641e598836.html.

26. "Live Results: New Hampshire 2020 Democratic Primary," *Washington Post,* February 19, 2020, accessed February 26, 2021, https://www
.washingtonpost.com/elections/election-results/2020-live-results
-new-hampshire-democratic-primary/.

27. "Exit and Entrance Polls," CNN Politics, accessed February 16, 2021,
https://www.cnn.com/election/2020/primaries-caucuses/entrance
-and-exit-polls/iowa/democratic.

28. "Election2016: New Hampshire Exit Polls," CNN Politics, accessed February 25, 2021, https://www.cnn.com/election/2016/primaries/polls
/nh/dem.

29. Elena Schneider, "Buttigieg Drops Out of Presidential Race," *Politico,*
March 1, 2020, https://www.politico.com/news/2020/03/01/buttigieg
-dropping-out-of-presidential-race-118489.

30. Courtney Vinopal, "Sanders Banked on Young Voters. Here's How the
Numbers Have Played Out," *PBS NewsHour,* March 11, 2020, https://
www.pbs.org/newshour/politics/sanders-banked-on-young-voters
-heres-how-the-numbers-have-played-out.

31. Mike Damiano, "Massachusetts' Other Senator," *Boston,* October 1,
2017, https://www.bostonmagazine.com/news/2017/10/01/ed-markey/.

32. Michael Graham, "Unremarkable Ed Markey Could Make Joe K III a
Left-Over," *Boston Herald,* July 30, 2020, https://www.bostonherald
.com/2020/07/30/unremarkable-ed-markey-could-make-joe-k-iii-a
-left-over/.

33. Andy Metzger, "Kennedy Holds 17-Point Lead over Markey in Poll,"
CommonWealth, August 29, 2019, https://commonwealthmagazine.org
/politics/kennedy-holds-17-point-lead-over-markey-in-poll/.

34. Nik DeCosta-Klipa, "How Ed Markey Became the First Person to Beat a
Kennedy in Massachusetts," Boston.com, September 3, 2020, https://
www.boston.com/news/politics/2020/09/03/how-ed-markey-beat
-joe-kennedy.

35. Damiano, "Massachusetts' Other Senator."

36. "Massachusetts Senate—Democratic Primary," *RealClearPolitics,* September 1, 2020, accessed February 23, 2021, https://www.realclearpol-
itics.com/epolls/2020/senate/ma/massachusetts_senate_democratic
_primary-6946.html#polls.

37. Michelle Goldberg, "How the Green New Deal Saved a Senator's Career," *New York Times,* September 4, 2020, sec. Opinion, https://www
.nytimes.com/2020/09/04/opinion/ed-markey-young-progressive
-voters.html.

38. Joanna Weiss, "How 74-Year-Old Ed Markey Is Stealing the Youth Vote from a Millennial Kennedy," *Politico,* accessed August 18, 2020, https://www.politico.com/news/magazine/2020/08/18/ed-markey-ad-youth-vote-kennedy-397351.

39. Ed Markey, @EdMarkey, Tweet: "When the government abandons its people, it's up to us to rise up and make a revolution. We're fighting for dignity, for justice, and for our future. Join us at http://edmarkey.com/events. #GreenNewDealmaker," Twitter, August 13, 2020, https://twitter.com/edmarkey/status/1293986122318610435.

40. "Ed Markey: The Green New Dealmaker," Ed Markey for Senate, August 13, 2020, https://www.youtube.com/watch?v=DDg5glIt_0A.

41. Martha Hayes and Erica Buist, "'It's Not About Your Age, It's About Your Ideas': The Teen Power List," *The Guardian,* December 10, 2016, http://www.theguardian.com/lifeandstyle/2016/dec/10/the-teen-power-list.

42. Adam Best, @adamcbest, Tweet: "This quote from Ed Markey perfectly encapsulates why Joe Kennedy's generational change argument is nonsense: 'It's not your age. It's the age of your ideas that's important,'" Twitter, July 28, 2020, https://twitter.com/adamcbest/status/1288209605001125890.

43. DeCosta-Klipa, "How Ed Markey Became the First Person to Beat a Kennedy in Massachusetts."

9. I Hear You

1. Brittany Renee Mayes et al., "Exit Polls from the 2020 Democratic Super Tuesday Contests," *Washington Post,* March 30, 2020, accessed July 5, 2021, https://www.washingtonpost.com/graphics/politics/exit-polls-2020-super-tuesday-primary/.

2. John Whitesides, "After Big Wins, Biden Makes Appeal to Young Sanders Voters: 'I Hear You'," Reuters, March 18, 2020, https://www.reuters.com/article/usa-election/after-big-wins-biden-makes-appeal-to-young-sanders-voters-i-hear-you-idUSL1N2BB08A.

3. Isabella Grullón Paz, "Read Bernie Sanders's Full Speech on Ending His Campaign," *New York Times,* April 8, 2020, sec. U.S., https://www.nytimes.com/2020/04/08/us/politics/bernie-sanders-concession-speech.html.

4. Joe Biden, "Statement from Vice President Biden," Medium, April 8, 2020, https://medium.com/@JoeBiden/statement-from-vice-president-biden-5de128a935ac.

5. "President Trump Job Approval," *RealClearPolitics,* accessed February 27, 2021, https://www.realclearpolitics.com/epolls/other/president_trump_job_approval-6179.html.

6. "How Popular Is Donald Trump?," *FiveThirtyEight*, accessed March 17, 2017, https://projects.fivethirtyeight.com/trump-approval-ratings/.

7. Katelyn Burns, "The Racist History of Trump's 'When the Looting Starts, the Shooting Starts' Tweet," *Vox*, May 29, 2020, https://www.vox.com/identities/2020/5/29/21274754/racist-history-trump-when-the-looting-starts-the-shooting-starts.

8. Ella Nilsen, "'The Presidency Is a Duty to Care': Read Joe Biden's Full Speech on George Floyd's Death," *Vox*, June 2, 2020, https://www.vox.com/2020/6/2/21277967/joe-biden-full-speech-george-floyd-death-trump.

9. "CNN/SSRS Poll," CNN, May 13, 2020, http://cdn.cnn.com/cnn/2020/images/05/13/rel5c.-.2020.pdf.

10. Sunrise Movement 🌅, @sunrisemvmt, Tweet: "Here's a thought, @Joe-Biden. Maybe your climate policy advisor shouldn't be somebody who has taken a million dollars from the fossil fuel industry. Otherwise your commitment to averting the climate crisis sounds like a bunch of . . . well, malarkey.," Twitter, December 5, 2019, https://twitter.com/sunrisemvmt/status/1202664144585023495.

11. Lisa Friedman and Katie Glueck, "Biden's Big Climate Decision: Will He Embrace His Task Force's Goals?," *New York Times*, July 6, 2020, sec. U.S., https://www.nytimes.com/2020/07/06/us/politics/joe-biden-climate-change.html.

12. Alexandria Ocasio-Cortez, @AOC, Tweet: "Today the 6 Biden-Sanders Unity Task Forces are unveiling final language. The Climate Task Force accomplished a great deal. It was an honor to serve as co-chair w/ Sec. @JohnKerry. Among the notable gains: we shaved *15 years* off Biden's previous target for 100% clean energy.," Twitter, July 8, 2020, https://twitter.com/AOC/status/1280964109098455043.

13. Michael M. Grynbaum, "The TV Divide: Convention Ratings Surge on MSNBC as Fox News Dips," *New York Times*, August 21, 2020, sec. Business, https://www.nytimes.com/2020/08/21/business/media/democratic-convention-ratings.html.

14. Joe Biden, "The Honorable Joe Biden, Democratic Nominee for President of the United States, Democratic National Convention, Remarks as Prepared for Delivery," August 20, 2020, https://s3.documentcloud.org/documents/7041461/Biden-Speech.pdf.

15. "Election Week 2020: Young People Increase Turnout, Lead Biden to Victory," CIRCLE (Center for Information & Research on Civic Learning and Engagement), November 25, 2020, https://circle.tufts.edu/latest-research/election-week-2020.

16. Charlotte Alter, "The 2020 Election Was a Breakthrough Moment for Young Voters," *TIME*, May 18, 2021, https://time.com/6049270/2020-election-young-voters/.

17. Rob Griffin, William H. Frey, and Ruy Teixeira, "America's Electoral Future: The Coming Generational Transformation," Center for American Progress, October 19, 2020, https://www.americanprogress.org /issues/politics-and-elections/reports/2020/10/19/491870/americas -electoral-future-3/.
18. Craig Helmstetter, "Who Voted in Georgia's Runoff Elections?," APM Research Lab, American Public Media, January 7, 2021, https://www .apmresearchlab.org/blog/who-voted-in-georgias-runoff-elections.

10. To the Future

1. Kim Parker, Rich Morin, and Juliana Menasce Horowitz, "1. America in 2050," Pew Research Center, March 21, 2019, https://www .pewresearch.org/social-trends/2019/03/21/america-in-2050/.
2. Seth G. Jones et al., "The War Comes Home: The Evolution of Domestic Terrorism in the United States," CSIS Briefs, Center for Strategic & International Studies, October 22, 2020, https://www.csis.org/analysis /war-comes-home-evolution-domestic-terrorism-united-states.
3. A. C. Thompson, Ali Winston, and Jake Hanrahan, "Inside Atomwaffen As It Celebrates a Member for Allegedly Killing a Gay Jewish College Student," ProPublica, February 23, 2018, https://www.propublica.org /article/atomwaffen-division-inside-White-hate-group?token=l0i8Jn dZRzf9U7hmG1DlFV6RjLJo1zYf.
4. WBAY News Staff, "Neenah Man Arrested at Green Bay Protest Has Ties to Antifa," WBAY, August 31, 2020, https://www.wbay.com /2020/08/31/neenah-man-arrested-at-green-bay-protest-has-ties-to -antifa/.
5. Clare Hymes, Cassidy McDonald, and Eleanor Watson, "500 Arrested so Far in Capitol Riot Case, Including 100 Charged with Assaulting Federal Officers," CBS News, accessed June 30, 2021, https://www .cbsnews.com/news/capitol-riot-arrests-latest-2021-06-30/.
6. Chief Investment Office, GWM Investment Research, "The Food Revolution: The Future of Food and the Challenges We Face," UBS, July 2019, https://www.ubs.com/global/en/ubs-society/our-stories/2019 /future-of-food.html.
7. Ibid.
8. "The United States Meat Industry at a Glance," North American Meat Institute (NAMI), accessed July 6, 2021, https://www.meatinstitute .org/index.php?ht=d/sp/i/47465/pid/47465.
9. Emily Jed, "Aramark Brings Gen Z Food Trends to Life on College Campuses Nationwide," Vending Times, August 12, 2018, https://www .vendingtimes.com/news/aramark-brings-gen-z-food-trends-to-life -on-college-campuses-nationwide/.

10. Victoria Campisi, "Gen Z's Influential Food Preferences," The Food Institute, July 27, 2020, https://foodinstitute.com/focus/gen-z-preferences/.

11. Derek Thompson, "The Capitalist Way to Make Americans Stop Eating Meat," *The Atlantic,* January 10, 2020, https://www.theatlantic.com/ideas/archive/2020/01/why-2020s-will-be-peak-meat-america/604711/.

12. Hiroko Tabuchi and Nadja Popovich, "Two Biden Priorities, Climate and Inequality, Meet on Black-Owned Farms," *New York Times,* January 31, 2021, sec. Climate, https://www.nytimes.com/2021/01/31/climate/black-farmers-discrimination-agriculture.html.

13. Matt Haines, "Pandemic Worsens 'Food Deserts' for 23.5 Million Americans," Voice of America, May 19, 2020, https://www.voanews.com/usa/pandemic-worsens-food-deserts-235-million-americans.

14. Horus Alas, "Will Other Countries Continue to Outpace the U.S. in Voter Turnout?," *U.S. News & World Report,* October 30, 2020, https://www.usnews.com/news/best-countries/articles/2020-10-30/these-countries-have-had-the-highest-voter-turnout.

15. Archon Fung, "Archon Fung: We Voted," Harvard Kennedy School, Policy Topics: Democracy & Governance, Winter 2020, https://www.hks.harvard.edu/faculty-research/policy-topics/democracy-governance/archon-fung-we-voted.

16. Michael Waldman, "Voting in America: A National Perspective on the Right to Vote, Methods of Election, Jurisdictional Boundaries, and Redistricting," The Committee on House Administration, Subcommittee on Elections, U.S. House of Representatives, June 24, 2021, https://docs.house.gov/meetings/HA/HA08/20210624/112806/HHRG-117-HA08-Wstate-WaldmanM-20210624.pdf.

17. Ciara Nugent and Charlie Campell, "The U.S. and China Are Battling for Influence in Latin America, and the Pandemic Has Raised the Stakes," *Time,* February 4, 2021, https://time.com/5936037/us-china-latin-america-influence/.

18. Liza Lin, "Xi's China Crafts Campaign to Boost Youth Patriotism," *Wall Street Journal,* December 30, 2020, sec. World, https://www.wsj.com/articles/xi-china-campaign-youth-patriotism-propaganda-11609343255.

19. Vicky Xiuzhong Xu, "China's Youth Are Trapped in the Cult of Nationalism," *Foreign Policy,* October 1, 2019, https://foreignpolicy.com/2019/10/01/chinas-angry-young-nationalists/.

INDEX